The English Jacobin Novel on Rights, Property and the Law

Critiquing the Contract

Nancy E. Johnson
State University of New York
New Paltz

First published 2004 by
PALGRAVE MACMILLAN
Houndmills, Basingstoke, Hampshire RG21 6XS and
175 Fifth Avenue, New York, N. Y. 10010
Companies and representatives throughout the world

PALGRAVE MACMILLAN is the global academic imprint of the Palgrave Macmillan division of St. Martin's Press, LLC and of Palgrave Macmillan Ltd. Macmillan® is a registered trademark in the United States, United Kingdom and other countries. Palgrave is a registered trademark in the European Union and other countries.

ISBN 1–4039–3573–4

This book is printed on paper suitable for recycling and made from fully managed and sustained forest sources.

A catalogue record for this book is available from the British Library.

Library of Congress Cataloging-in-Publication Data
Johnson, Nancy E., 1956–
    The English Jacobin novel on rights, property, and the law: critiquing the contract / Nancy E. Johnson.
        p. cm.
    Includes bibliographical references and index.
    ISBN 1–4039–3573–4 (cloth)
        1. English fiction–18th century–History and criticism. 2. Law and literature–History–18th century. 3. Literature and society–Great Britain–History–18th century. 4. English fiction–French influences. 5. Social contract in literature. 6. Human rights in literature. 7. Jacobins–Great Britain. 8. Property in literature. 9. Law in literature. I. Title.
PR858.L39J64 2004
823'.6093554–dc22   2003066578

10   9   8   7   6   5   4   3   2   1
13   12   11   10   09   08   07   06   05   04

Printed and bound in Great Britain by
Antony Rowe Ltd, Chippenham and Eastbourne

For my parents, Harriett R. and Lester E. Johnson

Contents

Acknowledgements

This is a project that has long been in the works; therefore, there are numerous friends and colleagues to acknowledge. I am indebted to Alex Gold, Jr., who first introduced me to the English Jacobins, and Michael McKeon, who started me on the road to interdisciplinary studies in the eighteenth century. I owe a special thank you to David Hensley for his inspiration, counsel, and exceptionally comprehensive readings; he set by example extraordinarily high standards of scholarship and writing. I am appreciative, as well, to Ian Balfour, Mike Bristol, Mette Hjort, James Tully, and Bill Walker for their valuable direction on this project in its early stages, and to Pamela Clemit whose excellent suggestions have made this a much improved book.

I am grateful to my friends and colleagues at SUNY New Paltz, who have been generous with advice and encouragement: Jerry Benjamin, Stella Deen, Ernelle Fife, Dan Kempton (many thanks for repeated readings), Tom Olsen, Chris Robins, Jan Zlotnick Schmidt, Yoni Schwartz (many thanks), Harry Stoneback, Pauline Uchmanowicz, and Bob Waugh.

For truly sustaining friendship, I thank Steven Bruhm, Stewart Cooke, Kate Chisholm, Bill Donoghue, Richard Drake, Pat Dorfman, Theresa Egan, Mike and Wendy Klein, Dawn Morgan, Genice Ngg, David Ogawa, Peter Schwenger, Josephine Shannon, Xianmei Shen, Brigham Taylor, Jason Taylor, and Karen Valihora.

For their professional guidance and friendship, I thank Nancy Armstrong, Bob DeMaria, Nick Hudson, Claude Rawson, Alvaro Ribeiro, Peter Sabor, Lars Troide, Gordon Turnbull, and Peter Walmsley.

Finally, I extend my heartfelt thanks to my family – my parents, Karl, Chris, Judy, Bill, Hayley, and Juliana – for their enduring and unwavering support, and to David, for years of generous emotional support and intellectual guidance. I could not have completed this project without you.

Introduction

A final scene of Charlotte Smith's novel *The Young Philosopher* (1798) casts the sober, erudite Mr. Armitage (who bears a striking resemblance to William Godwin) in an intense discussion with a weary veteran of radicalism, Mr. Glenmorris, about the most effective way to live out one's political convictions and promote the happiness of others. Both are familiar with the political, legal, and economic corruption in their contemporary England, and both are cognizant of power as a function of property. But they disagree about the remedy, about the most appropriate response to rampant injustice. Mr. Glenmorris is ready to embrace exile in America, where, he believes, he and his family could participate in the creation of a new society, while Mr. Armitage suggests that remaining in England is preferable because it is still possible to transform the nation. This philosophical exchange certainly provides Smith with a vehicle for censuring the "haughty mother country" (England) and the wretchedness and misery she has nurtured – an overriding concern in the novel. Yet it also points to the ambivalent state of radicalism at the end of the eighteenth century. The debate between these two formidable characters hovers around a common goal – to shape an equitable social contract – however, the proper means to that end is obscured by uncertainty.

   I open with this novelistic reference from a rather late English Jacobin text because the uncertainty that plagues Smith's *Young Philosopher* was particularly influential, early on, in shaping this sub-genre of the novel.[1] It was a generative force behind what I will propose in this book is the contribution of the English Jacobin novel to political theory in late eighteenth-century Britain: a critique of the social contract, based on a reassessment of a theory of rights. Novels by Charlotte Smith, Robert Bage, William Godwin, and Mary Wollstonecraft, among others, have long been regarded by critics as a source of support for the rights campaign of the 1790s, and indeed they were.[2] With the exception perhaps of Godwin, the Jacobin authors embraced the transition away from monarchy and toward a government formed by consent and agreement. They endorsed, in general principle, the shift of political authority from a sovereign figure to a body of laws and a legislative system. And, they supported the notion of inalienable individual rights that are derived from natural law, precede civil society, and cannot be violated by government or legal institutions. All agreed that "things as they are" are intolerable and that a socio-political transformation is necessary.[3] However, as I will argue in this book, the English Jacobin authors approached these tenets of contract theory with a significant degree of skepticism.[4] Even as they aligned themselves with late eighteenth-century contractarians and opposed the idea of a traditional constitutional monarchy that binds each generation to the past, they also critiqued the notion of the social contract as it was being formulated by contractarians. This collection of novels was not just an unquestioning advocate of "the rights of man", nor merely an amanuensis to a political campaign. Rather, it was an active, challenging participant in the political debates of the period and in the development of contractarianism at the end of the eighteenth century.

The fiery discourse on rights that precipitated in the 1790s was spearheaded by the "pamphlet wars", in which leading intellectuals fired volleys at each other through published writings.[5] Under dispute was the paradigm of the social contract and the rights that would sustain it. While adherents to the "ancient constitution", such as Edmund Burke, wished to preserve a notion of English rights contained in the Magna Carta of 1215 and most recently revised and reaffirmed in the Declaration of Rights, 1689, reformers such as Thomas Paine hoped to reconstitute the English concept of guaranteed liberties and model it on the American Bill of Rights, 1789, and the French *Déclaration des droits de l'homme et du citoyen* of 1791. At the same time, the novel quickly surfaced as an additional site of inquiry and debate. Essayists turned to the novel, as William Godwin explains, to veer the dialogue on rights away from "refined and abstract speculation" and toward "a study and delineation of things passing in the moral world".[6] The result was an expansive narrative investigation of concerns central to political debates. Some authors, such as Mary Wollstonecraft, identified British law as the source of trouble for women in society and anticipated legal reforms, whereas others, such as Elizabeth Inchbald, criticized in more general terms the impositions of civil society and social customs on the individual. In sum, all of the English Jacobins strove to outline the figure of the legal subject of the social contract and redefine the relationship between the citizen and the law.

At the heart of the Jacobin novel's contribution to the debate on rights and its critique of the contract was the elucidation of the powerful connections between rights, property, and the law. As the novel expounds on the complex and multivalent "relationships" of the contract – on what it means to participate in the "mutual rights and duties" required of citizens – it demonstrates that to be engaged in civil society, one has to be a legal subject endowed with rights, and those rights are a function of property.[7] The very term "enfranchisement" specifies the conflation of the political, legal, and economic domains in defining agency. According to the *Oxford English Dictionary*, enfranchisement refers, first, to the "[l]iberation from ... political subjection", second, to "the citizenship of a state; admission to political rights", and, third, to "[t]he action of making lands freehold", of releasing one from "obligatory payments" or "legal liabilities". To "alienate", the term used to designate the violation or negation of a right, means "to transfer to the ownership of another".[8] Thus, to enjoy admission to political rights, one has to establish a "personal freehold"; one has to claim financial independence.

Locke's concept of the "right of property" also points to the economics of citizenship that is embedded in contractarianism. When in his *Two Treatises of Government* (1690), Locke determines the right of property to be a foundation for enfranchisement, he both continues a tradition of tying legal subjecthood to economic status and promotes a change in the conception of property. The property of which Locke writes is grounded in an assumption of self-determination based on self-ownership. In other words, the chief property necessary to enfranchisement is the property one claims in oneself. For those who could assert self-ownership, the recognition of natural rights that the individual retains when entering into civil society locates the source of political authority in the citizenry and renders its participants "legislators" rather than subjects or victims of the law. However, while Locke's "right of property" would seem to free enfranchisement from the requirement of wealth, it leaves participation in civil society contingent on another, more fundamental, form of proprietorship: self-possession.

Thus, the Lockean right of property was for some a liberating prospect. But for others, it signified a darker side of what Mary Wollstonecraft called "the iron hand of property", as it burdened and

obstructed women, younger brothers, and others who found themselves propertyless.[9] Not everyone was considered a free, rational agent
qualified to participate in a social contract. As the idea of the citizen
was reinterpreted and the borders of the individual reconsidered, the
economically dependent were denied a full array of rights and
excluded from the enjoyment of political agency in civil society. These
concerns were to inform English Jacobin fiction as powerfully as its
support of inalienable rights. The optimistic zeal of those Jacobin texts
that envisage a golden age of egalitarian societies was palpable.
Notably, in the work of Robert Bage and Thomas Holcroft, the social
critique in these most idealistic of texts is every bit as penetrating as
the bleakest analysis by Mary Wollstonecraft or Charlotte Smith. Yet,
when the confident idealism eventually gives way to the harsher realities of the mechanics and limitations of change, the English Jacobin
novel betrays a wariness of the continued dependence of agency on
property.

Enabling the novel's participation in political debates was the
significance of law to the form and substance of political authority in
the eighteenth century, which according to David Lieberman and
E.P. Thompson was "England's century of law".[10] In the political
theory of contractarians, such as John Locke, Algernon Sidney, and
Jean-Jacques Rousseau, law emerges as the foundation to political
authority and legal subjecthood as a requirement to citizenship.
Additionally, the concept of law itself was undergoing a transition.
When Sidney wrote in 1698 that the law and its intentional meaning
are "purely human ordinances", he signaled a shift in perceptions of
legal authority.[11] What was once deemed to be a force sustained by a
divine correspondence and legitimization, was now regarded as a
secular institution that was characterized by confusion, manipulation
and abuse. Such fallibilities led to efforts to clarify the law because, as
James Harrington observed, "[t]hat law which leaves the least arbitrary
power to the judge or judicatory is the most perfect law".[12] It also
meant that establishing rights to protect the individual against legal
abuses was a vital endeavour.

In addition to the increasing concern with law in the eighteenth
century was a growing interest in the literariness of the law, which,
especially by the 1790s, invited critical analysis by the novel. The "glorious uncertainty" or the "equivocal spirit" of the law – phrases that were
often repeated in the discourse of the period – underscored the interpretive quality of the law and its transactions.[13] Jeremy Bentham writes lib-
erally about law as a "species of discourse" and a product of the

"imagination", as well as about lawyers who "can no more speak at their ease without a fiction in their mouths".[14] Increasingly, trials were seen as rhetorical performances, permeated with the machinations of language and comprised of stories that were often fragmentary or contrived and always directed by lawyers and judges.[15] An especially revealing example can be found in the highly publicized London Treason Trials of 1794, in which the intention of political reformers was subject to speculation and interpretation by both the prosecution and the defense. The jury was asked to "imagine" the potential outcome of actions taken by the defendants and to decide on whether or not the defendants were "imagining" the king's death.[16] Consequently, when the law gradually began to move center stage and claim its place as the primary locus of political authority under government by contract, the ambiguity associated with the law brought with it both a crisis and an opportunity. It thrust political authority into the realm of interpretation (because law is an interpretive discourse), and it afforded a chance to reestablish the relationship between the individual and the law and to reconstruct the new citizen. The "uncertainty of the law", now associated with government, could indeed be construed as "glorious" because it enabled a potential transformation of the body politic.

Scholars of the 1790s have often commented that the debates on rights were to a great extent about language.[17] They were about defining natural and civil rights, interpreting the social contract, employing rhetoric to evoke optimism or fear, buoyant confidence or betrayed passion. The authority of language, its persuasive and its performative power, brought political theorists and novelists into the same arena. They were all engaged in inquiry, determined by contractarians to be a natural right, and they were all writing about what contemporary theorist Carole Pateman calls a "political fiction": an originating social contract. The agreement of a nation to establish a civil society, which is a foundation of government by contract, is according to Pateman, "[t]he most famous and influential political story of modern times".[18] Although a political essay could certainly argue the details of such a "story", the novel was in a unique position to respond to the fictions of politics.

*

The history of the English Jacobin novel is a political as much as it is a literary history, and a great deal of the story was defined and told by its opposition. The rubric "English Jacobin" was itself a product of the self-proclaimed "Anti-Jacobin" movement, whose mission was to prevent specific reforms within Britain. To refer to the work of authors such as Thomas Holcroft, Mary Hays, William Godwin, and Mary Wollstonecraft as "Jacobin" was to associate their ideas with the dangerously provocative and seductive French *philosophes* and the most extreme and volatile party of the French Revolution, the Jacobins. Although Holcroft, Hays, Godwin, Wollstonecraft and their fellow writers repeatedly disavowed violent revolution and promoted gradual change in a decade simmering with impatience, Anti-Jacobin assaults continued.[19] "Jacobinism" is boldly cited in the prospectus to the *Anti-Jacobin; or Weekly Examiner*, a periodical devoted to saving Britain from French ideological trends, as the culprit responsible for seditious activities: "Of all these and the like principles, – in one word, of JACOBINISM in all its shapes, and in all its degrees, political and moral, public and private, whether as it openly threatens the subversion of States, or gradually saps the foundations of domestic happiness, We are avowed, determined, and irreconcilable enemies".[20]

The attacks on English Jacobinism were relentlessly severe and hyperbolic, but they were responses to the very real potential for a reconfiguration of the body politic: the move away from the subjecthood of monarchy toward citizenship in a social contract.[21] They also proved to be indicative of the direction of political discourse. The link between "the subversion of States" and "the foundations of domestic happiness" points to the central role the family played in national politics and explains the attention received by the family in the debates on rights and, consequently, in the novel. Anti-Jacobinism adopted the political tradition of formal patriarchalism in which private obedience and domestic order were thought to be necessary for public peace and the fostering of loyal subjecthood. The reciprocal support between devotion to a father and veneration of a king was considered essential to the stability of the family, the most basic unit of society.[22] Protecting Britain meant protecting the British family.

The title "English Jacobin" was of course a red herring. Although war with France was a lingering threat that did materialize later in the decade, Anti-Jacobin fears were directed not so much at French infiltration as at reform efforts within Britain.[23] An essay on "The Rise, Progress, and Effects of Jacobinism" in the *Anti-Jacobin Review and Magazine* is an example of this phenomenon. The text begins with a discussion of the French Revolution but quickly shifts its focus to "the model of political perfection" among British radicals. The topic of the essay, one quickly realizes, is not French infiltration but internal British politics. "Their [British radical's] writings, for many years", the author argues with a tone of exasperation,

> shewed that what they held up as the model of political perfection, bore no resemblance to this constitution. They had attacked its establishments, they had attacked its principles, they had taken their plans of polity from their own visionary fancies, and not from experience. They conceived that the French doctrines coincided with their own ideas on *the origin of civil and religious liberty, and the first principles of government*. They opened in praises of the new order of things. From them and their votaries, whether preachers, pamphleteers, club haranguers or book-makers, came the first systematic exertions in favour of the French revolution.[24]

The French doctrines, however, did not merely "coincide" with the English. The theories of individual rights that fueled the French Revolution had been brewing in English political thought for more than a century, and the events in France may have been exacerbated by, or been the result of, English controversies and developments, rather than vice versa.[25] The Dissenters – Protestant Non-conformists who dissented from the authority of the Church of England – were the immediate, local threat because they were asking for the repeal of the Test and Corporation Acts, legislation that prohibited them from holding public office.[26] The Anti-Jacobin propensity to associate Dissenters (especially its leaders, Dr Richard Price, Dr Joseph Priestley, and Dr Andrew Kippis), with the revolutionary turbulence of France simply appealed to British fears, intensified xenophobia, and disguised the real source of animosity. Dr Price, in his incendiary sermon of November 4, 1789, *A Discourse on the love of our country*, argued that English principles derived from the Glorious Revolution were the catalysts for the American and French Revolutions.[27] The marquis d'Argenson, much earlier, confessed to the same when he wrote of France in 1751 that "there is a philosophical wind blowing toward us from England in favour of free, antimonarchical government... it is entering minds and one knows how opinion governs the world".[28] Moreover, Attorney William Fox in his pamphlet, *The Interest of Great Britain Respecting the French War* (1793), noted the heightening of international concern when English ideas were adopted on the continent, particularly in France.

> It is not the principles themselves, but it is those principles becoming *French*, which constitutes the danger; while they were confined

to this foggy island, while they were locked up in a language almost unknown on the continent, the monarchs of Europe were either strangers to their existence, or fearless of their effects. But when these principles are adopted by a nation, situated in the midst of happy, despotic monarchies; by a nation whose language is the universal language of Europe; and whose writers, by their genius, their wit, their learning, and their taste, had almost monopolized the literature of Europe; then it was that these principles excited their alarm, and threatened danger.[29]

Far from being a consequence of the French Revolution, the movement toward a recognition of inalienable rights in the social contract in Britain was a gradual one, and it was well under way before the fall of the Bastille and by the time the dialogue on rights became a fevered public debate.

*

There are a number of novels in and around the 1790s that are identifiably "English Jacobin" on ideological grounds. I found it necessary, therefore, to be highly selective in my choice of texts for this study and to use the criterion of a clear contribution to the development of a theory of rights in the social contract, for selection. I also chose what I thought to be the best examples of those contributions. The authors I discuss are easily identifiable as English Jacobin novelists, with the exception perhaps of Maria Edgeworth. I include her early novel *Castle Rackrent* (1800) because it engages with the dialogue on individual rights and elucidates an important dimension of progressive fiction: moral agency. Both Robert Bage and Thomas Holcroft wrote other novels that pertain to the present subject, most notably, Bage's *Man As He Is* (1792) and Holcroft's *Adventures of Hugh Trevor* (1794–97). For the most part, however, these two novels corroborate the philosophical premises entertained in Bage's *Hermsprong; or, Man As He Is Not* (1796) and Holcroft's *Anna St. Ives* (1792). There are, in addition, many novels by women, such as Helen Maria Williams' *Julia* (1790), Elizabeth Inchbald's *A Simple Story* (1791), and Mary Robinson's *Walsingham, or the pupil of nature* (1797), that I have not included in my discussion of the new citizen or women and agency. The sheer number of appropriate narratives by women has prevented me from covering them all. Finally, I have limited my study of Godwin's fiction to *Things As They Are; or, the Adventures of Caleb Williams* (1794) because it reveals, more than any of his other novels, the complexities of the English Jacobins' critique of contractarianism.

The early part of this book addresses the theoretical and historical foundations for my readings of English Jacobin fiction. In the first chapter, I consider how the novelists used the authority of narrative to conduct an inquiry into the theories of rights in a social contract and to investigate the intersections of rights, property, and the law. In the second chapter, I discuss the debate over natural and civil rights culminating in the 1790s as the social and political context of the English Jacobin novel. The overall layout of the textual analysis that follows the first two chapters is organized to show three major focal points and trends in the critique of the contract: the buoyant and optimistic envisaging of the new citizen, the sobering analysis of exclusion from the body politic, and a reassessment of the state of radicalism and reform at the end of the eighteenth century. Chapter 3 explores the English Jacobins' use of sentimentalism to celebrate the figure of the propertied, self-governing member of the commonwealth. Chapter 4 addresses the denial of rights (particularly in regard to women and servants) that leads to a quest for political agency, and Chapter 5 examines two late English Jacobin novels that search for a stable center to the movement for social transformation and ponder the future of radicalism.

There are a number of terms in my discussion of political theory that it would perhaps be helpful to define. "Contract" is a particularly ambiguous word in seventeenth- and eighteenth-century writing because it was used by both sides on the issue of the origins of political authority. "Contractarians", "contract theorists", or "*a priori* theorists" were those who believed political authority to be derived from agreement and consent of the people. "Royalists" or "absolutists" also recognized a compact, but it was between monarchs and subjects. "Democracy" is a closely related term that was sometimes used to indicate subversive activity or an interest in overthrowing the British government. In its purest sense, democracy means government by the people, either directly or through representation. But I use it sparingly because the English Jacobin authors give little indication of just how they envisaged the mechanics of government by the people.

"Republicanism" is another label that was occasionally used in regard to the Jacobins. Meaning government by law, republicanism was established in contrast to monarchy and indicates the predominance of law in government. This is perhaps the most accurate term to describe the form of government imagined by contractarians because it emphasizes citizen participation, social obligations, and the common good. For "jurisprudence", I use Adam Smith's definition because it emphasizes theory and the connection between law and government. "Jurisprudence", Smith writes, "is the theory of the rules by which civil governments ought to be directed."[30] "Inalienable rights" are those liberties that the individual does not surrender when entering into civil society, such as the right to self-governance, intellectual inquiry, and political reform. "Natural rights" are those that one holds in a state of nature; some are given up and some retained when one forms a community with others. "Civil rights" are the protections of law. They exist only within civil society, and they frequently refer to the preservation of property in "goods" and the "person". "Civil society" refers to the formal organization of a nation; it is contradistinguished from a state of nature and subjecthood. The "franchise" denotes the rights of citizenship, participation in the public sphere, and, at times, voting privileges. (It is not always clear just what form Jacobin authors imagined political agency might take; it is rarely defined as specifically as voting privileges.) The "public sphere" designates that realm of society that involves civic participation based on political agency, whereas the "private sphere" is a place characterized by passivity and lack of political agency; in the private domain, one is subjected to the decisions of the public and the political but one cannot participate in making those policies.

*

The novel's inclusion in the rights debates of the 1790s was both remarkable and not so. Fiction, particularly the novel, was suspect. But this "new" genre, which was freeing itself somewhat from the formal literary conventions of "high art", was reaching a broader and more democratic audience, and it set itself up in opposition to the traditional literary forms of the early eighteenth century, such as the satiric, georgic, and tragic, that dominate Burke's writing and are directed toward a social and political elite.[31] Moreover, the 1790s was a notable time for a blurring of boundaries. Burke's *Reflections on the Revolution in France* (1790) was as replete with theatrical displays of sentiment as any piece of fiction, and a novel like Holcroft's *Anna St Ives* functioned, in part, as a rigorous philosophical argument. The English Jacobins' response to the literariness of the law not only illuminated the "glorious uncertainty of the law", but it gave vent to the emotional and imaginative elements of political development. It became a vehicle through which we *read* the law that is comprised in a system of rights. The late Robert Cover, a former Yale law professor who studied hermeneutics and legal discourse, rejoiced in what he saw as the most intimate of connections between law and literature. "No set of legal institutions or prescriptions", he concluded, "exists apart from the narratives that locate it and give it meaning. For every constitution there is an epic, for each decalogue a scripture".[32] After considering the contribution of the Jacobin novel to notions about the form and distribution of rights in a social contract, I would here like to extend Cover's remark and suggest that "for every bill of rights there is a novel". English Jacobin fiction tells the tale of how the novel, in one critical moment of history, located and gave meaning to a theory of rights that became a foundation of modern democracy.

1
Narrativizing a Critique of the Contract

In his investigations of the hermeneutic interdependence of literature and the law, Robert Cover observes how literature initiates, and contains the stories of, historical change. Cultural transformations occur, he explains, when hegemonic forces encounter alternative narratives that act against the "universalist virtues" that inhere in dominant precepts.[1] All such movements take place in a *nomos*, a "world of law" that is comprised of "a system of tension between reality and vision".[2] The role of literature is to negotiate this tension between what is, what should be, and what might be, and it does so by revealing the realities of material conditions and placing them against visions of alternate possibilities. Literature acts as a catalyst for change and absorbs into its narrative codes the adjustments of historical development.

The English Jacobin novel was just such an agent of transformation that embodies the changes taking place in the *nomos* of late eighteenth-century Britain. These progressive narratives mediated a major historical event – the advancement of a theory and system of rights in a social contract – and they provide accounts of what transpired in the process. Of particular value is their elucidation of the complexities, discrepancies, nuances, and disagreements in the defining of political principles.[3] By the 1790s, for example, the "contract" was firmly in place as the paradigm for social organization, but its definition remained unsettled. For Edmund Burke, the social contract was the "great primeval contract of eternal society".[4] It was an agreement infused with spiritual authority and based on prescription; each generation was obliged to consider the wishes of its predecessors and yield to ancient wisdom. For Thomas Paine, however, civil society was to be based on an originating contract that would be reconsidered by each generation. He regarded the covenant between governors and the governed as a civil agreement only (thus allowing for modifications by succeeding ages), and he saw it as a means of obtaining social equity. One would expect the English Jacobin authors to embrace the version presented by contractarians, yet as Ian Balfour notes, "philosophies of the social contract did and do not always divide neatly along party lines".[5] In his *Enquiry Concerning Political Justice* (1793), Godwin takes issue with notions of "consent" and the "acquiescence" required by a political constitution. Predictably, he challenges Burke and asks rhetorically, "if I be obliged to submit to the established government till my turn comes to assent to it, upon what principle is that obligation founded? Surely not upon the contract into which my father entered before I was born?"[6] However, Godwin also contests Locke's idea that a "tacit consent" to the social contract obliges one to obey the laws of the government, whereas to be a member of the commonwealth requires "positive engagement and express promise and compact." "A singular distinction!" Godwin responds, "implying upon the face of it, that an acquiescence, such as has just been described is sufficient to render a man amenable to the penal regulations of society; but that his own consent is necessary to entitle him to its privileges".[7] Instead, Godwin proposes his own notion of "private judgment", the "duty" to decide one's conduct by individual conviction.[8]

Destabilizing hegemonic categories and mediating historical events, according to Michael McKeon, has long been a function of the novel.[9] But in the 1790s, the novel was an especially significant force because the personal was increasingly seen as political, largely due to Godwin's social thought, and the novel was a narrative site where the politics of individual lives could be explored most effectively. The English Jacobin authors saw the novel as a didactic force that exemplified and encouraged political inquiry, which was an essential function for preparing and maintaining the social contract. They also used the novel to explore subjectivity because a discrete self was essential to participation in civil society and because domestic matters were of national concern. While the novel has traditionally been engaged in exploring the parameters of the self, in the debates on rights, the individual's liberties in relation to familial restrictions was a central point of dispute. Citizenship was bound up in subjectivity, and that assertion of the self meant extricating oneself from the limitations of the family. The novel, which so often represented the domestic sphere, became a crucial site for examining the politics of the domestic and the shaping of the individual into a legal subject. In addition, striving for a unified narrative to counter those of law, which are characterized by fragmentation, the Jacobin novel asserted itself as a mechanism for mediation and critique, a place where one might envisage a future in an equitable social contract.

In his preface to *Caleb Williams*, which was omitted from the first published edition because it was thought to be too inflammatory, Godwin makes an observation about fiction that was perhaps the single most important idea informing the English Jacobin novel: "It is now known to philosophers that the spirit and character of the government intrudes itself into every rank of society. But this is a truth highly worthy to be communicated to persons whom books of philosophy and science are never likely to reach". It is through the "invention" of fiction that one might reveal "the modes of domestic and unrecorded despotism, by which man becomes the destroyer of man".[10] Godwin's remarks, which anticipate more recent comments such as Fredric Jameson's sweeping claim that "everything is 'in the last analysis' political", not only welcome the novel into political dialogues, but they also imply that the novel might be a preferred method of exploring a domestic despotism that is, in fact, national.[11] For Godwin, the idea of a public/private divide – a struggle that was an undercurrent of cultural tensions in the late eighteenth century – was an illusion.[12] Expanding the compass of his inquiry to include the domestic was also a way in which Godwin distinguished himself from traditional contractarians, such as Sidney, Locke and Paine. At the very start of *Political Justice*, Godwin argues that while "[t]hey have been prompted in their exertions rather by a quick sense of justice and disdain of oppression", he has been guided by an awareness of "the intimate connection of the different parts of the social system, whether as it relates to the intercourse of individuals, or to the maxims and institutes of states and nations".[13]

Godwin's views reverberate through the prefaces of other English Jacobin authors when they write of their motivations and intentions for using the novel as a vehicle to illustrate reality and vision, the way things are and the way things ought to be. Mary Wollstonecraft, in the preface to *Wrongs of Woman; [or] Maria* (1798), declares that her "main object" is "the desire of exhibiting the misery and oppression, peculiar to women, that arise out of the partial laws and customs of society".[14] The novel enabled her to reveal the impact of legal abuses on women who are unprotected by rights and to reach an audience that might not have exposure to essays such as her *Vindication of the Rights of Men* (1790): the public readership of novels, largely made up of women.[15] Similarly, Mary Hays suggests in the preface to the *Memoirs of Emma*

Courtney (1796) that it is the job of the novelist to look behind the "sacred and mysterious veil" of morality and philosophy to discover truth. She accomplishes this goal by "tracing consequences, of one strong, indulged, passion or prejudice", and hence "afford[ing] materials, by which the philosopher may calculate the powers of the human mind, and learn the springs which set it in motion".[16] Thomas Holcroft asserts that the novel deserves our "esteem" because it has "the power of playing on the fancy, interesting the affections, and teaching moral and political truth".[17] In the preface to *Memoirs of Bryan Perdue*, Holcroft outlines the didactic intent in each of his novels. "Whenever I have undertaken to write a novel", he explains, "I have proposed to myself a specific purpose. This purpose, in Anna St Ives, was to teach fortitude to females; in Hugh Trevor, to induce the youth (or their parents) carefully to inquire into the morality of the profession which each might intend for himself". For *Bryan Perdue*, his goal was "to induce all humane and thinking men, such as legislators ought to be and often are, to consider the general and the adventitious value of human life, and the moral tendency of our penal laws".[18]

The quality of didacticism that inheres in Godwin's prefatorial position and in the Jacobin novel generally was, according to J. Paul Hunter, one of the "cultural contexts" of the novel at its origin in the English tradition and throughout the eighteenth century. The urgency, the authorial stance of certainty, and the faith in the effective value of language – all features of the didactic tradition – certainly distinguish the progressive novel.[19] The practice of acquainting readers with the text's intention, Hunter also explains, was "part of the process of living through a radical historical change in the writer-reader relationship, in going from a language of familiarity among friends to a language designed to communicate with strangers".[20] This is indeed also true for the Jacobin novel, but its didacticism is of a decisively politicized form, inseparable from a campaign to expand the franchise and endow individuals with rights. The "strangers" are the populace who should be readying themselves for their place in the social contract, and the novelists are the educators, working in the tradition of philosophical sentimentalism, which sees human nature as essentially good and casts evil as mere error. Providing instruction was part of the novelist's social obligation.

The English Jacobin authors understood the novel to be, as James Boyd White characterizes narrative, an "action in the world" – and the nucleus of that activity was "inquiry".[21] Their novels were social and philosophical investigations into abusive prejudices, institutional tyranny, and the possibilities of reform. They became examples, for the populace, of the value of careful scrutiny, and they encouraged a rational analysis of personal situations. Godwin articulates these concerns and responsibilities when, in response to accusations in *The British Critic* that *Caleb Williams* is full of legal errors, he explains his purpose in writing the novel. It was not his intention, he argues, simply to reveal the specifics of the unjust laws of England. "The object is of much greater magnitude", he writes. "It is to expose the evils which arise out of the present system of civilized society; and, having exposed them, to lead the enquiring reader to examine whether they are, or are not, as has commonly been supposed, irremediable; in a word, to disengage the minds of men from prepossession, and launch them upon the sea of moral and political enquiry".[22]

In the campaign to expand the franchise, inquiry was presented as an imperative, as the intellectual activity that must precede actual change and must continue to maintain a commonwealth. The Jacobins wrote of inquiry with a faith in reason and a belief that the novel could reveal truth; their visionary world was one in which intention and action, soul and deed are integral. Holcroft, when he wrote for *The Monthly Review*, consistently used the measure of a character's or situation's relation to "real life" to comment on the merit of the literary work because verisimilitude would encourage attention to "real life" problems. In one of his reviews, Holcroft takes issue with the *Arabian Tales; or, a Continuation of the Arabian Nights Entertainments* (1793) because the stories "have a tendency to accustom the mind rather to wonder than to inquire; and to seek a solution of difficulties in occult causes instead of seriously resorting to facts". Tales of the marvelous have far less "moral utility", according to Holcroft, than "those which originate in true pictures of life and manners".[23]

For similar reasons, Holcroft disparaged gothic fiction. In a review of the anonymously published *Castle of St. Vallery* (1792), he writes of the genre that

> [o]f all the resources of invention, this, perhaps, is the most puerile, as it is certainly among the most unphilosophic. It contributes to keep alive that superstition which debilitates the mind, that ignorance which propagates error, and that dread of invisible agency which makes inquiry criminal. Such stories are in system neither divine nor human, but a strange mockery of both.[24]

The gothic was counter-instructive. It excited fear and pessimism at a time when reform movements needed the spirited energy of hope and sanguinity. "[W]e rise from reading", Holcroft writes in another review, "not with that animation which should make us happy in ourselves and useful to others, but with a sensation of the wretchedness of human existence".[25] In addition, the gothic novel threatened to distract readers from the actual terrors at hand with pleasurably provocative, spine-tingling stories; and it did so just at the moment when the nation needed attention and clear-headedness. Holcroft's conclusion that it is far better to depict "man as he really is", even in a utopian narrative, became a fundamental maxim for the Jacobins.

The English Jacobin novel's "action in the world" – its didacticism and its insistence on the freedom of inquiry – was largely about the shaping of subjectivity. The novel was busy constructing images of the new citizen because subjectivity was emerging as a crucial claim for all forms of agency. A discrete, independent self was a pre-requisite to citizenship, to proprietorship in the social contract, to the avoidance of a subjecthood that was a carryover from formal patriarchalism. As Martha Minow and Robin West have both observed, subjectivity has long been the criterion for asserting one's full array of rights as a citizen; it has definitively established one's relationship to legal institutions and ultimately determined one's vulnerability (as a dependent figure) to denial, abuse, and violation.[26] In the writings of contractarians such as Locke, Sidney, and Rousseau, in the Putney Debates of 1647–49, and in discussions in the National Assembly of France, segments of the population were being excluded from key political advancements, based on subjectivity. Those who were deemed economic dependents and therefore not full subjects, such as women and servants, were ultimately not considered beneficiaries of all natural and civil rights in the body politic. While these exclusions can be gleaned from the texts of political theory, when represented in the novel, they stand out far more as egregious denials with wide-ranging implications. By encoding political principles and controversies in narrative events and characterizations, the English Jacobin authors were able to show the dire need for everyone (but especially the most vulnerable) to claim individual, inalienable rights because everyone requires protection against a government comprised of the fallible systems of law.

Because subjectivity was essential to enfranchisement, private history became an important component of the English Jacobin novel. When Maria Edgeworth explains why she chose the narrative form to elucidate a bit of Irish/English history in her preface to *Castle Rackrent*, she points to the significance of private history and defends the public's interest and delight in "anecdote". Unlike critics who deemed such indulgence anti-intellectual, she finds this enjoyment "an incontestible proof of the good sense and profoundly philosophic temper of the present times". History, she argues, is contrived and uncertain at best. The story, particularly in the form of "secret memoirs and private anecdotes", can, in contrast, show us what lies behind carefully constructed facades and lead us to philosophical truth.

> We cannot judge either of the feelings or of the characters of men with perfect accuracy from their actions or their appearance in public; it is from their careless conversations, their half finished sentences, that we may hope with the greatest probability of success to discover their real characters.... . We are surely justified in this eager desire to collect the most minute facts relative to the domestic lives, not only of the great and good, but even of the worthless and insignificant, since it is only by a comparison of their actual happiness or misery in the privacy of domestic life, that we can form a just estimate of the real reward of virtue, or the real punishment of vice.[27]

Hunter identifies this movement of the "intimate and precise world of privacy" into the public sphere as an early eighteenth-century phenomenon and another cultural context of the novel. When ideas of "selfhood, personality, subjectivity, [and] propriety" began to predominate, the private story began to take on a new authority. It often served as an exemplum and a form of witnessing.[28] Correspondingly, the novel, which was also emerging as a distinct genre at this time, began to examine the individual life and "the interpretive mind bent on sorting human experience".[29] Out of a similar interest much later in the century, the Jacobins turned to the "biography" and the "memoir" to tell the philosophic tale. Their assumption in doing so was that the private story is political, and it is of public use. Edgeworth presents *Castle Rackrent* as a biography of the Rackrent family and as a means of edification for the public at a time when Irish/English unification was a visible and contentious issue on the minds of Irish and English alike. With a similar gesture of biographical exemplification, Robert Bage offers a twofold narrative structure in *Hermsprong* to demonstrate the common benefits of the "rights of man". His narrator, Gregory Glen, conveys an entertaining biography of the legendary "Hermsprong" and interweaves into the tale his own private story – the history of "the son of nobody" – to show the impact of a model of enfranchisement on a man who has been denied agency.

The Jacobin novel is "biography", however, only in the way that Georg Lukács claims the novel in its "outward form" is "essentially biographical" – as a construct that objectivized "[t]he fluctuation between a conceptual system which can never completely capture life and a life complex which can never attain completeness because completeness is immanently utopian". The novelistic character, according to Lukács, is vital "only by his relationship to a world of ideals", and the world is actualized "only through its existence within that individual and his lived experience".[30] In a like manner, the Jacobins were concerned with the agency of the subject but always in a dynamic relation to the world. The inner workings of perhaps the most psychologically aware Jacobin character, Caleb Williams, are significant because they provide a negative example – a picture of things as they are – and a rationale for reform. At times, as in the case of Holcroft's *Anna St. Ives*, Jacobin characters seem rather hollow figures who function only as concepts and thus lose what Lukács regards as the product of the interaction between personal lives and the world in the novel: a sense of the "problematic individual" that gives the novel its inner form. Yet in Godwin's *Caleb Williams*, Wollstonecraft's *Wrongs of Woman*, Hays's *Memoirs of Emma Courtney*, and Smith's *Young Philosopher*, for example, the protagonists are of political interest precisely because they represent the complications of individual agency, citizenship, and human passion.

The memoir, because it is both personal and public and it affirms identity,[31] was a popular form for political novelists of the 1790s, conservative and progressive alike.[32] Borrowing much from the confessional mode of Samuel Richardson, the Jacobins used personal histories to bear witness to public dilemmas. Mary Hays offers a memoir of a young woman, Emma Courtney, who indulges in excessive passion to show that reason is the faculty required for social reform, and Mary Wollstonecraft constructs the stories of Maria and Jemima, which are told as memoirs, to expose the victimization of women by the law. The Jacobins embraced, as well, the memoir's reaffirmation of the self-directing subject firmly placed in the world. He or she arbitrates the tension between the "individual will" and "social and interactive values" but does so from a position of empowerment.[33] Most of the fictional memoirs of the Jacobins are the stories of those who are battling to claim a discrete self: women and servants. Women had a uniquely complicated struggle because, as Patricia Meyers Spacks observes, "[t]he identities they define derive mainly from their exploration of vulnerabilities: sexual, social and psychic". However, the mere "declaration of the self implicit in the writing process", is an asssertion of personal "integrity".[34] Women and servants are also those who are most involved in private life. Servants, as Mikhail Bakhtin suggests, are "the most privileged witnesses to private life"; they have a "distinctive, embodied point of view on the world of private life without which a literature treating private life could not manage".[35] (Godwin's *Caleb Williams*, who is a servant, provides an illuminating example of Bakhtin's observation when his intimate knowledge of his "Master's" affairs propels him toward a tragic end.) Nonetheless, Felicity Nussbaum reminds us that a private existence, beyond the influence of "the state and the economy" belies "the way that the production of a rich and complex inner life is itself a political practice".[36] That "political practice", the English Jacobins narrativize in their novels.

When the exploration of subjectivity collided with the Burkean notion of "inherited" liberties in the debate on rights, the resulting tension determined to some extent the direction of narrative analysis in the novel.[37] It necessitated a study of the individual in relation to the family and the family in relation to the nation. A woman's domestic identity, for example, as wife, mother, or daughter, became a particularly important focus because it was a means to showing the devastating effect of "inherited rights" on dependents. For women, who were so often left out of the inheritance process, or who quickly lost property to a husband, inherited rights restricted their liberties. But, as mentioned earlier, women were also in danger of being excluded from the political advancements of contractarians. English Jacobin authors therefore strove to demonstrate how women might be enfranchised, how women might claim the same "birthrights" as men and therefore not be limited by their place in the family. In the visionary world of fiction, a reconstruction of natural and civil rights might result in protective privileges that could, in turn, guarantee a relationship with the law that transcends the limitations of a woman's familial role. For instance, a wife could claim a legal identity separate from her husband's based on her own autonomy; a woman could enter into a contract, other than marriage, without the intervention of a male member of the family, a guardian, or trustee. In novels such as Holcroft's *Anna St Ives*, social obligation requires that the young female protagonist succumb to filial disobedience, step outside of her domestic confinement and declare her individual agency. To fulfill her role as a citizen and exercise her rights, Anna St Ives must shift her loyalty from her father to the community. Not surprisingly, the attempt to claim the rights of man for women stirred its own particular controversy. It was seen by the *Anti-Jacobin Review and Magazine* as an attack on the British family, and a stable family was essential to the security of the nation. In its review of Mary Hays's *Memoirs of Emma Courtney* (also written in response to *The Monthly Review*'s article on the same novel), the *Anti-Jacobin* poses a choice between rights and decency for women. The two could not co-exist.

[T]he plain question is – Whether it is most for the advantage of society that women should be so brought up as to make them dutiful daughters, affectionate wives, tender mothers, and good Christians, or, by a corrupt and vicious system of education, fit them for revolutionary agents, for heroines, for Staels, for Talliens, for Stones, setting aside all the decencies, the softness, the gentleness, of the female character, and enjoying indiscriminately every envied privilege of man?[38]

The attack on the oppressive structure of the family, which is a trademark of the English Jacobin text and is intimately linked with the theory of rights they supported, creates a rather unique form of the domestic novel. Most domestic fiction, Nancy Armstrong explains, "actively sought to disentangle the language of sexual relations from the language of politics and, in so doing, to introduce a new form of political power", which is that of the domestic woman.[39] In addition, the domestic novel was able to "represent an alternative form of political power without appearing to contest the distribution of power that it represented as historically given".[40] In contrast, when the Jacobin novel represented the family, it was engaged in a direct struggle with political power, and it was determined to transform that power rather than offer an alternative. Moreover, the success of this mission was dependent on revealing the politics of the domestic in the formulation of inherited rights and resisting a separation of the private and public spheres. The English Jacobins used stories of private life to demonstrate that domestic authority was an illusion that, even if it could be defined in a positive manner, would not be the equivalent of political power defined by inalienable rights and the franchise. It would not equal the force deriving from property ownership, self-governance, the power of intellectual inquiry, and legal subjecthood.

As they told their stories of the legal subject, the Jacobin novelists were responding to other narratives of legal and political theory. They took advantage of the "fluidity and indeterminacy of social categories" in this turbulent time of the 1790s and offered reconstructions for a more equitable social contract.[41] By engaging in a dialogue with political, legal, and economic discourses, the Jacobin novels were to conduct significant inquiry into the development of a theory of rights; and by functioning as formal exempla, they were to ready the populace for citizenship. The Jacobin text now also provides an important insight into the inevitable conflation of the narrative of cultural critique with the performative language of law and politics. Jacobin fiction contributed to the formation of legal and political thought much as it was imagined the individual might enter into a contract. It was engaged in a self-reflexive empowerment. The Jacobin novelists assumed the ability to critique the social contract just as an individual strengthened by inalienable rights was enabled, theoretically, to be a party to a civil or legal agreement. The assumption of power was manifest in the insistence of contractarians that the source of civil authority be located in the individual. It gave credence to private judgment, and it realized the potential of the person as a guardian of law, once endowed with rights.

The novel for the English Jacobins was a means of edification, a vigorous and influential tool of inquiry, and a vehicle for defining subjectivity in the social contract. It was also a way to represent a vision of the future, while also navigating history. Bakhtin describes literature as a mechanism to "'embody' the world, to materialize it, to tie everything in to spatial and temporal series, to measure everything on the scale of the human body". But it is also a device "to construct" and to do so "on that space where the destroyed picture of the world had been – a new picture".[42] Art of the revolutionary period, Ronald Paulson notes, was about representing the "unprecedented", the "unknown" and the "unexperienced", at the same time that it was dependent on a historical referent and saw itself as "altering political action by the action of art".[43] It had to steer a course from the familiar to the unfamiliar.[44] The progressive novel in the 1790s was offering a critique that was also negotiating new possibilities and had to do so while acknowledging historical change and maintaining steadfast foundational principles.

The English Jacobin novel was contingent on a policy of perpetual re-evaluation according to historical circumstances, which was in direct contradiction to the ideological policy of prescription that held each age accountable to the traditions of preceding ones. As fiction that dealt in the future, in the possible, in the realm of "what if", and as a relatively new genre, the novel was a powerful ally for Paine's assertion that government is a function of continuous "creation" rather than "generation".[45] Moreover, by maintaining a tension between the macrocosm and the microcosm, the novel was able to present an argument *as if* the principles it was espousing arose from a specific moment in history and a given set of circumstances. In *Hermsprong*, Robert Bage is able to place a truly monolithic, mythical figure who embodies the best of the entrepreneur and landowner, the mediator and rebellious leader, the enfranchised man and the good husband all at the core of a historically and geographically specific configuration. By doing so, Bage was not only able to make this superman, at least for a fleeting moment, seem like an actual possibility, he was also able to elucidate the multifaceted and multivalent dynamic of the family and the self, in relation to property, such that the reader becomes aware of the status-delineated and gender-specific reality of property. His microcosms of familiar referents and indices of the everyday strategically infuse the chimerical vision of an enfranchised man with the promise of political realization.

While many of the Jacobin novelists argued their positions in political treatises, the novel offered them an opportunity to humanize, to particularize, to concretize the abstract, to explore further the influence of government on the nation, and challenge assumptions made about the extent of juridical authority. The use of narrative seemed, in many ways, the most obvious and necessary means of analyzing what Holcroft, echoing Godwin, called "one of the most palpable of truths" revealed by the French Revolution: that political institutions "essentially influence the morals and the happiness of the people, and that these institutes are capable of improvement".[46] As fictional representation, the novel was able to complicate the rigid ideological structures of political debate and occupy the space between the polarized points of the theoretical essay. There it could grapple with the messy contradictions otherwise hidden in the well-reasoned tract, delve into assumptions and premises of competing arguments, or (like the fiction of the contract), deftly place the politicized ideal within reach. It could also shift the logic of debate or discourage formal reasoning altogether. The novel required that one think inductively, beginning with the particular and moving toward general principles, or it forced one off the safe track of the syllogism into pockets of doubt where one was persuaded to consider the multifaceted dimensions of concepts such as property, contract, and self-determination. In either case, the novel was able to compromise and negotiate in ways that the persuasive essay was not.

A study of the English Jacobin novel's contribution to political theory of the late eighteenth century is one example of the novel's participation in the development of a bill of rights in modern culture. While fiction played a critical role in narrativizing advancements, it was not without its skeptics. Bentham warned that "the pestilential breath of Fiction poisons the sense of every instrument it comes near".[47] Thomas Paine implicates fiction in his criticism of Burke. Paine protests that Burke's *Reflections* "degenerates into a composition of art, and the genuine soul of nature forsakes him. His hero or his heroine must be a tragedy-victim expiring in show, and not the real prisoner of misery, sliding into death in the silence of a dungeon".[48] Art as artifice was dangerous and seductive, particularly in the rhetoric of the French Revolution (both for and against). But narrative was pervasive, and lines between fiction, narrative, and legal and political discourse were obscured. Paine himself follows his criticism of Burke's use of the literary arts with a gripping narrative of his own that describes events in France. Faced with the "equivocal spirit of law", the Jacobins sought to clarify the influence of natural and civil rights on life in the commonwealth by narrativizing the tragic consequences of things as they are, if they continue to be. But they also tried to show through fictional inquiry the expanse of human potential.

2
Debating Rights, Property, and the Law

The debate over natural and civil rights was a furious, ubiquitous exchange that dominated public discourse in the 1790s. Much was at stake in defining personal liberties and public duties: the configuration of the body politic and the direction of the modern state. One particular conflict that prevailed in the ensuing battle was a struggle between the family and the self-contained individual as the image and, more importantly, the site of political authority. From the essays of Sir Robert Filmer and John Locke on patriarchalism and government to the treatises on the social contract by Algernon Sidney, James Harrington, Jean-Jacques Rousseau, Edmund Burke and Thomas Paine, the exploration of the individual's relation to the state maintained a vibrant momentum that peaked in the excitement of the French Revolution. By the 1790s, the notion of liberty was either safely protected in the "inherited rights" of Burke's design or boldly redistributed to the "individual inalienable rights" advocated by Paine. One conception of rights was meant to contain the franchise, the other to extend it.

Royalists and absolutists invoked the image of the family as a symbol of government to legitimate monarchical and patriarchal rule. Sir Robert Filmer, in *Patriarcha: A Defence of the Natural Power of Kings against the Unnatural Liberty of the People* (c.1620–42),[1] bestows divine, natural, and historical authority on the absolute dominion of the monarch. The basis of his argument is the reciprocal support between the male head of household and the king. By "natural right of a supreme father", the sovereign commands allegiance, and correspondingly, by "natural right of regal power", our "obedience to kings is delivered in the terms of 'honour thy father' [Exodus, xx, 12] as if all power were originally in the father".[2] One form of paternal authority justifies the other. In a response to Hugo Grotius's *De Jure Belli ac Pacis* (1625), in which Grotius argues for a "primitive will" of the people, Filmer establishes the authority of the patriarchy through his characteristic reliance on Adam and a genetic theory of government.[3] Filmer maintains "the natural and private dominion of Adam to be the fountain of all government and property .... The ground why those that now live do obey their governors is the will of their forefathers, who at the first ordained princes – and in obedience to that will the children continue in subjection".[4]

Much of Filmer's discussion in *Patriarcha* revolves around the unlimited legislative power of the monarchy. The idea that the citizenry could legitimately rebel against a sovereign was preposterous because it implied a law superior to that of the king. According to Filmer, the sovereign was the principal lawmaker who is above and beyond his own laws, as a father is in his own home. "For as kingly power is by the law of God, so it hath no inferior law to limit it. The father of a family governs by no other law than by his own will, not by the laws or wills of his sons or servants".[5] Filmer's argument for the predominance of the king's law is dependent on the sovereign's commitment to the well-being of the community. But the assumed benevolence and good will that Filmer argues would monitor a sovereign's behaviour came under especially harsh attack by contract theorists and Jacobin novelists alike. *Noblesse oblige*, they retorted, does not offer the protection that individual rights, in theory, do because it provides no guarantee nor a means of contest and reparation. Political liberties, which Filmer attributes to the king's "grace", had to be extracted from what Filmer describes as a sacred contract between the king and his people "either originally in his ancestors, or personally at his coronation".[6]

While Filmer is often cited in explications of formal patriarchalism, and he himself claimed to be the source of the analogy between father and king, family and kingdom, scholars of Filmer's work are quick to point out that the comparison was hardly Filmer's innovation. *Patriarcha* was preceded by numerous other tracts on paternal authority, and, by the early seventeenth century, patriarchy was a common and familiar idea in royalist political theory.[7] Nonetheless, it was Filmer to whom Locke responded in his *Two Treatises of Government* (1690) and Algernon Sidney, in his *Discourses Concerning Government* (1698). *Patriarcha* offers a particularly vivid account of royalist thought and both marks the fading interest in absolute monarchy as a viable form of government and provides a source for the resurgence of concern for "the family" in the 1790s.

The image of the self-contained body emerged in contract theory to counter the influence of the family politically and economically. One of the more literal examples of the importance of the individual occurs in Rousseau's *Discourse on Political Economy* (1755), where Rousseau compares the body politic to the figure of an individual man. While drawing an analogy between government and the human body was, like formal patriarchalism, nothing new, it took on a renewed vigour in discussions of the social contract because it foregrounded a bounded self, comprised of several working parts, and illustrated an alternative vision of the individual's relation to the law. Rousseau explains:

> The body politic, taken individually, can be considered as an organized, living body and similar to that of a man. The sovereign power represents the head; the laws and customs are the brain, the center of the nervous system and seat of the understanding, the will and the senses, of which the judges and magistrates are the stomach which prepare the common subsistence; public finances are the blood that a wise *economy*, performing the functions of the heart, sends back to distribute nourishment and life throughout the body; the citizens are the body and members which make the machine move, live, and work, and which cannot be injured in any way without a painful sensation being transmitted right to the brain, if the animal is in a state of good health.
>
> The life of both together is the *self* common to the whole, the reciprocal sensibility and the internal connection between all the parts.[8]

One of the more interesting facets of Rousseau's description of the body politic is his version of reciprocity. The primary reciprocal relationship between king and father in royalist discourse gives way to a focus on the complex relationship between law, economics, and the citizenry.[9] Concern for the happiness of the multitude of body parts (the citizenry) and the belief that its well-being will have an impact on the brain (the law) indicates an altered conception of the relationship between the enfranchised populace and juridical institutions.[10] Interest in the authority of the citizenry does not deny the subjection of persons to the law; it does, however, suggest a more empowered position for them. The people's potential rebellion becomes a force that must be reckoned with, and their participation in the community as a whole will presumably be reflected in policy. Moreover, in Rousseau's portrait of the body politic, law emerges in the central role it holds in a republic. It has arguably the most significant function as the site of the understanding and will, and although it is encased in the sovereign/head, it bears no systematic relation to those trappings. The head is a mere vessel.

Rousseau's blueprint for the body politic has its roots in seventeenth-century contractarian discourse on the ascendancy of the juridical.[11] Locke, for example, also argued for the supremacy of law in the commonwealth – not the king's law, but law that has the consent of a citizenry. "The *legislative*", Locke explained, "is not only *the supreme power* of the common-wealth, but sacred and unalterable in the hands where the community have once placed it".[12] In *Two Treatises*, as Locke dismantled Filmer's argument, he worked to reconfigure the legislative and to establish the integrity of the individual distinct from the family. His motivation was twofold: an interest in obtaining both civil equity and religious toleration.[13] Locke is passionately persuasive about the inseparability of civil and religious liberty, and with good reason. Anti-toleration legislation was firmly in place, and it meant persecution and exile for Roman Catholics and Protestant Dissenters. The Corporation Act of 1661 required all office-holders to take "the sacrament according to the rites of the Church of England", and the Test Acts of 1673 and 1678 denied public office to anyone unwilling to renounce the Pope and the doctrine of transubstantiation. The second Test Act (1678) also specifically excluded Roman Catholics from membership in both Houses of Parliament.[14]

Passed in May of 1689, the Toleration Act offered some relief to non-conformist Protestants; they were allowed to meet publicly and worship. This act, however, still prohibited dissenting Protestants and Roman Catholics from holding public office, and it left the Corporation and Test Acts in place.[15] Locke, in his *Letter Concerning Toleration* (1689), argues the benefits of religious freedoms for the community.[16] He asserts the separation of church and state by maintaining that "the Power of Civil Government relates only to Mens Civil Interests, is confined to the care of the things of this World, and hath nothing to do with the World to come". In the skeptical tradition, he also justifies separation by refusing to acknowledge any single church as the consummate religious institution closest to the spiritual truth.[17] Furthermore, Locke relies on a respect for *personal* commitment, understanding, and faith. He defends the privilege of individual religious freedom in the face of the Anglican Church's attempt to reassert its strength: "Whatsoever may be doubtful in Religion, yet this at least is certain, that no Religion, which I believe not to be true, can be either true, or profitable unto me".[18] Locke first wrote his *Letter Concerning Toleration* while in exile in Amsterdam, driven abroad because of his participation in politically subversive activities between 1679 and 1683. His plea for toleration would certainly have served his personal interests, but, if taken in a practical vein, Locke's *Letter* went beyond self interest and offered the crown advice on the inefficacy of coercive allegiance.[19]

One of the cornerstones of *Two Treatises* and *A Letter Concerning Toleration* is the right to rebel and then dissolve government if necessary. In *Two Treatises*, Locke's stance largely counteracts Filmer's unwillingness to acknowledge any form of legitimate resistance to the crown. Filmer's position is consistent with his conception of absolute governance and obedience, but it was also a means of silencing religious/political dissent. As he does in his *Letter*, Locke gives advice about the expedience of toleration:

> [W]hen the *People* are made *miserable*, and find themselves *exposed to the ill usage of Arbitrary Power*, cry up their Governours, as much as you will for Sons of *Jupiter*, let them be Sacred and Divine, descended or authoriz'd from Heaven; give them out for whom or what you please, the same will happen. *The People generally ill treated*, and contrary to right, will be ready upon any occasion to ease themselves of a burden that sits heavy upon them. They will wish and seek for the opportunity, which, in the change, weakness, and accidents of humane affairs, seldom delays long to offer it self.[20]

The right to rebel is one of the principles that distinguishes contractarians from royalists or absolutists. In the latter traditions, the people are said to alienate their political power "absolutely" to a sovereign, whereas contractarians recognize some inalienable rights, for example, the ability to withdraw their support from a sovereign and confer political authority on another. Both Locke and Rousseau cite the inevitability of dissension and its rightfulness based on what Locke defines as the *"end or measure"* of government: the preservation of society, of "all Mankind in general".[21] Rousseau is particularly adamant about inalienable liberty. In a chapter of *On Social Contract* suggestively entitled "Slavery", Rousseau discusses what it means to "alienate"; it is "to give or to sell", he writes, and people do not willingly do so to subject themselves to the possible "insatiable greed" and "vexations" of a monarch. "To renounce one's liberty", he contends, "is to renounce one's humanity, the rights of humanity and even its duties". Any agreement requiring one to give up freedom of will and to submit to unlimited obedience is "vain and contradictory" and a form of slavery.[22]

Pivotal in Locke's discussion in *Two Treatises*, as well as in all contractarian arguments, is the separation of family and state. "[T]he *Paternal* is a natural *Government*", Locke concedes, "but not at all extending it self to the Ends, and Jurisdictions of that which is Political". "*Parental Power*", Locke continues, "is nothing but that which Parents have over their Children, to govern them for the Childrens good".[23] Through his insistence on distinguishing political from domestic constructs, Locke enables the emergence of political individualism. The subject as child, in royalist writings, gives way to the citizen as adult in contractarian discourse. Moreover, Locke's measurement of maturity is the person's ability to interact with the law in an aggressive way. The mark of having outgrown parental jurisdiction (by one's parents or the crown) is the ability to reason, understand the law, and govern oneself. The foundation of control that Locke establishes is in the individual who consents to bequeath his power – the political power one holds in a state of nature – to a designated legislative body in civil society, as if it were transferred to a "trust".[24] One may alienate certain authority to institutions, but what Locke is beginning to consider is the idea that one retains the privileges and responsibilities of self-governance in civil society.[25]

The origin of law in the consent of the community is a principle that Locke repeats throughout *Two Treatises*. Of particular interest in Locke's essays is his effort to keep the integral individual distinct from the law. In his chapter on the "Extent of the Legislative Power", as Locke discusses the limits of law, he explains that the power of the legislative "can be no more than those persons had in a State of Nature before they enter'd into Society, and gave up to the Community. For no Body can transfer to another more power than he has in himself; and no Body has an absolute Arbitrary Power over himself, or over any other, to destroy his own Life, or take away the Life or Property of another". The focus on an observable power in the self, that must not be tampered with, assumes an autonomy that is meant to offer protection from external and internal tyrannies. By outlining the boundaries of the self, Locke situates the parameters of law and the responsibilities of the individual toward himself. "A Man, as has been proved", Locke continues, "cannot subject himself to the Arbitrary Power of another.... It [legislative power] is a Power, that hath no other end but preservation, and therefore can never have a right to destroy, enslave, or designedly to impoverish the Subjects".[26] Rejecting arbitrary subject-hood, Locke insists on the following: in the state of nature one has dominion over no one but oneself, the first rule of intent is self-preservation and the preservation of mankind, and when one alienates one's power in entering a commonwealth it is to a legislative institution. The legislative takes the seat of authority left vacant by the monarch, and the individual is protected from tyranny of the law by certain rights to self-governance.

Another significant response to Filmer that helps to illuminate the figure of the individual in contract theory is Algernon Sidney's *Discourses Concerning Government*. Sidney also takes issue with Filmer's analogy of father and king. "I suppose it may be safely concluded", he writes, "that what right soever a father may have over his family, it cannot relate to that which a king has over his people".[27] In addition, he questions the viability of considering the king immune to the restrictions of law. If there is no means of correction for a king who transgresses his authority or neglects his job as caretaker of the kingdom, then what guarantee is there that he will look out for the best interests of his kingdom? If there is no means of redress, how can a body of people protect themselves against misuse? In Sidney's queries, certain assumptions about "the people" are clearly at work. He presumes, as Locke does, that the people have *agency*, a foundational ability to reclaim the political authority they alienate when entering into a community. He takes it for granted that persons elect to belong to a commonwealth, and that they do so because they consider it a profitable undertaking. Sidney describes the civil body as "a collation of every man's private right into a publick stock" driven by the belief that it will be beneficial. "[N]othing could induce them to join", he argues, "and lessen that natural liberty by joining in societies, but the hope of a publick advantage".[28] In passages that echo Hobbes, Sidney points to human weaknesses, the "fierce barbarity of a loose multitude, bound by no law, and regulated by no discipline". But his remedy calls for a collective response: "[t]he first step towards the cure of this pesti-lent evil, is for many to join in one body, that everyone may be pro-tected by the united force of all; and the various talents that men possess, may by good discipline be rendered useful to the whole".[29] The "united force of all" is manifest in a system of laws subject to change by a people who have not relinquished their agency.

The "freemen" who constitute Sidney's notion of "the people" are distinguished by the characteristics Locke also identified: economic independence, the capacity for rational thought, and self-governance.

The most important was self-governance because it marked the individual as a self-contained entity with agential powers and because it became both the reward of the commonwealth and the requirement for political participation. "[T]he liberty we contend for", Sidney explains, "is granted by God to *every man in his own person*, in such a manner as may be useful to him and his posterity".[30] The individual who is "led by reason which is his nature" is "his own judge".[31] Moreover, reason is what enables the newly empowered individual to temper the pursuit of personal success and consider the interests of the collective. "He that enquires more exactly into the matter may find", Sidney writes, "that reason enjoins every man not to arrogate to himself more than he allows to others, nor to retain that liberty which will prove hurtful to him; or to expect that others will suffer themselves to be restrain'd, whilst he, to their prejudice, remains in the exercise of that freedom which nature allows".[32] Sidney frequently reminds us (as Locke does), that the purpose of the commonwealth is an improvement of the community at large, and the desired result of forming a body politic and asserting individual freedoms is general prosperity.

The integral figure that emerges in these few excerpts from Rousseau, Locke, and Sidney worked, theoretically, to free persons from the bonds of familial structures. Hampering this liberation, however, were the restrictions built into these developments. Not everyone could meet the criteria of the discrete individual. The strong sense of self that was so much a *product* of Locke's idea of a commonwealth also became a *requirement* for activity in the commonwealth. The characteristics of reason, understanding, property, and self-governance that enabled one to be a citizen were not so easy to come by and immediately eliminated those who were financially dependent, and therefore politically dependent. What on one level seemed to be a gesture toward inclusion – an expansion of the franchise and a reconfiguration of the body politic – on another worked to marginalize those who could not meet the specifications of legal subjecthood. Who was to be included in the collective of "mankind" and who was to participate in the compact of government were among the questions debated throughout the long eighteenth century in the public domain of pamphlets, speeches, essays, and the novel.

Particularly telling, in the modern history of British enfranchisement, were the Putney Debates of 1647–49.[33] This exchange of ideas about what constituted political authority revealed that, in addition to gender, economic dependence limited one's access to civil liberties. The

Levellers' mid-seventeenth-century campaign for extended franchisement stirred discussion of exclusion in attempts to determine the "proprietors" of civil society. In the Debates, the Levellers presented an argument that, according to Keith Thomas, emerged from several years of parliamentary bids to widen civil participation.[34] The Levellers proposed that "freemen" be considered eligible for the vote, but what they meant by "freemen" is not entirely clear. Colonel Thomas Rainborough, a key player on behalf of the Levellers, seemed to be supporting universal manhood suffrage when he insisted that "the poorest he that is in England hath a life to live, as the greatest he; and therefore ... every man that is to live under a government ought first by his own consent to put himself under that government".[35] However, Sir William Petty, who was also a Leveller, acknowledged exceptions in what some critics have maintained was a compromise position put forward to pacify opponents.[36] Only "inhabitants that have not lost their birthright", he asserts, "should have an equal voice in elections". Those who are financially dependent are the ones who have surrendered their birthright and thereby forfeited political participation. "The reason why we would exclude apprentices, or servants, or those that take alms", Petty explains, "is because they depend upon the will of other men and should be afraid to displease [them]. For servants and apprentices, they are included in their masters, and so for those that receive alms from door to door".[37] Whatever the individual or collective intent of the Levellers, the result of the Putney Debates was a final version of the "Agreement of the People" in which servants and alms-takers were eliminated from the franchise because they were financially liable to another party.[38]

One of the key points of dissension in the Putney Debates, which re-emerged in the controversy over natural rights in the 1790s, was the role of natural law in a socio-political framework. Obedience to a legal authority (the king), Richard Gleissner contends, was of preeminent importance to Commissary General Henry Ireton and those interested in preserving the social order.[39] When Rainborough made his plea that franchisement be extended to "the poorest", Ireton cited the danger of recognizing inalienable liberties in a response that presages Burke: "if you make this the rule I think you must fly for refuge to an absolute natural right, and you must deny all civil right".[40] Only those who have "a permanent fixed interest in this kingdom", only "the persons in whom all land lies, and those in corporations in whom all trading lies", Ireton argued, should "choose the represeners for the making of laws by which this state and kingdom are to be governed".[41] Also anticipating Burke, Ireton feared that the acknowledgment of natural rights would inevitably lead to anarchy and a loss of property through a process akin to theft.

A similar desire (or perceived need) to circumscribe political liberty surfaced as well in works of later eighteenth-century contractarians. In his *Essay on the First Principles of Government* (1768), for example, Joseph Priestley both establishes himself as an important advocate of the social contract[42] and outlines some of its limitations. He embraces political equality as a first principle and bases his theory on a maxim "that *every government, whatever be the form of it, is originally, and antecedent to its present form, an equal republic*".[43] He also declares that in an ideal civil society every member of the commonwealth should have "a chance of arriving at a share in the chief magistracy".[44] Yet Priestley relinquishes the idea of a "perfect political liberty" through which all members of a community would have equal opportunities to participate in government.[45] While making claims to the existence of certain inalienable natural rights that would not "deny all civil right" as Burke argued, Priestley steps back from endorsing "perfect equality" which cannot be preserved "while some are more powerful, more enterprising, and more successful in their attempts than others".[46] He considers practical restraints on political liberty and concludes that

> none but persons of considerable fortune should be capable of arriving at the highest offices in the government; not only because, all other circumstances being equal, such persons will generally have had the best education, and consequently be the best qualified to act for the public good; but also, as they will necessarily have the most property at stake, and will, therefore, be most interested in the fate of their country.[47]

Moreover, Priestley somewhat hesitantly decides that those who are too dependent may have to be excluded from political participation. In a passage that echoes the concerns of Sir William Petty in the Putney Debates, Priestley suggests that "it may, perhaps, be more eligible, that those who are extremely dependent should not be allowed to have votes in the nomination of the chief magistrates; because this might in some instances, be only throwing more votes into the hands of those persons on whom they depend". As an alternative, Priestley proposes a kind of prorated system of participation that allows for some advancement. He suggests that "in every state of considerable extent, we suppose a gradation of elective officers, and, as they increase in wealth and importance, to have a share in the choice of persons to fill the higher posts, till they themselves be admitted candidates for places of public trust".[48] Priestley's concessions to a "practical" political and civil liberty are indicative of the kinds of limitations incorporated into the post-revolutionary social contract.[49]

The emphasis on property and its link to civil and political liberty that surfaced so strikingly in the Putney Debates re-emerged with a vengeance in the public discourse of the 1790s. Contractarianism was dominated by the idea, articulated most concisely by Locke, that property originates in an ownership of the self. In his *Two Treatises*, Locke establishes a natural right of property, derived from natural law;[50] he claims that "every Man has a *Property* in his own *Person*. This no Body has any Right to but himself. The *Labour* of his Body, and the *Work* of his Hands, we may say, are properly his".[51] "By *Property*", he reasserts, "I must be understood here, as in other places, to mean that Property which Men have in their Persons as well as Goods".[52] Locke's conception of property had enormous implications for political theory, such that it continues to be a thorny issue among contemporary scholars. There seems to be some agreement about James Tully's assertion that "property", in Locke's definition, refers not only to the property itself but also to the *right* of property.[53] Still, there is much disagreement about the ownership of property produced by one's labour. Locke's statement that "the Grass my Horse has bit; the Turfs my Servant has cut; and the Ore I have digg'd in any place where I have a right to them in common with others, become my *Property*", has led to a myriad of contentious interpretations because it seems that the servant, miner, and other similar workers are not able to claim the property of *their* labour. Some scholars, such as C.B. Macpherson, have read the latter passage as a statement of the bourgeois position on the profits of employment and an assumption that the wage relationship is natural.[54] Others have seen it as a response to a specific set of listeners; Richard Ashcraft, for example, contends that Locke was writing to an artisan audience.[55]

Two major points gleaned from Locke's thought were vital to public discourse in the 1790s. The first, discussed at length by James Tully, is that the term "property" in the seventeenth century referred, among other things, to "personal rights, especially religious and civil liberties".[56] When Locke writes that "[t]he great and *chief end*, therefore, of Mens uniting into Commonwealths, and putting themselves under Government, *is the Preservation of their Property*", he is referring not only to "goods" but more importantly to those civil and religious liberties that allow one to function in society as a full legal subject.[57] The second critical point is that the right of property is a natural, or an *a priori* right – that is, it precedes and exists independently of civil society – and it is transferred to a civil authority for protection, not alienation. Regarding the right of property as a natural right under-mined assumptions about the security of property and had the potential to toss the distribution of wealth and the transferal of wealth through inheritance into flux. It also indicated a primary shift in the basis for political authority.

By the end of the eighteenth century, Locke and other contractarians had already established that political authority "has its original only from compact and agreement, and the mutual consent of those who make up the community".[58] Discussing society as a contract was not exclusive to contractarians or proponents of natural rights; royalists were defending the "compact" of government that was the product of the Revolution of 1688.[59] At issue was the consent of the community and the constitution of the enfranchised populace. And at its core was the self-governing individual. "For what Compact can be made", Locke asks, "with a Man that is not Master of his own Life?"[60] The conditions that contract theorists were beginning to establish for the reconstitu-tion of the body politic offered a form of emancipation for Dissenters and others suffering from religious persecution. These conditions were not liberating, however, for those who could not claim to be masters of their own lives: women, servants, and beggars. Financial dependence kept them vulnerable, and, in the case of women, the belief that the female sex was deficient in reasoning powers prohibited them from making the claim that they could govern themselves. Mental stability in terms of "Truth and keeping of Faith", Locke contends, is one of the components of property – that is, capacities of self – that "belongs to Men, as Men, and not as Members of Society".[61] One could not be trusted to participate in government unless one had a sound mind.

Property maintained its central place in the discourse of contractari-ans throughout the late seventeenth and eighteenth centuries. It was the operative force in James Harrington's *Commonwealth of Oceana* (1656), a recommendation for restructuring English government into a commonwealth where political power is a direct function of owner-ship (particularly of land).[62] Harrington outlines two principles of government for his discussion: "internal, or the goods of the mind, and external, or the goods of fortune". Internal principles refer to "natural or acquired virtues", such as wisdom and courage, and they exact "authority"; external principles are "riches", and they command "power or empire". In *Oceana*, Harrington is primarily concerned with the economics of power, for example, the distribution of wealth and its corresponding alignments of political advantage. "[W]here there is inequality of estates", Harrington writes, "there must be inequality of power", and "where there is inequality of power, there can be no commonwealth".[63] Harrington also defines different forms of government in terms of their balance of property; for example, "[i]f one man be sole landlord of a territory, ... his empire is absolute monarchy".[64]

Assuming that monarchy is already an obsolete mode of government, Harrington envisaged a citizenry of "proprietors". His argument, extensively documented with historical evidence, often focuses on the military situation of a country – a situation he directly connects to its economic organization.[65] According to Harrington, the intense concentration of wealth that characterized the monarchy left a nation vulnerable to *coup d'états*. "Where a conqueror finds the riches of a land in the hands of the few, the forfeitures are easy, and amount to vast advantage". Conversely, the distribution of wealth among "the people" enhances national security. "[W]here the people have equal shares, the confiscation of many comes to little, and is not only dangerous but fruitless".[66] Moreover, to create a nation of subjects, as occurs in a monarchy, is to weaken the defense of the country. In the case of military threats from without, once the heads of power are removed, "the rest being all slaves you hold her without any further resistance". Regarding insurrections from within, an equal apportionment of property would quell disturbances because everyone would have an interest in securing peace. "Men that have equal possessions and the same security of their estates and of their liberties that you have, have the same cause with you to defend; but if you will be trampling, they fight for liberty".[67]

Harrington places more weight on the role of property in citizenship than Locke and other contractarians. For Harrington, property (perhaps more in terms of actual wealth than rights) protects one from the tyranny of others, and it is this freedom that makes one capable of functioning in a commonwealth. Yet *Oceana* and an additional essay on the commonwealth as political organization, *The Prerogative of Popular Government* (1658), raise significant questions about whom Harrington had in mind when he referred to "the people". Christopher Hill has argued that he meant what we would consider the middle class, "yeomen, merchants, gentlemen"; C.B. Macpherson has insisted that Harrington envisioned a "gentry-led commonwealth"; and J.G.A. Pocock defines "the people" in Harrington as "independent freeholders".[68]

Whatever the case, there is no evidence that Harrington meant to distribute wealth to absolutely everyone. His vision of a commonwealth assumes individual proprietorship for those considered part of "the people", and consequently it assumes the exclusion of certain segments of the population. The significance of property, in terms of personhood, individual liberties, and wealth, was crucial to Harrington, Locke, and those who were trying to mould the new commonwealth, and it became one of their most significant legacies.

The controversies, then, between seventeenth-century royalists, absolutists, republicans, and contractarians are revisited in the debate over natural and civil rights of the 1790s. At the heart of the late eighteenth-century dialogue was an interpretation of rights and an investigation of the individual's relationship to civil society. Sparked by Dr Richard Price's sermon *A Discourse on the love of our country*, delivered November 4, 1789 (the anniversary of the Revolution of 1688), a flurry of responses ensued that proved to be some of the most important documents written on the modern concept of rights.[69] In his sermon, Price advocated three resolutions that had been agreed upon by the Revolution Society: the right of the English people to choose their own governors, cashier them for misconduct, and form their own government. The resolutions were provocative enough, but Price also passionately congratulated France on her rebellion against tyranny at the fall of the Bastille and indicated that he saw France as heralding a new order for Europe. He stated his support of the French Revolution, however, only at the close of his sermon and in a congratulatory address drawn up by the Revolution Society at a meeting in the London Tavern after the sermon was over. The focus of Price's texts was the development of a policy of individual rights that he regarded as the legacy of the Glorious Revolution. Price considered it the business of Dissenters and other reformers to continue the work implied in the principles established by the English revolution – principles that began to consider the extension of enfranchisement. The celebrated resolutions Price articulated were in fact drawn from the Dissenting tradition; as recently as the previous year, 1788, the Revolution Society passed similar resolutions after listening to a sermon by the Reverend Dr Andrew Kippis.[70] In addition to the three primary resolutions on government were others that asserted a liberty of conscience in theological matters. The declaration of religious freedom was a direct reference to the penal laws that continued to restrict the access of Dissenters to public office. One of the benefits Protestant Dissenters realized from the Glorious Revolution was the right to worship, authorized by the Toleration Act of 1689, yet they did not enjoy the full range of rights available to Anglicans. Repeal of the Test and Corporation Acts had been debated in Parliament from 1787 until 1790 when the third application for repeal failed to pass.[71] This was one of the pieces of unfinished business that Price insisted must be addressed. In his sermon, therefore, he encouraged further attempts at repealing the Test and Corporation Acts that continued to prohibit Dissenters from holding office.[72]

Responses to Price's sermon were swift and passionate. Edmund Burke's fervid rebuttal, *Reflections on the Revolution in France* (1790), strategically shifted the focus away from the controversy over religious freedom in England to the events in revolutionary France. Although Burke had at one time courted the electoral support of Dissenters, he abstained from earlier votes on the Test and Corporation Acts, and he eventually opposed its repeal because he saw it as a precursor to an outright attack on the Church of England.[73] Fully cognizant that the conflict with Dissenters was an issue of British legislation, Burke, in his response to Prices' sermon, still played on British fears of the French Revolution to exaggerate the danger of reform.[74] Despite Burke's attempt to cloud the issue at hand, the exchange of essays that followed illuminated the critical controversy over the definitions of "natural" and "civil" rights. What emerged was that both sides considered liberty to be "property", and both sides desired the protection of that property, but they defined the mechanism for achieving this end in different terms. Burke regarded liberty as prudently contained in "inherited rights", while Paine, Wollstonecraft, and other respondents to Burke's *Reflections* conceived of liberty as necessarily redistributed to "individual inalienable rights".

In *Reflections*, Burke is concerned only with civil rights – liberties that exist within the confines of civil society. He denies the existence of individual natural (*a priori*) rights that one retains in civil society and rejects the contractarian idea that liberty is contained in a birthright. Instead, Burke proposes that liberty is an "entailed inheritance", bequeathed to us by our forefathers and intended to be transmitted to posterity.[75] Our rights are likened to an "estate", and through "a constitutional policy, working after the pattern of nature, we receive, we hold, we transmit our government and our privileges, in the same manner in which we enjoy and transmit our property and our lives". The guarantees and privileges contained in rights are therefore subject to the legal framework of inheritance, the family, and the control of wealth. In addition, Burke borrows the term "natural" from proponents of *a priori* rights and endows his concept of inherited liberty with the validity of natural law by claiming that it is a system patterned after and conforming to nature. "This [constitutional] policy", Burke comments, "appears to me to be ... the happy effect of following nature, which is wisdom without reflection, and above it". The inheritance of "privileges, franchises, and liberties, from a long line of ancestors" renders the political system "in a just correspondence and symmetry with the order of the world". That "order" is a biological one of "perpetual decay, fall, renovation, and progression", and as such the "method of nature" can be found "in the conduct of the state".[76]

Burke confers natural (and eventually divine) authority on his system of rights, even though he relies on secular law for its protection. The most influential legal theorists of the eighteenth century, however, consistently stressed the civil basis of laws of inheritance. The Baron de Montesquieu, in his *Spirit of the Laws* (1748), agrees that "it is an obligation of the law of nature to provide for our children". "[B]ut", he continues, "to make them our successors is an obligation of the civil or political law". In other words, "the Order of succession or Inheritance depends on the Principles of political or civil Law, and not on those of the Law of Nature".[77] Similarly, Sir William Blackstone, in his *Commentaries on the Laws of England* (1765–69), distinguishes the management of liberty from the control of real property (land) and wealth. One of the basic divisions in the organization of his book is between the rights of persons and the rights of things. The right to private property is defined as a right of persons, but dominion over that property, including inheritance, is defined as a right of things. "[T]here is no foundation in nature or in natural law", Blackstone argues,

> why a set of words upon parchment should convey the dominion of land; why the sons should have a right to exclude his fellow creatures from a determinate spot of ground, because his father had done so before him; or why the occupier of a particular field or of a jewel, when lying on his death-bed and no longer able to maintain possession, should be entitled to tell the rest of the world which of them should enjoy it after him.[78]

One of the implications Burke draws from his own argument about a theory of rights patterned after nature is the resulting importance of what he calls the "unerring and powerful instincts" needed to strengthen the "fallible and feeble contrivances of our reason". For the protection of our rights and privileges, and to guarantee the tempering of an unwieldy "spirit of freedom" that threatened to undermine the stability of Britain, Burke turns his faith toward that which is in our "nature" and in our "breasts". He relies on our reverence in "the presence of canonized forefathers" rather than on the "speculations" or "inventions" of our reason.[79] In spite of his discomfort with an abstract concept of rights and the use of a principle as a foundation of government, Burke depends on abstractions of his own, such as the spiritual relationship in the continuum of generations. To Burke there had occurred an evolution from the Magna Carta to the Declaration of Right, producing a constitution based on the cumulative historical experience of the great "partnership" that spans generations. It is the *civil* social contract that emerged out of the Revolution of 1688 that Burke wished to defend[80] and to "naturalize" on the historical basis of its evolution and on the spiritual grounds of the collectivity it represents.[81] "Each contract", Burke writes, "... is but a clause in the great primeval contract of eternal society, linking the lower with the higher natures, connecting the visible and invisible world, according to a fixed compact sanctioned by the inviolable oath, which holds all physical and all moral natures, each in their appointed place", and society is a "partnership not only between those who are living, but between those who are living, those who are dead, and those who are to be born".[82] This omnipotent contract is the source of Burke's doctrine of prescription (authority based on possession and/or long usage), which is also a means of protecting property.[83] It is the origin of an inviolable law to which all must submit, and it renders other contracts merely "municipal corporations" subordinate to the "universal kingdom" of the eternal society. No reform is justifiable unless it works without a breach of this ahistorical (arguably divine) decree, and each generation remains answerable to a civil social contract as a power greater than itself.

Burke recognizes the "real" rights of men only within a municipal context. "If civil society be made for the advantage of man, all the advantages for which it is made become his right .... for I have in my contemplation the civil social man, and no other". For Burke the "rights of man" are expansive. "Whatever each man can separately do, without trespassing upon others, he has a right to do for himself; and he has a right to a fair portion of all which society, with all its combinations of skill and force, can do in his favour". However, they do not necessarily include governance. "But as to the share of power, authority, and direction which each individual ought to have in the management of the state", Burke argues, "that I must deny to be amongst the direct original rights of man in civil society".[84] Some elements of Burke's scheme echo contract theory: the concern with justice, the recognition of the right to the product of one's industry, and the acknowledgment of the ability to do what one desires as long as it does not impinge on the freedoms of others.[85] Yet there are decisive differences. One of the most fundamental is the suggestion that law is "beneficence acting by a rule".[86] Attributing juridical decisions to benevolence harks back to Filmer's reliance on the good will of a monarch, and it is a refusal to acknowledge rights that would protect one from charity gone awry.

Burke calls natural rights "metaphysic" and "primitive", rights that "undergo such a variety of refractions and reflections, that it becomes absurd to talk of them as if they continued in the simplicity of their original direction".[87] Convention must determine rights, according to Burke, and "limit and modify all the descriptions of constitution which are formed under it". All legislative and executory powers are "creatures" of that convention and can have "no being in any other state of things". But what is perhaps most striking about Burke's analysis of political authority is his rejection of self-governance: "One of the first motives to civil society, and which becomes one of its fundamental rules, is, *that no man should be judge in his own cause*. By this each person has at once divested himself of the first fundamental right of uncovenanted man, that is, to judge for himself, and to assert his own cause".[88] Society is a covenant of faith to Burke, and when the individual enters into a covenant, he relinquishes certain individual liberties, particularly that of private judgment and a jurisdiction over the self. Once under the necessary government of an external power, one then considers the *restraints* on liberty to be among one's rights.

Burke's faith in convention and the predominance of law is the basis of his acceptance of the English Revolution of 1688 and his passionate intolerance of the revolution in France. The only "principles" of the Glorious Revolution, Burke claims, are grounded in "the statute called the *Declaration of Right*", a "most wise, sober, and considerate declaration, drawn up by great lawyers and great statesmen, and not by warm and inexperienced enthusiasts". In the Declaration, furthermore, no mention is made of Kippis's and Price's resolutions, "not one word is said, nor one suggestion made, of a general right 'to choose our own *governors*; to cashier them for misconduct; and to *form* a government for *ourselves*'". Still in debate, however, is the origin of political authority. For Burke, the Declaration of Right places rights in a legal statute, and the conflicts over origins dissolve with the acceptance of prescription. But a sovereign will of the people would violate the civil social contract because it would be a claim of individual power existing outside of that contract. Also important in Burke's aversion to the resolutions of the Revolution Society is the threat to the succession of power as it is guaranteed by the Declaration of Right. To Burke, the rights of liberty and the political process of hereditary succession are "in one body, and bound indissolubly together".[89] Any human interventions threaten to transgress the "great primeval contract of eternal society" and the universal law identified by Burke.

The images of the family that were so important to seventeenth-century patriarchalism resurface in Burke's theory of rights. Burke argues that the benefits one derives from inherited rights "are locked fast as in a sort of family settlement" and are "grasped as in a kind of mortmain for ever". The state maintains "the image of a relation in blood", Burke continues, by "binding up the constitution of our country with our dearest domestic ties; adopting our fundamental laws into the bosom of our family affections".[90] Yet Burke's use of the "family" is far more literal and descriptive than Filmer's in his analogy of father and king. Burke's arrangement goes well beyond comparison to point to a direct relationship between the benefits one derives from rights and the control and transmission of familial property. Liberty is, *in fact*, locked fast in family settlements and grasped in mortmains forever. The state is more than just an *image* of a family relation, it functions in direct socio-economic connection to the management of familial estates and the laws governing family property. The constitution of the country (constitution both in terms of content and political ordinance) *is* bound with domestic ties, and the laws of the state *are* at the heart of the family. Burke acknowledges and particularizes the intimate relationship between the family and the state when a bit later in his essay he writes of the strong links between the family and the structure of the government:

> The perpetuation of property in our families is the most valuable and most interesting circumstance attending it, that which demonstrates most of a benevolent disposition in its owners, and that which tends most to the perpetuation of society itself. The possessors of family wealth, and of the distinction which attends hereditary possession (as most concerned in it) are the natural securities for this transmission. With us, the house of peers is formed upon this principle. It is wholly composed of hereditary property and hereditary distinction; and made therefore the third of the legislature; and

in the last event, the sole judge of all property in all its subdivisions. The house of commons too, though not necessarily, yet in fact, is always so composed in the far greater part.[91]

Political power, then, is derived from the fundamental participatory requirement of family property. In the tripartite structure of power only the House of Commons functions outside of the process of familial inheritance, and even those elections are, by and large, controlled by the Crown and the House of Lords.[92] The family, for Burke, goes a long way to ensure national security. It guarantees the continuation of society by encouraging virtue and checking greed, it stabilizes government, and it monitors property. The tight control over property by modeling everything after the process of hereditary succession meant the containment of political power and the ability to stave off its disbursements into individual rights. The grand design of inheritance, as "the order of the world", legitimated certain positive laws governing the accumulation and transferal of property.[93] Burke's justification of large concentrations of wealth because of the political strength and stability they provide – "[l]et those large proprietors be what they will, and they have their chance of being amongst the best, they are at the very worst, the ballast in the vessel of the commonwealth" – easily authorized, for example, the practice of primogeniture that guaranteed the continuation of consolidated resources.[94] It sanctioned, as well, multiple restrictions on women's access to property, which in turn left women subject to the manipulations of other family members who expected to control the family's property. Within the maneuvers of property transactions, however, were the orchestrations of political authority and the opportunities to participate in economic, legal, and political life.

Price's sermon and Burke's *Reflections* together occasioned several more responses, especially by contractarians who endorsed inalienable rights and government by contract.[95] The theory of inalienable rights in the 1790s professed the existence of certain rights the individual retains when entering civil society. Like its seventeenth-century precursors in contractarianism, it located the source of political power in the individual, recognized the appropriateness of rebellion, and established the importance of self-governance. Liberty was again regarded as "property", but property in terms of both "person" and "goods" and the rights necessary to protect them. Ownership of the self was necessary to agency, and it was agency – always in the context of civic duty – that was largely at stake in the ongoing debates.

The strength of the contractarian movement continued to come from the Dissenting tradition.[96] Two of the leading radical spokespersons – Richard Price and Joseph Priestley – and two of the most influential publishers – Joseph Johnson and Ralph Griffiths – were prominent Dissenters. In addition, reformist organizations, such as the Society for Constitutional Information and the London Corresponding Society, boasted a large membership of religious non-conformists.[97] Their pervasive visibility has led critics such as Marilyn Butler to conclude that rational Dissenters were the most "coherent" body of reformers active in the late eighteenth century.[98] The conceptual interests and the political needs of Dissenters rendered them appropriate leaders of a "rights of man" campaign. Their beliefs in individual conscience, private worship and a separation of church and state would be well served by an official recognition of inalienable rights. Moreover, an atmosphere of tolerance might lead to a repeal of the Test and Corporation Acts and allow them full participation in civil society.

The work of the Dissenters is also a good reminder that the debates of the 1790s were about British politics, not French philosophy. In spite of attempts, sometimes on both sides, to deflect attention toward revolutionary France, British reform efforts persisted. While Burke looked to France to raise fears, Dissenters turned abroad for international support.[99] Dissenters, however, were not thoroughly enamored of the thinking of the French *philosophes*. As Seamus Deane points out, eminent non-conformists such as Joseph Priestley considered social change only within a Christian context. The libertinism, atheism, or overall secularization of thought that characterized the ideologies of the French Revolution was at odds with the doctrines that Dissenting ministers preached. Deane rightly describes the position of the Dissenters as "permanently compromised".[100] They could support the French Revolution for the system of rights it advocated, but they could not endorse much of the French intellectual tradition that had come to be associated with revolutionary activities. As a result, while they looked to France early on for the fiery blossoming of the "rights of man", they kept a clear focus on events in Britain and the development of civil and religious liberties for British people.

Although she never formally disavowed the Anglican Church, Mary Wollstonecraft was a regular within Dissenting circles and maintained friendships with Richard Price, Joseph Priestley, Thomas Paine, Joseph Johnson, and, of course, her fellow English Jacobin authors. Wollstonecraft was also one of the earliest respondents to Burke's essay on the French Revolution. Her rejoinder, *A Vindication of the Rights of*

Men, appeared in print within one month of the publication of *Reflections*. Wollstonecraft has often been applauded or condemned for her work on the rights of women, but she has frequently been overlooked as a political theorist.[101] *A Vindication of the Rights of Men* is a sagacious analysis of Burke's motives, and it places her at the core of the debates of the 1790s and contractarian thought of the eighteenth century.

The crux of Wollstonecraft's argument in her *Vindication* is the recognition of "birthright" as an inalienable possession. Reminiscent of the Putney Debates, birthright emerges as a foundation for individual liberties and a means of opening a rift in the bastion of hereditary wealth and power. Wollstonecraft defines the term as simply "such a degree of liberty, civil and religious, as is compatible with the liberty of every other individual with whom he is united in a social compact".[102] Birthright entitles one to the "rights of humanity", those "rights which men inherit at their birth, as rational creatures, who were raised above the brute creation by their improvable faculties". Furthermore, they receive these rights "not from their forefathers but, from God, prescription can never undermine natural rights".[103] There exist, then, according to Wollstonecraft, certain *a priori* liberties that one does not surrender to civil society and that guarantee the individual a basic security against the encroachments of corrupt power. The recognition of these "natural rights" is a "first principle" upon which the organization of society – legally, economically, and politically – is founded.

In her response to Burke, Wollstonecraft attacks the paradigm of inheritance and the English obsession with property. She focuses much of her criticism on laws that govern the control and transmission of wealth and privilege. She condemns hereditary succession in government because, as evidenced by historical example, it has meant instability and opportunism rather than divine order and national security in the Burkean continuum of society. In a surprising turn to the authority of law, Wollstonecraft quotes Blackstone on the legality of hereditary succession.

> The doctrine of *hereditary* right does by no means imply an *indefeasible* right to the throne... . It is unquestionably in the breast of the supreme legislative authority of this kingdom, the King and both Houses of Parliament, to defeat this hereditary right; and, by particular entails, limitations, and provisions, to exclude the immediate heir, and vest the inheritance in any one else.[104]

Much like Locke and early contract theorists, Blackstone features "the legislative" in his perspective on political authority. Likewise, Wollstonecraft draws on contractarian assumptions about the ascendancy of law in society to support her advocacy of inalienable rights. She is careful, however, to distinguish institutional law from a theory of rights and not to accept the absolute sovereignty of legal systems; she is adamant that "a blind respect for the law is not a part of [her] creed". She insists that *the people* have not just a prerogative but a "right" to elect their king and remove him from the throne if necessary. By the same token, laws are fallible and subject to change.

"[H]ereditary property" and "hereditary honours", Wollstonecraft continues, have obstructed the progress of civilization. Adherence to prescription has bred "artificial monster[s]" and stifled personal ambition and creativity. The alternative figure – the one who would generate growth – is the individual "with a capacity of reasoning" who "would not have failed to discover, as his faculties unfolded, that true happiness arose from the friendship and intimacy which can only be enjoyed by equals". The paradigm of inheritance, according to Wollstonecraft, is problematic because it lacks a ruling "first principle" that provides "coherence", "order" and "certain[ty]".[105] While Burke condemns the notion of such abstract premises because they tend toward dangerous abstractions, Wollstonecraft tries to prove that they are essential to social order. Using the example of Edward III's reign, which Wollstonecraft (quoting Hume) depicts as a dissipated government,[106] Wollstonecraft looks to the authority of history to find evidence that natural rights would provide a social anchor and are necessary to the coherence of society and government. She attempts to demonstrate that the system of heredity, which Burke argues is patterned after nature, is actually chaotic and contrived. By proving that it is artificially constructed, Wollstonecraft is able to conclude that it is merely an institution subject to reform.

The control of property through inheritance elicits even more censure from Wollstonecraft. She astutely observes that protection of property serves to concentrate and conserve political authority. "I beseech you to ask your own heart", Wollstonecraft requests of Burke, "when you call yourself a friend of liberty, whether it would not be more consistent to style yourself the champion of property". Security of personal wealth may be "the definition of English liberty", but it is also the means of guaranteeing the continuance of privilege. Furthermore, the definition of property is political. "[I]t is only the property of the rich that is secure; the man who lives by the sweat of his brow has no asylum from oppression". A working man's property is "in his nervous arms", but because his arms and their labour are not protected by rights, they remain subject to the "surly command of a tyrannic boy, who probably obtained his rank on account of his family connections, or the prostituted vote of his father".[107] It is here that the importance of the Lockean notion of locating property in the self becomes evident. If one considers the definition of property to include religious and civil liberties, and if one deems self-governance to be a natural and inalienable right, then the individual, regardless of gender, familial role, status, and wealth, would maintain some degree of personal security in the face of imperfect governments and juridical systems.

Finally, Wollstonecraft objects to the "imprisonment" of children through the perpetuation of wealth in the family. The image of the family as a model for government, its importance in the tripartite structure of government and its function as a pretext for the concentration of wealth come under attack by Wollstonecraft, who represents the family as a tyrannical institution. She laments the "brutal attachment to children" by "parents who have treated them like slaves, and demanded due homage for all the property they transferred to them, during their lives". The almost frenzied concern for dominion "has led them to force their children to break the most sacred ties; to do violence to a natural impulse, and run into legal prostitution to increase wealth or shun poverty; and, still worse, the dread of parental malediction has made many weak characters violate truth in the face of Heaven". The practice of primogeniture, moreover, leads to an unjust and unproductive sacrificing of younger children to the eldest. They have been "sent into exile, or confined in convents, that they might not encroach on what was called, with shameful falsehood, the *family* estate". The life of a "child" is hardly one of safety and the home is anything but a sanctuary. Echoing Locke and Rousseau, Wollstonecraft pleads for the recognition of citizens as adults. "It appears to be a natural suggestion of reason", she observes, "that a man should be freed from implicit obedience to parents and private punishments, when he is of an age to be subject to the jurisdiction of the laws of his country".[108] Release from the family was necessary for the individual to blossom into the citizen endowed with rights and legal subjecthood.

Wollstonecraft sees in Burke's reverencing of antiquity, and in his faith in inheritable rights, the simple desire to conserve an arrangement of property acquisition and transmission beneficial to a few. As an alternative to allow individuals of talent and merit an opportunity to enjoy the benefits of society, Wollstonecraft suggests that property be "fluctuating". Scorning the ambition and avarice that have accompanied efforts to concentrate wealth, she argues that dissemination of property should be based only on "the natural principles of justice" that would assume acknowledgment of inalienable rights. As the powerful image of the family crumbles, Wollstonecraft replaces it with the crystalline figure of the productive individual who warrants the protection of his property in "goods" and "person". Wollstonecraft explains: "The only security of property that nature authorizes and reason sanctions is, the right a man has to enjoy the acquisitions which his talents and industry have acquired; and to bequeath them to whom he chooses".[109] Thus, the paradigm of inheritance is dismantled, and the power in the transfer of property is distributed to the rights of individuals.

Another response to Burke's *Reflections*, Sir James Mackintosh's *Vindiciae Gallicae* (1791), was well-regarded at the time of its publication but has since been largely forgotten. The reason for its obscurity may have to do with Mackintosh's public retraction of his defense of the French Revolution, and his support of Burke in 1801.[110] Nonetheless, *Vindiciae Gallicae* is one of the most cogent and well-informed answers to Burke, and, unlike many other rejoinders, it provides a historical discussion of the origins of the French Revolution while detailing the day-to-day political activities of the new regime. The first point Mackintosh makes is one which nearly all other respondents have observed – the excessive emotion of Burke's essay. Of *Reflections*, Mackintosh writes:

> All was invective: the authors and admirers of the Revolution, – every man who did not execrate it, even his own most enlightened and accomplished friends, – were devoted to odium and ignominy. The speech did not stoop to argument; the whole was dogmatical and authoritative.... It [*Reflections*] is certainly in every respect a performance.... Argument every where dexterous and specious, sometimes grave and profound, clothed in the most rich and various imagery, and aided by the most pathetic and picturesque description, speaks the opulence and the powers of that mind of which age has neither dimmed the discernment, nor enfeebled the fancy.[111]

Yet Mackintosh, more clearly than most, reveals the politics of Burke's rhetorical style and its antithesis, rational discourse. One of the motives behind the widespread support of "reason" by contract theorists was its ability to "level" and to recognize individual talent and merit. "Analysis and method", which is what Mackintosh claims to offer as an alternative to Burke's immoderate passion, are "like the discipline and armour of modern nations". They "correct in some measure the inequalities of controversial dexterity, and level on the intellectual field the giant and the dwarf".[112] Meanwhile, the unpredictability of human passions was a rationale for not extending the franchise, to women in particular, and it was soon to be associated with the violence of the French Revolution. To be able to charge Burke with dangerous sentimentality was considered a victory for proponents of natural rights.

A related observation Mackintosh makes is the effect of the expanded use of printing on the intellectual playing field. Trying to explain how philosophy and truth work their way into the public consciousness, Mackintosh notes that the art of printing has succeeded in "provid[ing] a channel by which the opinions of the learned pass insensibly into the popular mind". While he argues that the people cannot be "profound", he is convinced that "[t]he convictions of philosophy insinuate themselves by a slow, but certain progress, into popular sentiment". The people cannot read "the great works"; however, the "substance passes through a variety of minute and circuitous channels to the shop and the hamlet". In a valiant attempt to explain the process of absorption, Mackintosh turns to an analogy with nature:

> The conversion of these works of unproductive splendour into latent use and unobserved activity, resembles the process of nature in the external world. The expanse of a noble lake, – the course of a majestic river, imposes on the imagination by every impression of dignity and sublimity: but it is the moisture that insensibly arises from them which, gradually mingling with the soil, nourishes all the luxuriancy of vegetation, and adorns the surface of the earth.[113]

The "engine" behind this quiet and unobserved growth, Mackintosh claims, is "the press". It is their discussion of "great truths" that has found its way into legislation and "prepared a body of laws for the National Assembly". The dispersal of knowledge "has *almost* prepared a people to receive them; and good men are at length permitted to indulge the *hope*, that the miseries of the human race are about to be alleviated".[114] Intellectual inquiry, moreover, is both a benefit of the new society envisaged by rights theorists and necessary to its success.

Like his fellow contractarians, Mackintosh reproved the policy of concentrated wealth and its accompanying power and urged the replacement of hereditary distinction with personal excellence. But while others were cautious about advocating revolution over the process of gradual change, Mackintosh tried to show why, in the case of France, revolution was necessary. To advocates of moderate reform, Mackintosh argued that the incorrigible institutions of the French government "would have destroyed Liberty, before Liberty had corrected their spirit". Contained measures would only exacerbate the wrongs because "[p]ower vegetates with more vigour after these gentle prunings. A slender reform amuses and lulls the people: the popular enthusiasm subsides; and the moment of effectual reform is irretrievably lost". "No important political improvement", he concludes, "was ever obtained in a period of tranquility".[115] Mackintosh's very reasoned approach to why revolutionary change is appropriate is characteristic of his attempt to present a rational defense of the events in France. It posits him as a calm observer and thoughtful reporter, and it renders him the image of the new citizen – a man capable of "governance".

Mackintosh also directs his argument toward the main point of contention between Burke and his adversaries. He astutely notes that the basis of the revolution and its new government is "the assertion and protection of the natural rights of man", and it is this concept that Burke so ardently opposes. The existence of natural rights, Mackintosh claims, is indisputable. What he is concerned about is "the object for which a man resigns any portion of his natural sovereignty over his own actions". The only reason why a person surrenders a degree of self-governance is to obtain protection from abuse of "the same dominion in other men".[116] One therefore subjects oneself to the law with the expectation that one will be guaranteed certain personal securities. Mackintosh also contends that relinquishing some individual sovereignty to the law does not diminish the integrity of natural rights. Law is "restrictive" rather than "permissive" precisely because its function is to protect natural rights, and it is a service to the people rather than a burden because these rights are "not the boon of society, but the attribute of their nature".[117] (437). Mackintosh's rebuttal to Burke's *Reflections* was very much a challenge to the populace to take responsibility for the liberties they were demanding.

The most well known and controversial response to Burke, Thomas Paine's *Rights of Man*, is more pointedly political and activist-oriented than Wollstonecraft's, and it is rather more intoxicating than Mackintosh's. To counter Burke's theory of rights and, like Wollstonecraft, to destroy the prevailing operative model of inheritance, Paine develops the concept of the *birthright* into the idea of natural, individual, and inalienable rights. He contends that "all men are born equal, and with equal natural rights" that are granted "in the same manner as if posterity had been continued by *creation* instead of *generation*". "[C]onsequently", he continues, "every child born into the world must be considered as deriving its existence from God".[118] By shifting the focus of origin from one's worldly father (and his social rank) to God, Paine moves "birth and family" from its secular association to a divine and natural one and thereby levels status. The extent to which Paine's observations about birthright and equality at birth were revolutionary is evident in his own provocative metaphor of "a wilderness of turnpike gates" at the barriers of prescription and hereditary authority:

> It is not among the least of the evils of the present existing govern-ments in all parts of Europe, that man, considered as man, is thrown back to a vast distance from his Maker, and the artificial chasm filled up by a succession of barriers, or sort of turnpike gates, through which he has to pass. I will quote Mr. Burke's catalogue of barriers that he has set up between man and his Maker. Putting himself in the character of a herald, he says – 'We fear God – we look with *awe* to kings – with affection to parliaments – with duty to magistrates – with reverence to priests, and with respect to nobility'. Mr. Burke has forgotten to put in '*chivalry*'. He has also forgotten to put in Peter.[119]

Since the punishment for trespassing a turnpike gate was hanging, the image Paine evokes is one of terror and the implications he forces us to consider are the life-threatening stakes involved in the debate over natural and civil rights. To transgress or actually remove the "barriers of succession" was to subvert the government and hegemonic percep-tions of civil society and to weaken the protection of the existing dis-tribution of property (including the right of property). The seriousness of the threat was soon borne out in the drama surrounding the publi-cation of *The Rights of Man* and Paine's exile from England. The ori-ginal publisher, Joseph Johnson, withdrew the release of Part One set for 22 February 1791 out of a fear of reprisal. It was published a month later, on 16 March 1791, but that event only set further wheels in motion. Because *The Rights of Man, Part the Second* cost a mere six-pence and therefore could be read by literate members of the lower classes, and because it quickly became a popular text in France and England, Paine was charged with "seditious libel" in 1792. By November of that year, Paine had become the target of public attacks; consequently, he fled to France and was tried and found guilty *in absentia*.[120]

Paine's support of the contract as the prototype for government was in itself hardly revolutionary. He corroborates the theories of Locke, Sidney, Rousseau, and other contractarians by describing the origin of political authority as a consenting contract. "[T]he *individuals themselves*", Paine asserts, "each in his own personal and sovereign right, *entered into a compact with each other* to produce a government: and this is the only mode in which governments have a right to arise, and the only principle on which they have a right to exist".[121] But Paine's emphasis on the continuation of society as a process of *creation* rather than *generation* establishes the basis for one of the most important aspects of contractarian thought. Each successive generation, according to Paine, must be able to amend the social contract. In direct contradiction to Burke's notion of the "great primeval contract", Paine affirms the historical relativity of law:

> It requires but a very small glance of thought to perceive, that altho' laws made in one generation often continue in force through succeeding generations, yet that they continue to derive their force from the consent of the living. A law not repealed continues in force, not because it *cannot* be repealed, but because it *is not* repealed; and the non-repealing passes for consent....
>
> The circumstances of the world are continually changing, and the opinions of men change also; and as government is for the living, and not for the dead, it is the living only that has any right in it. That which may be thought right and found convenient in one age, may be thought wrong and found inconvenient in another. In such cases, Who is to decide, the living, or the dead?[122]

Paine's answer to this question is easy to discern. Yet the implications of his answer for the relationship of the individual to the law are perhaps more profound than they initially appear. The legislature remains the primary form of authority within government; however, as he situates each component in the process of creating a government, it becomes clear that law is less prominent than in earlier theories of the contract. Paine explains that the people first comprise a "nation". In that form, they create a constitution, followed by a government that is bound to the principles of the constitution. Likewise, "[t]he court of judicature does not make the laws, neither can it alter them; it only acts in conformity to the laws made".[123] In this particular discussion, Paine does not clarify exactly who does "make the laws", but presumably it would be some construct of the people or its representatives. The end result, in any case, is a historicization of the law as it is removed from the origin of power and is placed, theoretically, under the control of the individuals who form a nation. Not only does Paine's perspective counter Burke's transformation of the constitution and the law into an omniscient entity, it also endorses the recreation of government anew and justifies stepping outside of the law when necessary, or when "a nation" chooses to do so.

The one aspect of law that is not subject to change is the concept of natural rights. According to Paine, the rights one does not surrender when entering into civil society are those that one exercises as an individual (for example, intellectual and religious rights). The natural rights one does yield are those, the exercise of which is not beneficial to the individual without the advantage of civil society. The importance of Paine's distinction inheres in the premise that the relinquishment of rights occurs for the betterment of the individual, as opposed to Burke's contention that one concedes all natural rights when entering into a social compact for the benefit of society and out of social duty. Paine reasons that "[m]an did not enter into society to become *worse* than he was before, not to have fewer rights than he had before, but to have those rights better secured". One's natural rights are, moreover, the "foundation" of civil rights.[124]

In Paine's *Rights of Man*, the individual is a stalwart figure. "Society *grants* him nothing", Paine insists. "Every man is a proprietor in society, and draws on the capital as a matter of right".[125] Paine also very precisely locates the origin of political authority within the individual: "as there is but one species of man, there can be but one element of human power; and that element is man himself".[126] He endows the new citizen with the responsibilities of self-governance but always with the aid and under the watchful eye of the society in which he has a vested interest. "A man, by natural right", he argues, "has a right to judge in his own cause; and so far as the right of the mind is concerned, he never surrenders it". But, Paine continues, "what availeth it him to judge, if he has not power to redress? He therefore deposits this right in the common stock of society, and takes the arm of society, of which he is a part, in preference and in addition to his own".[127] The liberty of self-governance is not an absolute freedom but subject to the jurisdiction of a collective of which the citizen is a participating member. Paine's challenge to Burke's theory of the origin of rights walks a fine line between endorsing divine law and surrendering it to history. In his notion of the birthright, one might argue that Paine is asserting a form of divine power. But Paine equivocates and says of the birthright, and resultant natural rights, "[i]f this be not divine authority, it is at least historical authority, and shews that the equality of man, so far from being a modern doctrine, is the oldest upon record".[128]

Current scholarship on the contract has rightly shown that the story of an originating covenant is indeed a fiction, that the equality at birth cited by Paine immediately dissolves into a trap of "ubiquitous hierarchies" and that the notions of consent and freedom of contract are utopian myths. It has also demonstrated that the glorification of the autonomous individual (itself an illusion) and inalienable rights has overshadowed the exclusion of some persons from the benefits of the contract and has often overlooked the needs of the community at large.[129] But in the context of the late eighteenth century, the idea of the contract was undergoing a transformation, and it was certainly regarded as the promising alternative to inherited wealth and privilege. By mid-century, contract law itself was concerned more with "customary practices and traditional norms" than with fulfilling an obligation or promise. By the 1790s, it became more widely associated with economic transactions and the ownership of land and capital.[130] In both instances, however, contract law and participation in government and commercial life were informed by theories of rights. The imagined relationship of the individual to the law came to determine the individual's ability to function in civil society, and hence the establishment of those rights became a crucial endeavour. The tremor of change most profoundly generated by Thomas Paine's *Rights of Man* was seen by the disenfranchised as an opportunity to acquire political, legal, and economic agency. Dissenters such as Thomas Holcroft and women like Mary Wollstonecraft saw in the potential reconstitution of the individual's relationship to the law, through a comprehensive theory of rights in a protective social contract, a strengthening of the individual distinct from the family and preparation of the individual endowed with agency for political participation.

3
Envisaging the New Citizen

Thomas Holcroft's *Anna St Ives*, Charlotte Smith's *Desmond*, Elizabeth Inchbald's *Nature and Art*, and Robert Bage's *Hermsprong* are among the most optimistic of the radical texts published in the 1790s. They impart the keen hopefulness of the discourse on rights as it attempted to fashion the "new citizen" – the legal subject of the contract – and prepare the populace for activity in the commonwealth. In their enthusiasm, these texts begin to define a new kind of literary hero who represents the enfranchised individual characterized by property that originates in ownership of the self and is sustained by access to economic opportunities that are released from the exclusive control of the family. The empowerment afforded by these qualities derives from the ability to claim inalienable, natural rights, which precede and exist independently of the government. Yet the individual narrativized by English Jacobin authors was not an isolated, egocentric figure retreating from humanity and responding to a blind self-interest; such was the criticism they received from their political adversaries. The image of a new citizen required responsible participation in the public domain and attentiveness to the well being of the community. Individual liberties were a mere foundation to the greater vision of a society comprised of a strong, enfranchised citizenry that is distinguished by self-determination and social obligation.

Narratives by Holcroft, Smith, Inchbald, and Bage are also characterized by their use of sentimentalism to portray an explicit political idealism. According to Marilyn Butler, sentimentalism was the "inheritance" of radical authors. Tracing the tendency to view human nature as good back to the latitudinarian divines and their reaction against "Puritan pessimism", she notes the association of political liberalism with this "kindly" opinion about humanity.[1] Indeed, the perception that the individual is inherently benevolent, sympathetic, and capable was a crucial premise that justified political reform and the establishment of a power base in the citizenry. Whereas the Hobbesian view of humanity evoked a picture of warring parties and thereby helped to justify monarchy, the Jacobin perspective, based in part on sentimentalism, was that of a populace whose strength is yet undiscovered but knows few bounds. Informed by the secular humanism of Shaftesbury and Hutcheson, in particular, the Jacobins regarded humanity as (potentially) naturally progressive and benevolent.

At times the English Jacobins entertained extraordinary ideas of human capability, especially early in the 1790s. Godwin argues in *Political Justice* that "[t]here is no characteristic of man, which seems at present at least so eminently to distinguish him, or to be of so much importance in every branch of moral science, as his perfectibility".[2] After a discussion informed by Lockean epistemology, of humanity in its original state when it acquired "the first elements of knowledge, speaking and writing", Godwin poses a series of rhetorical questions that look to an unlimited future: "Is it possible for us to contemplate what he [man] has already done, without being impressed with a strong presentiment of the improvements he has yet to accomplish? There is no science that is not capable of additions; there is no art that may not be carried to a still higher perfection. If this be true of all other sciences, why not of morals?"[3] Moreover, while Godwin invests humanity with an apparently unlimited expansion of aptitude, he also speculates on the ability of the human mind to alter physical experience. He poses as a truth, that physical "indisposition" becomes "formidable" only "in proportion as it is seconded by the consent of the mind" and that "our communication with the material universe is at the mercy of our choice".[4] The power of the mind in Godwin's text is an unexplored resource.

This faith in human development was complemented by a corresponding belief that evil is mere error. In his *Letter to the Right Honourable William Windham*, Holcroft rails at Windham's neglect of the economic consequences of war on the poor, but he still presents the source of Windham's crime as a lack of knowledge. "Ignorance is the source of your impotence", he writes to Windham. "Ignorance is the origin of all the errors of which I or the world can accuse you".[5] Similarly, in his *Narrative of Facts, relating to a Prosecution for High Treason*, Holcroft explains that one of the chief principles by which we live is "that man is happy in proportion as he is truly informed ... in proportion as he advances in the knowledge of facts, he will increase the means of happiness".[6] Wollstonecraft, as well, argues that no one "chooses" evil; rather, they "mistake" it for the good they seek. To be enlightened is not to resign oneself to one's fate, but to correct one's errors and endeavour to elicit human happiness.[7] In *Political Justice*, Godwin also asserts that "[a]ll vice is nothing more than error and mistake reduced into practice, and adopted as the principle of our conduct"; however, his analysis extends to a criticism of government, which "gives substance and permanence to our errors. It reverses the genuine propensities of mind, and, instead of suffering us to look forward, teaches us to look backward for perfection". By embracing prescription, government impedes progress; "it prompts us to seek the public welfare, not in innovation and improvement, but in a timid reverence for the decisions of our ancestors, as if it were the nature of mind always to degenerate, and never to advance".[8]

Much of the manner in which the Jacobins transformed their humanistic ideals into a political agenda for a reformed society can be traced back to Shaftesbury's examinations of virtue. In his *Characteristicks of Men, Manners, Opinions, Times* (1711), Shaftesbury indicates the possibility of the universe being in "good Order, and the most agreeable to a general Interest that is possible". If a society is not the best that it can be, Shaftesbury refers to its weaknesses as an "illness". Whether caused by "design" or "chance", the notion of social "illness" presumes an underlying foundation of good from which the community has deviated.[9] Correspondingly, Shaftesbury argues that there is a definable right and wrong state for each individual, and the right one is naturally sought and promoted.

> There being therefore in every Creature a certain *Interest* or *Good*; there must be also a certain *END*, to which every thing in his Constitution must *naturally* refer. To this *END* if any thing either in his Appetites, Passions, or Affections be not conducing, but the contrary; we must of necessity own it *ill* to him. And in this manner he is *ill, with respect to himself*; ... . Now if, by the natural Constitution of any rational Creature, the same Irregularitys of Appetite which make him ill *to Others*, make him ill also *to Himself*; and if the same Regularity of Affections, which causes him to be good in *one* Sense, causes him to be good also in *the other*; then is that Goodness by which he is thus useful to others, a real Good and Advantage to himself. And thus *Virtue* and *Interest* may be found at last to agree.[10]

Shaftesbury's assessment of the human condition as one in which virtue and self-interest coalesce became something of a creed for the English Jacobin novel. In nearly all of these texts, heroes and heroines are characterized by the ability to reason about what is morally right and what is beneficial to the community at large. In the most sanguine of the Jacobin novels, the benefit to society is reinforced by the belief that humanity has a natural propensity toward an astute conscience and, accordingly, sound judgment. Much as Shaftesbury claimed that a sense of right and wrong is a "natural Affection" and "a first Principle in our Constitution and Make", the Jacobins represented sound judgment as a capacity of the new citizen that should be cultivated and rendered insusceptible to the whims of "speculative Opinion, Persuasion or Belief". It is marked by an endurance and a steady strength; "'[t]is impossible", Shaftesbury writes, "that this can instantly, or without much Force and Violence, be effac'd or struck out of the natural Temper, even by means of the most extravagant Belief or Opinion in the World".[11] An unshakeable reason, then, combined with a sense of obligation to the community was to become the cornerstone of the new society envisaged by the English Jacobin authors.

In their analysis of social forces and structures, Jacobin sentimentalism concludes that circumstances determine the development of the individual. From this premise, the Jacobin authors justified numerous proposals for reform, including the very possibility of change and improvement. Humanity's ignorance, Holcroft contends, "is not a fault but a misfortune" because one's knowledge correlates with one's exposure to information. With similar conviction, both Wollstonecraft and Godwin look to Locke's articulation of a *tabula rasa* to argue that virtue may be acquired by experience; it may be reasoned, and it may be taught. "Children are born ignorant", Wollstonecraft writes, and "the passions, are neither good nor evil dispositions, till they receive direction".[12] The ability of individuals to obtain virtue is an important basis of her argument for inalienable rights in *A Vindication of the Rights of Men* and in her proposal to educate women in *A Vindication of the Rights of Woman*. For Godwin, external circumstances are a powerful determinant of personal identity. Godwin devotes much of Book I of his *Political Justice* to explaining and outlining the influence of political institutions on the development of the individual and his/her situation. He too asserts that "[w]e bring into the world with us no innate principles". As a result, "we are neither virtuous nor vicious as we first come into existence", but we will be shaped by our experiences, and

many (if not all) of those experiences will be determined by the political institutions that govern our lives.[13] A "sound political institution"
can be "the most powerful engine for promoting individual good";
likewise, "an erroneous and corrupt government" can be "the most formidable adversary to the improvement of the species".[14] Our behaviour, our "virtues and vices", Godwin continues, "may be traced to the
incidents which make the history of our lives". Thus, "if these incidents could be divested of every improper tendency", he optimistically
concludes, "vice would be extirpated from the world".[15]

Even when the central figure of the contract endowed with rights is
the propertied man, as is the case in Smith's Desmond and Bage's
Hermsprong, there remains a robust confidence about the freeing of
liberty and political authority from the hands of patriarchalism, from
the bonds of "inherited rights" in all of these early novels. By drawing
on the traditions of sentimentalism to present a political ideal and by
casting the evils of the world as errors, the English Jacobins paved the
way for reform. They embraced the individual formed by circumstances and authorized by the rights of ownership to surpass the stric-
tures of positive law and become empowered participants in civil
society for the benefit of the commonwealth.

Thomas Holcroft, *Anna St Ives*

Shaftesbury's assessment of the human condition as one in which
virtue and self-interest coalesce became something of a creed for
Holcroft in *Anna St Ives*. As Holcroft imagines a new society distinguished by the idea that individual needs will coincide with what is
best for the community, he represents the individual as moving in the
direction of his/her "correct" state of being. The main protagonists,
Anna and Frank, must strike a balance between their emotional and
political responsibilities and demonstrate that virtue is attainable only
in the context of an equitable society. They succeed by putting their
superior physical and moral strengths to good use, by undergoing and
sharing with others a process of intellectual and social enlightenment,
and by exhibiting a virtuous understanding of property. The value of
Anna's and Frank's discoveries about their own unlimited potential
appears in their respective roles as models for others. In a civil state, "it
is *Example*", Shaftesbury writes, "which chiefly influences Mankind,
and forms the Character and Disposition of a People".[16] It is also,
according to Shaftesbury, the responsibility of leaders to remember
that their effectiveness is dependent on their ability to serve as an

example to the populace. While the obligation of example was common in reference to the monarchy, Holcroft's requirement that an "ordinary" man and woman set a precedent for others was a revolutionary replacement of the monarchical figure at the center of society with that of the enfranchised citizen.

Selfishness is the avowed enemy of Holcroft's Anna and Frank. As representative leaders of the future commonwealth, they must dissociate themselves from self-aggrandizement and yet not negate the new-found power of the individual. Personal good and public good must be consonant. Shaftesbury and Hutcheson provided early ammunition against the accusations of selfishness that plagued the campaign for inalienable rights. "Self-Good", Shaftesbury writes, "however *selfish* it may be esteem'd, is in reality not only consistent with publick Good, but in some measure contributing to it; ... 'tis so far from being ill, or blameable in any sense, that it must be acknowledg'd absolutely necessary to constitute a Creature *Good*".[17] It is our duty, therefore, to be strong, socially responsible individuals and to exercise reasonable, well-grounded private judgment. Similarly, Hutcheson denies that self-love is the motivation behind all of our actions. He argues that we have "a *moral faculty* ... truly disinterested, terminating upon the happiness of others, and often operating when we have no reference of it in our minds to any enjoyment of our own".[18] Hutcheson's position translates easily into a commitment to universal benevolence. The "grand determination" to achieve "the greatest general good" is as powerful a *modus operandi* in *Anna St Ives* as is the need to free oneself from the constraints of family, gender, and status.[19] Anna's and Frank's union is possible only because it is socially beneficial.

Holcroft wished to see philosophy at work in society and considered his novels a contribution to social advancement. He hoped that his literary work would endure beyond his lifetime and continue to instruct the populace and "promote the general good".[20] In his review of Robert Bage's *Man As He Is*, Holcroft defends the social role of the novel: "When we consider the influence that novels have over the manners, sentiments, and passions, of the rising generation – instead of holding them in the contempt which, as reviewers, we are without exception said to do, – we may esteem them, on the contrary, as forming a very essential branch of literature".[21] William Hazlitt, who completed Holcroft's memoirs (first begun by Holcroft himself), remarked that "Holcroft's politics were never any thing more than an enlarged system of morality, growing out of just sentiments, and general improvement".[22] Indeed, Holcroft saw the mission of the author as a social one, functioning with moral responsibility. In *The Monthly Review*, Holcroft wrote that

> the labours of the poet, of the historian, and of the sage, ought to have one common end, that of strengthening and improving man, not of continuing him in error, and, which is always the consequence of error, in vice. The most essential feature of every work is its moral tendency. The good writer teaches the child to become a man; the bad and the indifferent best understand the reverse art of making a man a child.[23]

Holcroft's *Anna St Ives* is an example of this sort of moral endeavour, as it guides us toward, and educates us about, the qualities necessary for a healthy citizenship: a sound and secure development of the self and a commitment to civic duty. Anna St Ives and Frank Henley constitute an idealized couple who learn to become good citizens. Anna is the daughter of a baronet and Frank is the son of the steward who oversees the St Ives estate. Together they cross numerous boundaries. They turn traditional notions of gender upside down when they reveal their tendencies toward passion and reason. Anna must learn to moderate her over-inclination toward "masculine" reason, while Frank must learn to curb his "feminine" emotions, which approach excessiveness. In addition, they challenge the wisdom and competencies of their parents' generation. Sir Arthur St Ives and Abimelech Henley mismanage property either through inattentiveness, purposeful deceit, or obsessive cultivation, whereas Anna and Frank radically re-conceive ideas about ownership. The right of property they establish is manifest in the evolution of a moral code that both enhances individual growth and contributes to the general welfare. Finally, they defy class when they unite in marriage at the end of the story and become models of what is possible in a new society. Honour and virtue, once considered innate characteristics of the nobility or qualities exhibited through chivalric acts, become vehicles of truth – a social, political, and economic reality that need only be investigated and revealed.

Anna St Ives was published in 1792 and, like Smith's *Desmond*, was written just before the French Revolution took a definitively violent turn and France began its invasions of other nations. It is an earnestly optimistic text as it looks forward to the New Jerusalem and celebrates the notion of French *fraternité* as a model for government. It is one of the few Jacobin texts that actually try to narrativize a utopian culture. Marilyn Butler notes that Holcroft had originally planned to end the novel tragically with the principal characters, Anna, Frank, and the villainous Coke Clifton, rendered victims of an oppressive society. Godwin, however, advised him to conclude with an affirmation of the possibility of social transformation.[24] Holcroft does so, but his attempt to illustrate the political idealism of the kind that Godwin discusses in *Political Justice* exacerbates a frequently noted weakness of *Anna St Ives*: the hollowness and flatness of the characters. Hazlitt deemed Anna and Frank unnatural because they seem to be mere "machines put into action ... to shew how these general principles would operate in particular situations".[25] Indeed, just as the story opens, Anna and Frank seize hold of an autonomy of behaviour that other Jacobin characters only dream about, and the process of obtaining self-governance remains opaque. Rather than illustrate the necessary and difficult steps toward liberty explored in later Jacobin texts, Holcroft demonstrates the extraordinary capacity of women and men when they are allowed to assert their independence and exercise their own judgment. While the convictions of Anna and Frank do seem miraculously void of self-doubt, painful sacrifices, and other human complexities, the novel itself wrestles with the appropriate means of reform, the reconciliation of passion with reason, and the definition and appropriate use of property. As Patricia Meyer Spacks observes, at issue in *Anna St Ives* is agency, is the definition of who has the right and ability to evoke change and determine its form.[26]

Frequently, *Anna St Ives* is labelled a sentimental novel because it tries to depict human perfectibility. In the novel, Holcroft insists that humanity's vice is due only to error and that proper instruction and information will eventually eliminate corruption, duplicity, and other social ills.[27] "The march of knowledge is slow", Anna writes, "impeded as it is by the almost impenetrable forests and morasses of error. Ages have passed away, in labours to bring some of the most simple of moral truths to light, which still remain overclouded and obscure".[28] Holcroft uses the sentimental not to prey on the sensibilities of his readers or to pique interest in the power of feeling but to present a political supposition that is itself dependent on an assumption of goodness and redemptive qualities in human nature. Holcroft also regards the belief in continual improvement to be at the foundation of his system of morality. In *Anna St Ives*, the reformative activities are dependent on the premise, also articulated by Godwin, that the discovery of true principles will lead to proper conduct. The assumption that one may voluntarily behave in a productive manner and in concert with the needs of the community implies the self-determination of an enfranchised individual.

The plot of *Anna St Ives* relies heavily on novelistic conventions, many of them borrowed from Richardson. Frank, akin to Sir Charles Grandison, is the doer of endless good deeds. When he, Anna, and Sir Arthur encounter robbers on the road to Paris, Frank exhibits his heroism by rescuing them all from the treacheries of theft. In addition, when Coke Clifton hits his head on a rock after diving into a lake, Frank saves him from drowning. Anna is a character constructed in the tradition of Clarissa. She wrestles with questions of filial obedience and the warring factions of head and heart when choosing a husband. She is immersed in conflict over her dowry (dissension not of her own making) and watches as money takes its central place in the marriage game. Anna is eventually abducted and, in a scene vividly reminiscent of *Clarissa*, is locked in an apartment and threatened with rape. Anna's abductor is Coke Clifton, a Lovelacean rake, who quickly realizes that Anna's interest in him is generated by her devotion to reforming his behaviour. Resistant to any such ideas of personal improvement, Coke begins to plan the demise of both Anna and Frank (between whom he realizes there is a strong affection) and contrives situations to entrap them. His duplicitousness is played out in a gothic world of overspent emotion and dangerously misguided passion.

But Holcroft overtly politicizes his novelistic conventions. First, he burdens heroic behaviour with the duties of reform. Frank's heroism is not complete when he saves Anna and her father from robbers; his objective is fulfilled only when he later meets one of the robbers and rehabilitates him. Similarly, it is not enough to have saved Coke Clifton's physical life; Frank is also obligated to see to the betterment of Coke's conduct. Second, Holcroft breaks down the gendering of victimization and provides his characters with the means of altering the usually devastating fates of young women forced into marriage for financial gain. When Anna is abducted and threatened with rape, her exceptional strength of mind and body enables her to resist Coke's advances, scale the walls of her prison, and secure her own freedom. "Courage has neither sex nor form", she reminds us (423). Moreover, Anna is not the only one to suffer at the hands of Coke. Frank is also abducted, and while he too is endowed with special physical powers and able to fend off three large gangsters single-handedly, he experiences the trauma so many women do in eighteenth-century texts. He is exposed to a firsthand understanding of what it is like to have one's agency denied. Finally, social obligation replaces filial obedience as the moral force behind marital decisions. In Anna's choice of a husband, she veers from the well-trodden path and eventually reaches a solution that enables her to be true to her own heart and her social mission at the same time. She first thinks she must betroth herself to Coke in order to convert him, but that proves to be both unnecessary and insufficient. It takes the combined power of the loving couple of Anna and Frank to be effective in reform. By choosing Frank, Anna walks away from the demands of filial obedience and economic control by the family, and she asserts her self-governance by trusting her own judgment.

In *Anna St Ives*, Holcroft depicts the convergence of an old world mired in corruption and the misuse of property with a new world of enfranchised individuals who strive to be better caretakers of public and private domains. Both Anna and Frank take a great deal of interest in the workings of property. Anna's earliest letters to her friend Louisa Clifton are filled with concerns about her father's management of the family estate. She worries about the influence that her father's steward, Abimelech Henley, wields over his employer in decisions about property. Furthermore, she gives advice to her brother when he tells her about an estate that had been entailed to him (and a disagreement with his father over the matter); she reminds him of "the true use of money" and suggests that unless he has found "the art of employing it worthily" he should not take possession of it (22). Still, the predominant focus on property in the hands of an outdated aristocracy is that of "improvement", the "turning of land to better account", the "cultivation and occupation" of real property.[29] Anna likens "a taste for improvement", when it becomes a "passion", to "gaming" because both can be "ruinous" (5). In reference to her father's unceasing endeavours to cultivate his estate, urged on by his steward, Anna remarks, "I doubt whether there be an acre of land in the occupation of Sir Arthur, which has not cost ten times its intrinsic value to make it better" (6).

Improvement becomes a focal point of Holcroft's novel because it goes to the heart of property issues, and correct and careful management of property defines the ideal of the new citizen. As Frans de Bruyn has shown, "improvement" was an important part of Burke's life, his politics, and his literary interests. It suited Burke's theory of social and political conservation, of maintaining continuity with the past rather than embarking on radical transformations that require the tearing down of ancient structures.[30] The improvements of Sir Arthur exemplify what de Bruyn calls "a peculiarly eighteenth-century mode of conspicuous consumption", the "expensive aesthetic improvements in houses, gardens, and estates" that, in their most outrageous forms, sometimes required the "relocation of entire villages" and the "rerouting of roads" for design purposes.[31] While Sir Arthur's and Abe's improvements have not quite reached these excesses, they have resulted in isolation. "[W]e are now all within ourselves", he writes in a letter to Abe (28). After twenty years of cultivation, he comments, "I believe, there are no grounds in all England so wooded and shut in as those of Wenbourne-Hill. We are surrounded by coppices, groves, espaliers, and plantations. We have excluded every vulgar view of distant hills, intervening meadows, and extensive fields; with their insignificant green herbage, yellow lands, and the wearisome eternal waving of standing corn" (28). Those "insignificant" and "wearisome" lands are, of course, the properties that sustain the population with fuel and food. Yet, cut off from the rest of his community, Sir Arthur concerns himself more with the pleasure he receives from seeing others admire his "temples, and groves, and terraces, and ascents, and descents, and clumps, and shrubberies, and vistas, and glades … (28). His maxim is "[t]he love of fame is a noble passion", and his ambition is that his estate, Wenbourne-Hill, be "one of the most beautiful spots in the three kingdoms, ay or in the whole world!" (29).

Sir Arthur's and Abe's self-centered and frivolous use of property is countered by their children: Anna and Frank. In addition to questioning the sense of their fathers' unceasing strategies for improvement, they challenge the validity of private property altogether. Frank, in a letter to his friend Oliver Trenchard, casts doubt on the very idea of ownership. "Still, this money, Oliver", he writes, "Prithee be at the trouble to examine the question, and send me thy thoughts; for I have not been able to satisfy myself. What is the thing called property? What are *meum* and *teum*? Under what circumstances may a man take money from another?" (36). Anna and Frank entertain but somewhat temper the Lockean idea that labour creates individual rights of property and Blackstone's definition of ownership as the right of persons over things by stressing the duties between people in respect of both "things" and the general welfare. Describing their moment of sociopolitical epiphany, Anna explains,

> Frank was present; and his imagination, warm with the sublimity of his subject, drew a bold and splendid picture of the felicity of that state of society when personal property shall no longer exist, when the whole torrent of mind shall unite in enquiry after the beautiful and the true, when it shall no longer be diverted by those insignificant pursuits to which the absurd follies that originate in

our false hearts give birth, when individual selfishness shall be unknown, and when all shall labour for the good of all! (278)

Anna and Frank also take on the entire system of familial property and inheritance as they begin to construct their political agenda. In a letter to her friend Louisa, Anna makes a remark that resonates throughout the text: "each family is itself a state" (209). Anna's observation not only points to the intimate connection between economic control and the family; it also addresses the controversial view of relationships proposed by both Holcroft and Godwin in which family loyalties must be sublimated to the welfare of the state. As she contemplates an idyllic future, Anna implicates the family in the demise of national politics. In reference to anticipated critics of her ideas, she defies a Hobbesian view of community:

> ... let them look round, and deny, if they can, that the present wretched system, of each providing for himself instead of the whole for the whole, does not inspire suspicion, fear, disputes, quarrels, mutual contempt, and hatred. Instead of nations, or rather of the whole world, uniting to produce one great effect, the perfection and good of all, each family is itself a state; bound to the rest by interest and cunning, but separated by the very same passions, and a thousand others; living together under a kind of truce, but continually ready to break out into open war; continually jealous of each other; continually on the defensive, because continually dreading an attack; ever ready to usurp on the rights of others, and perpetually entangled in the most wretched contentions, concerning what all would neglect, if not despise, did not the errors of this selfish system give value to what is in itself worthless". (209–10)

The mixture of political and domestic language used by Anna in her assessment of the state of the nation belies the separation of family and state and instead points to the demise of both in their current economic embroilments. The answer to this dilemma, Anna proposes, is "to arm ourselves with patience, fortitude, and universal benevolence" (210). The solution is also to reconfigure the basis of relationships. To come of age, Anna must allow rationality to regulate her relationships with family and friends. Echoing Godwin, Anna proclaims that "reason and not relationship alone can give authority" (264). Holcroft, like Godwin, attempted to establish morality as the foundation of law, including the maxims by which we live. Designating both virtue and contribution to society as touchstones for measuring an individual's worth, Holcroft and Godwin subordinated the importance of sentiment and familial loyalty. To illustrate his idea on individual worth in *Political Justice*, Godwin poses a hypothetical situation involving a fire and the ability to save only one of two persons – the "archbishop of Cambray" and "his chambermaid" from death. The ethical dilemma is how one decides which of these people to rescue. According to Holcroft's and Godwin's principle, "that life ought to be preferred which will be most conducive to the general good". Therefore, even if the less worthy life were that of one's family member, one would be obligated to save the life that is most valuable to all. "We are not connected with one or two percipient beings, but with a society, a nation, and in some sense with the whole family of mankind". Expressing faith in the rationality of moral law, Godwin denies the power of sentiment and emotional affinity. "What magic", he asks, "is there in the pronoun 'my', to overturn the decisions of everlasting truth? My wife or my mother may be a fool or a prostitute, malicious, lying or dishonest. If they be, of what consequence is it that they are mine?"[32] While Holcroft does not depict such an extreme dilemma, in *Anna St Ives* familial loyalties are frequently at odds with relationships between non-related persons that prove to be supportive and productive. If Frank had only his father to rely on, he would never have been educated. If Anna succumbed to her father's wishes, she would have married for money rather than virtue.

The universal benevolence that Anna also cites as a weapon against the errors of a corrupt social system was, as Evan Radcliffe has noted, a "politically charged" concept in the late eighteenth century, and it was a significant point at which the English Jacobin novel diverges from the tradition of sentimentalism is in its representation of benevolence.[33] While still endorsing, even insisting on, the promotion of universal benevolence, the Jacobins warned of the dangers involved in private charity. Carefully dissecting the notion of benevolence inherited from Shaftesbury and Hutcheson, they revealed personal patronage to be morally devastating because it creates an unnecessary dependence and clouds one's natural abilities. In addition, the Jacobins were cautious about the activity of sympathy as the primary catalyst for good works because, as Chris Jones notes, sympathy was often a means of protecting the normative.[34] For example, in his discourse on sympathy in *The Theory of Moral Sentiments* (1759), Adam Smith claims that the admiration we feel for persons of wealth and rank supports the order and stability of society. Of the prosperous, he writes, "[w]e are eager to assist them in completing a system of happiness that approaches so near to perfection".[35] Of the powerful, we hesitate to disturb their authority. "That kings are the servants of the people, to be obeyed, resisted, deposed, or punished, as the public conveniency may require, is the doctrine of reason and philosophy; but it is not the doctrine of Nature".[36] Ultimately, "the peace and order of society is of more importance than even the relief of the miserable".[37] The predominance of localized affection over universal benevolence, promoted by Smith as well as Hume, posed a formidable threat to reform efforts. As Evan Radcliffe has also observed, support of universal benevolence was essential to reform in the 1790s because primary identification with one's family, class, and country was used by English Anti-Jacobins to devalue events in France and strengthen British patriotism.[38]

For Anna and Frank, universal benevolence is a moral imperative by which they live and evidence of their being self-governing participants in the public domain. Yet it is a deceptively simple concept in *Anna St Ives*. Their devotion to the plight of others is also a political statement that aligns them with supporters of the French Revolution and British reformers. One of the basic tenets of the new philosophy was the ability and the moral responsibility to care for humanity; that empathy, however, was considered a "voluntary action" – one that implies individual will and a powerful self. The credo of opponents of revolution and reform was private philanthropy and local, as opposed to international, alliances. While universal benevolence, according to Radcliffe, "came to stand for a subversion of everything local and consequently the destruction of human nature itself",[39] in *Anna St Ives* concern for the general welfare is a means of assuring civic duty and an indication of a stronger, more explicitly defined human nature. The actual threat that the notion of universal benevolence posed was a challenge to the family as the means of economic control.

Holcroft proposes *fraternité* as the paradigm for government and society. Its antithesis – egoism – was considered a counter-revolutionary force during the French Revolution and a threat to the brotherhood envisaged by reformers.[40] Coke Clifton, presumably a reference to jurist Sir Edward Coke, embodies egoism, and his downfall exemplifies the destructiveness of such self-interest Holcroft makes a critical distinction between the kind of self-determining "voluntary action" that Anna and Frank enjoy and the manipulative contrivances for self advancement of which Coke is guilty. Anna and Frank glean their strong sense of self from their assumption of civic participation and their commitment to the welfare of others. Coke's flawed morality and self-will prevent him from enjoying the same. Coke's maneuvers, and by extension the activities of legal institutions, are driven by greed, revenge, and coercion – all of which have no place in the new brotherhood. *Fraternité* indicates an end to dark deceptions, oppressive law, and the victimization of others, and, in the text, it eventually works to everyone's advantage. Coke (and the law) are shown to be receptive to reform, and the enfranchised individual is revealed as a source of extraordinary power.

The difficulty in trying to narrativize an ideal relationship between the individual and the state, as well as the simple moral truths to which Holcroft was so devoted, is evident in the frequent criticism that *Anna St Ives* is a mere vehicle for political or moral philosophy. Indeed, the novel does illustrate key concepts in Godwin's *Political Justice*. Yet, Holcroft was most interested in showing those philosophical premises at work in society. While his novel does not consider the often severe difficulties involved in political reform – especially a massive and very gradual campaign to reconstitute the body politic – it ponders the often perplexing alliance between the self and the collective that endures through the period of modernity. Anna and Frank plan to marry at the end of the novel, but the wedding never actually takes place within the course of the story. Holcroft makes a decisive break with the family as a powerful social institution and embraces the individual as citizen. In addition, Holcroft identifies property as an essential component in the constitution of an enfranchised member of the commonwealth, but he also diminishes the importance of private ownership over and above the concerns of the community.

Anna St Ives seems innocuous in what now appears a naive idealism, but the form of the novel alone presents a model for a methodology of critique that embodies the democratic impulses behind English Jacobin fiction. *Anna St Ives* functions as an epistolary colloquium. Exchanges between characters give them each a chance to explore the motivations behind reform – foundational principles, abstract concepts, visions of the future – as well as the topics of reform: property, class relations, labour, education, and marriage. They are able to investigate, for example, marriage to reform a rake, for the benefit of the community, and ultimately for love that also benefits the community. They discuss the culture of filial obedience and the effect it has on young men and women; they consider the choices made in courtship and the consequences of their decisions. We have Anna's record of trying to transform Coke Clifton and her own process of self-realization when she discovers that she can marry the man she loves and still be socially responsible. Dialogue is a mode instruction, a means of enlightenment that welcomes those of diverse rank, economic status, profession, and education. Dialogue is also the means by which the reader may engage in inquiry and critique him/herself. It allows for and even elucidates the Bakhtinian idea of "a multiplicity of social voices" present in a text, of the "dialogism" that insists on the consideration of context, an interaction of meanings, and a competition of definitions.[41]

Charlotte Smith, *Desmond*

Charlotte Smith's *Desmond* (1792), composed in the heady first years of the revolution, is infused with the visionary, erudite critique that informs most early Jacobin novels. Though not of the inner radical circle of Holcroft, Godwin, and Wollstonecraft, Smith did become acquainted with Helen Maria Williams in Paris in 1791, and she was undoubtedly well read in history and the political discourse of the 1790s, as evidenced by her integration of this material in her novel.[42] In the developments of the French Revolution, Smith imagines the possibility of a New Jerusalem where, as her protagonist Desmond has seen in Paris, the "'people of fashion'" are replaced by "the philosopher, the philanthropist, [and] the citizen of the *world*".[43] This last figure of the new society exercises a "comprehensive mind [that] takes a more sublime view of human nature than he can obtain from the *heights* of Versailles or St James's, rejoices at the spectacle which every where presents itself of newly-diffused happiness, and hails his fellow man, disencumbered of those paltry distinctions that debased and disguised him" (I:111). Desmond, as his name indicates, is Smith's version of "the citizen of the world" (du monde). He is not of noble birth. His ancestors "were never above the rank of plain country gentlemen" and, he admits, "towards the middle of the last century, lose even that dignity in a miller and a farmer" (I:231). But Desmond is educated, and he is propertied.

In this epistolary novel, political discussions blend with a romantic narrative and together they take us through the debates of patriarchalism and contractarianism, from Filmer and Locke to Burke and Paine. Smith directs us to the central texts of the debates and demonstrates the grave consequences of patriarchalism and the promises of egalitarian reform. Desmond, however, our primary guide through these territories is notably bolstered by a liberal education, which is one of the natural rights that enables inquiry and critique, and by his financial independence, which allows him, in the very least, the freedom to travel to France to witness the revolution. His "considerable fortune", he himself admits, is a "passport" to society with "men of high birth" and "eminent consideration" (I:230). Thus, while Desmond's view of the transformation of a nation is not limited to "the *heights* of Versailles or St James's", it certainly includes access to those perspectives. Though we are instructed in the ways of equality, it is neither his footman nor his beloved Geraldine, but Desmond, an educated and propertied man already enjoying certain rights, who is poised to be the central figure of the social contract. Consequently, a shrewd reader will see not only the damage done by patriarchalism but also the limits of contractarianism.

One of Desmond's most significant responsibilities as "citizen of the world" is that of a foreign correspondent who reports on the state of French politics and society during the years 1790–92. In letters to Erasmus Bethel, his mentor and former guardian, Desmond describes what he sees in the streets of Paris, relays information he gleans from his friend the *ci-devant* Marquis Montfleuri, and repeats conversations he overhears in public and private venues. The topics of these communiqués are precisely those dominating the British reaction to the French Revolution in the years immediately following the fall of the Bastille: the elimination of rank and title, the confiscation of Church property, and the cries for equality. Desmond's interest in witnessing events of the revolution immediately identifies him as a progressive thinker; it also aligns him with the English Jacobin authors themselves, who wished to observe first hand the extraordinary event of the emergence of a new society. Thomas Holcroft traveled to France in 1789, Helen Maria Williams in 1790, Charlotte Smith in 1791, and Mary Wollstonecraft in 1792.[44] Desmond's function as a correspondent from France also contextualizes him in a particular journalistic practice in the 1790s, providing intelligence about revolutionary proceedings unfolding across the Channel. Although much of it was coloured by partisan sentiments, news from France was regularly featured in periodicals as wide ranging in political sympathies and constituencies as *The Anti-Jacobin Review*, *The Gentleman's Magazine*, and *The Monthly Review*. Additionally, perhaps the most well known collection of letters, Helen Maria Williams's *Letters written from France in the Summer of 1790*,[45] seems present in what Nicola Watson calls the "documentary" quality of Desmond's letters and further, Watson argues, "seem designed to replicate the impact of Williams's *Letters from France*".[46]

Smith's particular twist on the epistolary form – using letters as journalistic intelligence – provides an example of the fluid borders of the English Jacobin novel and its participation in public debates. Desmond's reports from France (as well as Geraldine's in Volume III) are not mere fiction; they are meant to convey reliable information, quell fears, and assert the truth about revolutionary developments in the face of propagandistic reports intended to raise British anxiety about mob rule and violence. Janet Altman, in her study of the epistolary novel, notes that the letter calls attention not only to the reader/recipient of the letter within the novel but also to the reader of the novel itself.[47] Numerous letters address, quite directly, the misinformation appearing in the British press and circulating in public discourse. In Volume I, Desmond's French companion Montfleuri tries to make sense of the British opposition to developments that he believes have benefited his country. He expresses his concern about false impressions and acknowledges his disbelief that "Englishmen of mature judgment and solid abilities [are] so lost to all right principles as to depreciate, misrepresent, and condemn those exertions by which we have obtained that liberty they affect so sedulously for themselves" (I:139). He surmises a certain "political jealousy" and "prejudices of papal superstition" at work, and he suggests that perhaps Englishmen "fear for their own nation the too great political consequence of ours, when our constitution shall be established; or know and dread, that the light of reason thus rapidly advancing, ... will make, too evident, the faults of their own system of government" (I:140). Desmond's letters provide Smith with a forum through which she can enter public dialogues about France and clarify the record. The novel, though she deferentially refers to its efforts as "slight skirmishing", she aligns with "the powerful efforts of learning and genius", and she uses it to reveal the hollowness of British opposition and underscore the hopes for reform that France has given to other nations (I–ix).

Desmond as hero embodies two concomitant passions: unwavering romantic love (for Geraldine Verney, a married woman) and ardent support of the French Revolution. The fusion of the personal and the political is a hallmark of Smith's novel, often cited in reviews and critical readings of the novel, whether the emphasis is Smith's feminism, political intent, or use of the epistolary form.[48] *The Monthly Review*, for example, concurs with Smith's novelistic assertion that "the great events which are passing in the world are no less interesting to women than to men, and that in her solicitude to discharge the domestic duties, a woman ought not to forget that, in common with her father and husband, her brothers and sons, she is a citizen".[49] The narrative tale of Desmond and Geraldine is where Smith demonstrates and reaffirms the urgency of the political situation, which is also a domestic one. Early in the novel, Desmond goes to France to divert himself from his passion for Geraldine; hence, he makes an initial mistake in assuming that the personal can be separated from the political and that one passion will override and displace the other. However, his journey through France, and even his subsequent one through the English countryside, becomes a process of enlightenment about the interconnectedness of the personal and political, the domestic and national, the private and public. Despite his attempt, Desmond cannot separate French politics from romantic love for a variety of reasons. First, his motivation for going to France is driven by his two passions: the revolutionary politics of France and a desire to please Geraldine by accompanying her brother Waverly, a young man as dithering as his name implies. Second, once in France, he befriends the enlightened Montfleuri, who both instructs Desmond on the state of affairs in France and encourages him in developing an affection for one of Montfleuri's sisters, Mme. de Boisbelle. Third, the novel's central villain is Geraldine's husband, Verney, who himself embodies the integration of the personal and the political in his role as a patriarchal figure.

Patriarchalism emerges in this novel with a resounding force and becomes the focus of Smith's political analysis. Desmond's reference to Filmer and Locke in one of his letters to Bethel reminds the reader of the tradition of formal patriarchalism and of the presence of the ubiquitous father/king analogy that contractarianism worked to displace. Appearing nearly mid-way through the novel, in Volume II, the mention of Filmer and Locke is pivotally placed. The reader must consider what has already occurred in the novel in a new, specifically, political light, and the reader's perspective for the rest of the novel is now firmly established. Moreover, the discussion of Filmer and Locke occurs immediately after a particularly egregious scene in which the debauched Verney behaves abominably toward his wife and children. "'[A]way with ye all', cried the worthless brute their father, 'there, get ye along to the nursery, that's the proper place for women and children'" (II:36). His companion, the dull, self-centered, and indolent Lord Newminster, also appears, and we are reminded that under the present conditions, under the practice of hereditary government, this man who admits, "Oh! The devil may take the British senate for me, ... I never put my head into it ... I don't care a curse for their damned politics" (II:41), is the future of British government; he is, as his name implies, the "new minister". These scenes are all conveyed by the reliable Bethel. Thus, when we read Desmond's response to Bethel in the very next letter, we are well prepared to see the foolishness of Filmer's argument for "unlimited government", for monarchies deriving their political authority from Adam, for the inheritance of political leadership (II:63). We are also ready to distrust Burke, precisely because Desmond has linked Burke's thought to Filmer's. In fact, it is in reading Burke's *Reflections* that Desmond is reminded of Filmer, and Burke's endorsement of inherited rights is seen as no more than a variation on Filmer's patriarchalism.

This extended political discussion, in which the specter of Filmer is raised, functions as a pivotal moment in the novel, as well, because it marks Desmond's assertion of his own analysis. Until this point in Volume II, Desmond has only occasionally articulated his own thoughts in conversations with others and largely restricted his political commentary to the conveyance of what others have said; he has been a reporter. Now, he is beginning comfortably to claim his agential role as an evaluator of world events by engaging in inquiry and critique – the responsibility and fulfillment of the new citizen. The two figures with whom he identifies are Locke and Paine. One of the first invocations of Locke occurs earlier, in Volume I, when Desmond is engaged in a heated argument about equality with the traditional French aristocrat Comte d'Hauteville (uncle to Montfleuri). Without naming Locke, Desmond voices a central, though especially controversial, notion of contractarianism – that one owns one's labour and employment is a contract between free men. Regarding his footman (a man the Comte refuses to consider an equal to Desmond who is a property owner), Desmond explains, if "I have occasion for his services, [and] he has occasion for the money by which I purchase them: in this compact we are equal so far as we are free. – I, with my property, which is money, buy his property, which is time, so long as he is willing to sell it" (I:237). The relationship between master and servant is transformed into an arrangement by contract. Desmond's comment insinuates that labour is property and that a man typically regarded as propertyless is actually a proprietor of himself and his work. Though Desmond cites Voltaire on equality, his observations are more indicative of Locke; they are in fact a concise articulation of Locke's conceptualization of the right of property. The relationship between servant and master that Desmond's assessment challenges is a feudal one, and it is also Burkean (although Burke, like Locke, is never mentioned).[50]

By Volume II, Desmond is immersed in the texts that debate contractarianism; he has been reading Locke's *Two Treatises*, Burke's

Reflections, Wollstonecraft's *Vindication of the Rights of Men*, and Paine's *Rights of Man*.[51] He uses Locke, Wollstonecraft, and Paine (though primarily Locke and Paine) to counter Burke's assertions and takes us through some of the central disputes explored in their treatises. He opposes Burke's notion of prescription and his conceptualization of the social contract as the "great primeval contract" that binds generations to posterity; he insists, by citing Locke, that government must have some means of correction.[52] He also comes to the defense of Thomas Paine, who is under fire for his publication of *The Rights of Man*, and finds in his text only the simple truth. Desmond's reading empowers him and then prepares him for one of the many political conversations that populate Smith's novel. Desmond holds his own in a debate with two Englishmen: Mr. Cranbourne, a lawyer and traveling companion to Lord Fordingbridge, a young man about to take his seat in the House of Peers. At the heart of their disagreeement are rights. Predictably, the future Peer finds the very idea of an extended franchise preposterous. Of the poor, he exclaims, *"They* rights! poor devils, who have neither shirts nor breeches! … They have no rights – they can have none, but to labour for their superiors" (II:121, 123). Desmond, who admits that in the past he has been reticent in voicing his opinion, now musters his courage and draws on his political readings. He speaks compassionately of the poor, and he talks knowledgeably about the assumptions of those in the British government. Having read Burke, he now knows his enemy and can anticipate Lord Fordingbridge's arguments. He even reconstructs the architectural metaphors that are a trademark of Burke's *Reflections*, such as "the Corinthian pillar of polished society" and the "edifice" of the gothic castle that represents British law (II:123, 129–30). He is eloquent on social obligation and defiant in the face of suggestions that misery is God's will. He tackles the poor laws that are "perverted" and ineffective, the penal laws that render property equal to human life, property law that leads to ruinous suits, and the very ambiguity of law – so remote from justice – that leads to endless delays and chronically protracted litigation.

The clash of the patriarch and the new citizen is played out in the narrative largely through Verney and Desmond. Verney is both a product of and a contributor to the old ways, partly a victim and partly a perpetrator. While hardly an innocent, Verney admits to being a "green-horn", a "raw boy from College" who was "drawn in by a pretty face, and a fine figure" and was persuaded by others to marry a young woman whom "all the young fellows of my acquaintance reckoned so confounded handsome" (II:39). Not encouraged or perhaps predisposed to make an intelligent, heartfelt decision about marriage, Verney is also an easy target for the machinations of a plotting mother – Geraldine's – who thought she saw a financial opportunity in this union and manipulated a marriage that was disastrous for both husband and wife. Smith's opposition to forced marriages is due, at least in part, to her own situation; she herself was a victim of such an arrangement. But in *Desmond*, in particular, the practice is a foundation to the political critique that considers personal ruin a manifestation of political ruin. Indeed, as patriarchalism suggests, the structure of authority in the home reflects the structure of authority in the nation. Instead of arguing, as Filmer and Burke do, that this reciprocity is necessary to social stability and national security, Smith demonstrates through her narrative just how disastrous, to the individuals involved, is this concept of rightful government. Moreover, by mirroring the situation in France – Montfleuri's sister Mme. de Boisbelle is also forced into an unhappy marriage while giving up the man she truly loves – Smith justifies the actions of the French Revolution on a domestic level, which is also a political one, and legitimates her calls for reform in Britain, lest the same revolt should happen there.[53] The situation in France reflects the situation in Britain, domestically and politically. If "every attempt to repair" the "structure" that is the British nation is prevented or prohibited, Desmond warns, we will proceed "till the building falls upon our heads, and let those who escape the ruins, continue to meditate on the prodigious advantage of this holy reverence, and to boast of the happiness of being Englishmen!" (II:129–30).

Following Desmond's conversation with Mr. Cranbourne and Lord Fordingbridge, the behaviour of Verney and his French counterpart, the Duc de Romagnecourt, becomes increasingly outrageous and reprehensible. Verney has now joined a group of exiled French aristocrats, which includes M. le Duc de Romagnecourt and Josephine's husband, M. le Chevalier de Boisbelle. This gesture alone is enough to implicate Verney as an enemy of the revolution and a misguided, hopelessly degenerate man. But we have also heard news of his gambling, so excessive that he has had to sell off nearly all of his estate, and his carousing, which goes far beyond the occasional sexual liaison. He has hosted parties for his companions and a score of prostitutes. The final gesture, which signifies his ultimate fall into complete debauchery, is the "selling" of his wife to the Duc de Romagnecourt, who has always found her attractive, in payment for a debt Verney has incurred with the Duc. What enables Verney in his plan is the socially, politically, and legally sanctioned proprietorship of wives by their husbands. Geraldine herself knows her predicament. "'On what pretence does he [the Duc] claim a right to molest you?'", Desmond asks her. "'On that,' she replied, 'of being sent by Mr. Verney'" (III:7). She realizes, as she succumbs to her sense of duty and travels to France according to her husband's wishes, that the small amount of money he has given her will ensure that she will soon be left vulnerable to Romagnecourt. Her financial dependency, and therefore her personhood – her sexuality, her affection, her loyalty, her obedience – will be shifted from Verney to Romagnecourt. In a letter to her sister, Fanny, Geraldine again acknowledges her dependent status when she refers to her husband as "the unfortunate man whose property I am" (III:148). She is merely a part of his estate that he uses to pay a debt.

In marked contrast to Verney and his patriarchal cohorts is the new citizen Desmond. He emerges in the third, and last, volume of the novel as a complete hero, though not a perfect one. Cognizant that Geraldine is in danger, Desmond follows her to France, where he intervenes when she is taken in and threatened by a group of "free-booters", men who had once been armed by aristocratic counter-revolutionaries but have since released themselves from their allegiance and are now running free and plundering the property of their former employers (III:283–84). He and his servant rescue her, and then accompany her on the rest of her journey. They eventually find Verney, and he is lying on his deathbed. In these final scenes, the personal and the political are now fully integrated and the narrative flows freely between political discussions and dramatic narrative. Volume I was preoccupied with political thought, Volume II with domestic drama, and now Volume III brings the two firmly together. Educated in politics and love, the enlightened and therefore empowered Desmond has gained the resolve and courage to act heroically for Geraldine. Desmond has also maintained an all-important disinterestedness throughout the novel that has proven to be vital both publicly and privately. What all the politicians in *Desmond* have in common is self-interest, and it leads to destructive policies. Lord Newminster confesses to be in politics only to "keep the reversion of the sinecures my father got for me, and two or three little snug additions I've had given me since for the borough interest I'm able to carry them" (II:41). Bethel's solicitor, Mr. Stamford, was driven by personal ambition to wield his way to a seat in Parliament and is rewarded by "[p]referments and fortune [that] crowded rapidly upon him" (I:43). As Sir Robert Stamford, MP, his modus operandi is strictly *quid pro quo* (III:170–71). Lastly, a Member of Parliament whom

Desmond encounters defends the slave trade – and happens to own an estate in the West Indies. These politicians are clearly not public servants. In her promotion of disinterestedness, Smith betrays her roots in sentimentalism. As in other Jacobin novels, the individual is elevated over and above the family in *Desmond*. The family is either absent (Desmond has none), partial (Bethel lives a simple domestic life with his two children but has lost his wife), or harmful (Geraldine's mother is greedy and manipulative, her useless brother the sole recipient of the family's estate). When in trouble, help comes to Geraldine not from her family but from a friend. In addition, Geraldine comes to question her sense of duty, which has been her motivation for continuing in an abusive marriage. In another letter to her sister, Geraldine reflects back on her decision to meet her obligations but also realizes unhappily that she has been a "complete martyr" and that duty is an insufficient motivation when compared to love (III:271). Geraldine begins to break away from her family when she is in France witnessing the changes brought about by the French Revolution and contemplating her own democratic sympathies. In jest, she maintains that if her husband be an aristocrat then she must be a democrat; however, in all seriousness, she takes her stand on the French Revolution. While her husband declares himself in sympathy with the aristocratic counter-revolution, she is "convinced, that every priniciple, all that we owe to God, our fellow creatures and ourselves, is clearly on the other side [of] the question" (III:132). Immediately after this statement, Geraldine begins to analyze and censure her family. On her father's regard for women, she explains, he "would not condescend to suppose that our sentiments were worth forming or consulting ... I cannot help recollecting that he was a very Turk in principle, and hardly allowed women any pretensions to souls". Her mother, she avers, was a slave to "domestic policy" (III:133).

Still, even as Geraldine begins to assert her individuality (though in actuality to a very limited extent; she remains faithful to her degenerate husband until he dies), selfhood in *Desmond* is not about selfishness. It is about altruism. Until the very end of the novel, Desmond remains convinced that Geraldine will never be his wife. He devotes himself to her financially and emotionally with little hope that he will glean anything, except her good will, from the relationship. And Geraldine does not contemplate marriage to Desmond; instead, she encourages her sister in that direction. The scene of Verney's death, however, brings the principle players together, and, oddly enough, their union is instigated by Verney himself. When Desmond and Geraldine find Verney, he is, as he had indicated, deathly ill. Deserted by his aristocratic friends, he faces death alone until Desmond and Geraldine arrive. On his deathbed, he acknowledges Desmond's love for Geraldine and encourages them to marry but only if that is what Geraldine wishes. He admits he has no inheritance left for his children and asks that Geraldine and Desmond be the legal guardians. The familial and political irony in this scene is unmistakable. The wealthy property owner, the type of man to whom Burke entrusts the liberty of a nation, has lost everything and has nothing to bequeath to his children. What happens then to the "inherited rights" that he is also charged with protecting and transferring to future generations? Is not the nation in grave danger when it leaves its liberty in the hands of those whose only qualifications are wealth and title, rather than to those who are trustworthy and are judged to be so based entirely on merit? That Verney realizes his own inadequacies and recognizes the worthiness of Desmond and Geraldine is a testament to his own victimization – that of the social practices of marriage and the politics of patriarchalism. In the end, Verney encourages Geraldine to make her own choice about marriage and he hands over what is left of his estate – his children – to those who really are the future of Britain: Geraldine, a woman freed from an oppressive marriage, and Desmond, a constituent of the new citizenry.

In spite of this victorious transferal of power to the new citizen, Desmond does not in the end emerge as an infallible figure, nor does Geraldine. In both cases of passion, Desmond's enthusiasm and devotion are set off against a backdrop of censure, which begins immediately when Bethel tries to wean him from his love for Geraldine. Throughout, Bethel is a voice of moderation, temperance, and, we can only now say, foresight. His concerns about the French Revolution, the lack of leadership and the lack of unanimity, proved to be prescient ones.[54] But in the end, Desmond is right to have devoted himself to Geraldine, and so far the turmoil in France seems to be the inevitable upheaval that must accompany change of any kind. What startles the reader most is discovering that Desmond has had a sexual liaison with Josephine Boisbelle, the married sister of his friend Montfleuri, and is the father of the child she has recently delivered. Contemporary reviewers saw this transgression as a flaw in the novel, as an inconsistency in the character of Desmond who is, otherwise, an exceptionally virtuous and self-sacrificing man.[55] Indeed, this encounter casts Desmond as a "real" hero rather than an "ideal" one. It also renders him another victim, like Verney and Geraldine, of a system of laws and customs that discourage true passions and commitments. Geraldine too bears the scars of the role she has borne as she has tried to be the dutiful daughter and wife. Though she boldly speaks her mind on such topics as novel reading, education, and the French Revolution, she seems excessively acquiescent when she agrees to go to France at her husband's order and endangers her own life to do so.

Nevertheless, these flaws may be considered "errors", and this perspective would render Desmond and Geraldine exemplary characters in the tradition of sentimentalism, especially because they realize their mistakes and embark on improvement. The promise of Desmond and Geraldine, like that of reform, is manifest only in the future. Whereas Fanny Waverly's marriage to Montfleuri, at the end of the novel, merges the long time enemies of England and France and brings with it a certain sense of accomplishment, Desmond's and Geraldine's union is still to come and its effects unknown. Fanny is not immersed in, and has not been as damaged by, the patriarchal practices that Geraldine has suffered. Her frank and ingenuous character is an appropriate match for a former nobleman of France who has transformed his peasants into workers and his estate into a site of industry, and has demonstrated that a new society is possible. For the British couple, still encumbered by duty – they cannot marry until Geraldine has seen through an appropriate period of widowhood – the consequences of their marriage remain uncertain. There are certainly indications of good things to come, signified by the couple's welcoming of Desmond's illegitimate child. But the future of Britain is perhaps too dubious in 1792 to close the novel with the traditional comedic and celebratory ending of a marriage for the central couple.

Like Holcroft's *Anna St Ives*, one of *Desmond's* most significant features is its literary form: the epistolary novel. Far more than *Anna St Ives*, Desmond is driven by conversation rather than dramatic action. As mentioned earlier, the epistolary form is certainly appropriate to the specific subject of correspondence from revolutionary France that strives to stem the tide of propaganda. The letter reinforces a sense of truth and authenticity and, as Altman observes, purposefully "blur[s] the distinction between the fictional world of the correspondents and the real historical worlds of the novelist-reader".[56] In *Desmond*, Smith goes a bit further; she does not just blur the distinction, she opens the borders of fiction, aims her philosophical discussions and her sociopolitical information directly at the reader, and as a result, "the real historical world" becomes present in "the fictional world" and the categories of "real historical" and "fictional" begin to break down.[57] The epistolary form is also suitable to Smith's political intentions because of its tradition in both philosophical and, more recently, political discourse. Bruce Redford points to Seneca and Shaftesbury as examples of those who have fashioned their philosophy in an "epistolary mode".[58] In Smith's more immediate context, *Desmond* fits into the proliferation of political essays that were cast as letters in the turmoil of the 1790s. Burke's *Reflections* is an especially important case in point, since much of *Desmond* is a reply to Burke.[59] He presents his essay as a letter written in response to one sent by Chames-Jean-François de Pont, a young man in Paris who solicited his thoughts on events in France in 1789. Numerous responses to Burke's *Reflections* were then framed as correspondence, such as Thomas Christie's "Letters on the Revolution in France" (1791) and Joseph Priestley's "Letter to the Right Honourable Edmund Burke" (1791). Beyond the specific quarrel with Burke, as political debate became more and more public, the letter form was frequently enlisted to argue rationally for reform, dispute British policy, and at the same time convey passionate and powerful sentiment, which the epistolary form allows.[60]

The emphasis on conversation in *Desmond* also works to a particular advantage in the development of contractarianism at the end of the eighteenth century. Smith draws our attention to conversation in the Preface to *Desmond* when she identifies it as a source. "As to the political passages dispersed through the work", she explains, "they are for the most part, drawn from conversations to which I have been a witness, in England, and France, during the last twelve months" (I:ii). Letter writing, especially *about* conversation and *as* conversation, is both an assertion of the self and of the community of dialogue. It is a form of the classical novel motif of "meeting" that simultaneously incorporates separation.[61] The letter, Altman contends, "can choose to emphasize either the distance or the bridge" between writer and recipient.[62] In *Desmond*, Smith does both and this is central to her assumptions about the figure of the new citizen. Emphasizing the distance reinforces the individual of the social contract who is a discrete entity acting as an agent. Authoring a letter is a singular exercise of agency that assumes some degree of autonomy and authority. The best letters, Redford maintains, create "a distinctive world at once internally consistent, vital, and self-supporting" and "project an identity" that "inhabits a microcosm it seeks to share with the reader".[63] We see Desmond engaging in this form of self-assertion from the start of the novel, though it is less forceful early on before he begins to voice his own political analysis. It is, however, in Geraldine that the affirmation of the self involved in letter writing becomes most clear. While she remains loyal to her husband and acquiesces to his wishes, she is bold, defiant, and self-assured when she writes. She defends novel reading, in no uncertain terms, when responding to her sister's concerns about her mother's restrictions, and she writes with a discerning and independent mind when she records what she sees in revolutionary France. In this epistolary novel, however, the distancing necessary to allow the individual to claim his/her autonomy is matched by the interaction with an "other". There is, as is so often the case in epistolary fiction, the opportunity to convey interiority through the letter. But correspondence in *Desmond* is not that of lovers engaged in seduction, it is the reporting of events – domestic and national – and the conveyance of critique.

Elizabeth Inchbald, *Nature and Art*

According to Inchbald biographer James Boaden, *Nature and Art* was originally called "satire upon the times", and although it was not published until 1796, Inchbald was preparing it for publication in January of 1794.[64] True to its original title, the novel captures the Jacobin concern for assessing the present state of the individual in society and for identifying that which has to be altered to allow the emergence of the new citizen. Both the published title, *Nature and Art*, and an apparent interim title, "The Prejudice of Education", evoke a Rousseauistic interest in what constitutes proper instruction (eventually defined as that which cultivates natural abilities and shatters the false ideas of civilization).[65] The title also depicts British society at a crossroads and establishes the two divergent paths available to each member of the community: that of artifice or that of innocence. Nature is, of course, the preferred route because the simple logic associated with a natural education promises to reveal both the problems behind the extreme economic disparities in society and the possible solutions.

Nature and Art has been criticized for what is seen as a non-revolutionary, compromise ending. Indeed, it closes with the pastoral image of a somewhat self-contained, loving family that is content with its humble existence. This sort of familial portrait frequently appears as the conservative ideal in Anti-Jacobin novels such as Elizabeth Hamilton's *Memoirs of Modern Philosophers* and Jane West's *A Tale of the Times*.[66] Inchbald's conclusion, as well as her emphasis on her heroes' sensibilities, has elicited comments such as Gary Kelly's that

"Mrs Inchbald was clearly more interested in sensibility than reform".[67] Granted, the final scenes of *Nature and Art* seem a hurried about-face from the radicalism of the rest of the novel, but they do not eclipse Inchbald's relentless condemnations of educational, religious, legal, and political institutions. These criticisms were severe enough to delay the printing of the novel for two years, to spark the ire of one of the Queen's attorneys-general, and to provoke the *Anti-Jacobin Review and Magazine* into calling *Nature and Art* "that most impudent, malignant, and audacious heap of absurdity" and Inchbald herself a "*scavenger of democracy*".[68] In addition, while it is true that a crucial facet of her heroes' development is an awareness of their emotions, the ability to understand the role feelings play in human conduct and the maturity to balance them with reason and responsibility add further dimensions to the Jacobins' reconception of citizenship. Throughout most of the text, Inchbald is sharply pointed in her commentary on social inequities.

To a theme both simple and at times complex, Inchbald also connects an analysis of the discrepancy between word and meaning, action and intention, what one is told about the state of the nation, and what one actually sees. Private charity, we are shown, will never furnish the guarantees of liberty that inalienable rights provide, and the law as the protectorate of the people is in actuality a protectorate of the wealthy criminal. The legal scene, which so incisively illustrates the victimization of women, summons the "new philosophy" and questions the absolute authority of law. Eleanor Ty's suggestion that Young Henry's comments on language are a challenge to masculine symbolism can also be read as an indication of a crisis of integrity.[69] The gap between word and intention is ominous, and while it is presented in the terms of what Gary Kelly calls a "sentimental comedy", it touches the chords of an unresolvable anxiety about the equivocal spirit of law and efforts to unveil a discernible truth about one's social reality and therefore to remedy it.[70] Inchbald's so-called "mild revolutionism" had severe implications; only an overhaul of the individual to release him or her from prejudice and a re-evaluation of the resources of Britain so that their distribution begins to approach equality would answer the needs of society.

Inchbald's novel attempts to decipher social problems through the comparison of two opposing forces. Two brothers and their two sons demonstrate the consequences of a life of artifice and greed as opposed to a life of honest and devoted love. One brother, William, and his son, Young William, are immersed in socially acceptable duplicities and schooled in the everyday deceptions of decorum and custom. Their lives, though superficially adorned in the drapery of wealth, devolve into vacuous symbols of success. The other brother, Henry, and his son, Young Henry, choose to live by courageous inquiry and unadulterated loyalty, both of which are guided by reason. Their decision to eschew the delusions and compromises of corrupt British society exiles them from others, but in the end their defiance of prejudice and openness to enlightenment shine through the stultifying conditions of poverty, grave misunderstandings, and consequent tragedies.

The topic of sensibility that informs *Nature and Art* was controversial in the 1790s and its representation widely variegated. Chris Jones identifies three views of sensibility in writings of the late eighteenth century: as (1) a self-centered indulgence of feeling, (2) an emotional development reared by the traditions of society, and, (3) an innate emotional desire to see a "beneficial social order" and the liberation of "individual energies". The first, he argues, was rejected by all; the second he attributes to conservatives; the third, he ascribes to radicals.[71] Excessive, self-absorbed thought and behaviour are indeed censured in Jacobin and Anti-Jacobin novels alike. For both, they tend to be signs of aristocratic dissipation. Likewise, proper feelings of compassion and pity guided by the traditions of society are advocated in conservative novels. The Jacobins, however, who should fit neatly into the last category, struggle with the role of emotion in their design of a new society and their portrait of the new citizen. Whereas they argue that the desires for freedom, autonomy, and empowerment are intrinsic, they also insist that most (if not all) of what we know and feel is learned and is therefore subject to change. If circumstances create the individual, then they must step very carefully around an endorsement of innate emotions. Moreover, sympathy was being used by opponents of the French Revolution to decry the rebellious atrocities and to rouse compassion for the displaced aristocracy. "Sensibility is the *manie* of the day", wrote an irate Wollstonecraft in response to Burke's *Reflections*, "and compassion the virtue which is to cover a multitude of vices, whilst justice is left to mourn in sullen silence, and balance truth in vain".[72] At risk in the emphasis on emotion was justice.

Inchbald, therefore, faced a difficult task when she attempted to represent the new citizen as having a proper sensibility. She had to counter any emphasis on emotion with a corresponding stress on reason. She did so by showing the benefits of emotional self-awareness, to the individual and the community at large, and by equating the responsible handling of one's feelings with maturity and a readiness for political agency. When the novel opens, the two brothers exhibit a thoughtful sensitivity as they mourn their father's death. Still untouched by the tests of adulthood and London life, their innocence is born of their country upbringing. On their way to London from their country village, one "weeps bitterly" while the other tries to be brave and holding back his tears, utters "with a voice almost inarticulate, – 'Don't say any more; don't talk any more about it. My father used to tell us that when he was gone we must take care of ourselves: and so we must'".[73] When Henry and William come of age, evidence of the depth of their humanity is their acceptance or dismissal of their own emotions. As William becomes more and more educated, he learns to suppress his feelings and perceptions. He marries for money and status rather than love and epitomizes all that is reprehensible in a social climber personally and professionally. He and eventually his entire family – William, his wife Lady Clementina, and their son William – succumb to pride and vanity and live in a world of appearances. As a theologian, William is unbothered by his own lack of integrity, by the discrepancy between his own cold, calculating behaviour and the Christian compassion he preaches, and by his dishonesty in writing pamphlets published under the bishop's name. It is here, in William's world, that we begin to see the disjunction between form and content that is soon deciphered for us by Young Henry as he begins to analyze words and their meanings.

The elder Henry, in contrast to William, is aware that his "art" (his talent at playing the fiddle) has a certain power, and he uses his ability to orchestrate emotion to the benefit of those he loves. He knows that his entertainment "had often charmed … an effeminate lord; or warmed with ideas of honour, the head of a duke, whose heart could never be taught to feel its manly glow". Even "Princes had flown to the arms of their favourite fair-ones, with more rapturous delight" at the sound of his music (1:11). Yet Henry never loses sight of the effect of his art, the feelings it generates, nor the reason behind his endeavour: his hope to obtain financial help for his brother's education and subsequent placement in a profession. Henry's loyalty to his brother is immense, but it is not immune to the workings of judgment. When Henry marries a woman of his own class, out of love, William and Lady Clementina rebuff her because she is a common public singer. Henry reveals his ability to guide his emotions with sound reasoning by refusing to condone his bother's reaction. For Henry, no amount of fraternal affection will correct the wrong of prejudice. He walks out of his brother's life, and a year later, after the death of his beloved wife, leaves him (and the British society he represents) altogether; he sails away to an African island.

A similar dynamic of art and nature is played out in the comparison of the brothers' sons, Young William and Young Henry. In accordance with the English Jacobin premise that circumstances create the individual, the contrasting environments in which William and Henry are raised determine their inclination toward pretense or simple truths, feigned emotion or an honest sensibility. The theme of education, which is a foundation of the novel comes to the fore as the narrator begins to explain the contrary upbringings of the two young cousins. Of Young William, we are told that

> this unfortunate youth was never permitted to have one conception of his own – all were taught him – he was never once asked 'what he thought?' but men were paid to tell him 'how to think'. He was taught to revere such and such persons, however unworthy of his reverence; to believe such and such things, however unworthy of his credit; and to act so and so, on such and such occasions, however unworthy of his feelings. (1:26–27)

It is on this passage (and the contrasting development of a "child of nature" in Young Henry) that so many commentaries on *Nature and Art* base their remarks about Inchbald's interest in depicting Rousseau's theories on education. Her insistence that traditional instruction meant being taught the ways of falsehood rather than cultivating natural abilities points to Rousseau's maxims at the end of *La Nouvelle Héloïse*, which are later developed in *Émile* (1762), that "one need only to learn to read the book of nature in order to be the wisest of mortals" and that "the true book of nature" is "the heart of man".[74] The mistake of Young William's education is evident in his "imitation" of "the manners of a man" and his utter lack of the content of adulthood. "He would grin and bow to a lady, catch her fan in haste if it fell, and hand her to her coach, as thoroughly void of all the sentiment, which gives grace to such tricks, as a monkey" (1:28). His education makes a mockery of "natural" sentiment, defined as a coherence between action and intention, word and meaning.

Young Henry, in comparison, embodies a union of sentiment and outward behaviour, as well as the hope of a youthful innocence that can be nurtured only beyond the borders of British society. Both his refined mind and his coarse language are attributable to his lack of education and protection from local British customs. Raised by his father on an African island, he was taught only "to love, and to do good to his neighbour, whoever that neighbour might be, and whatever might be his failings" (1:33). Most important, he was instructed in truth and warned to hold falsehood and vanity in contempt. In contradiction to the pride that characterizes William's family, when Young Henry meets his aunt, uncle, and cousin, he is not thinking "'what they thought of him'", but "'what he thought of them'" (1:36). The narcissism that was such a focus of conservative attacks on reformers is the fatal flaw of the characters who represent the self-aggrandizement of the social elite, not of the fictionalized proponents of individual rights. Although the emphasis in interpreting the autonomous citizen is on a powerful and clearly defined self, it is not intended to encourage egoism. This stricture is evidenced by Young Henry, who vows that he "'never will stoop to act or to speak contrary to [his] feelings'", and whose "whole faculties were absorbed in others" (1:36) when he enters the civilized world of London (1:66). It is a weak sense of self that, in Inchbald's text, places one in danger of becoming prideful. The excessively vain Lady Bendham, for example, lacks the integrity that would give her substance and as a result becomes a mere "chameleon" (1:68).

The sensibilities of Young Henry and Young William are put to the test when the cousins first encounter women and love. Their sense of responsibility in courtship and marriage becomes a measure of their character. The outcome is easy to predict. Whereas "William indeed was gallant, was amorous, and indulged his inclination to the libertine society of women, ... Henry it was who *loved* them" and learned from them. Henry reverenced women "and felt so tender an affection for the virtuous part, that it shocked him to behold, much more to associate with the depraved and vicious" (1:66–67). William seduces and impregnates a young country girl, Hannah Primrose (a beautiful but illiterate girl of very modest means), and forsakes her to pursue his career and eventually a financially prosperous, though emotionally empty, marriage.[75] Young Henry falls in love with the least attractive, but most virtuous, of a Parson's three daughters. He must leave her for several years to search for his father, but the strength of their love endures and the novel ends with their reunion.

Beyond his role as a model of responsible sentiment, Young Henry's function, as a child of nature, is in his analysis of social absurdities. Inchbald's satirical intent – why she once entitled her manuscript a "satire upon the times" – is most evident in the humorous yet biting exchanges between Young Henry and his uncle and cousin. They reveal everything from ridiculous popular habits to profound statements about relations between the wealthy and the poor. Underlying all, however, is a fundamental questioning of the connection between word and meaning. Henry's mission is not to divulge the indeterminacy of meaning; it is, rather, to show the possibility of alternative readings, to expose the ridiculous reliance on traditional associations of thought, and to unveil a social reality. He acts as a Socratic revealer of truth and dramatizes the English Jacobin belief that one need only lift the veil of intentional obscurity to reveal the actual state of our existence and ready it for reform. Young Henry steps into forbidden territory and exposes hidden secrets.

By exposing meaning through a Socratic process that employs observation, logic, and "common sense", Henry reveals the workings of a moral code, displays its chimerical qualities, and provides an explication to instruct and liberate. Henry frequently and "innocently" misuses words that are infused with political ideology. "[C]ompliments" he confuses with "lies", "reserve" with "pride", "war" with "massacre", and "prosecute" with "persecute". His intent is both to reveal the politics of language and to justify reforms; if the law persecutes rather than prosecutes, it warrants change. Similarly, Henry demonstrates the farcical nature of customs we endow with reverence and by doing so divulges the hollowness of authority. When Henry first encounters his uncle's great white wig (William is now a Dean and magistrate), he is frightened. Then upon learning that "they are worn to give an importance to the wearer" and to distinguish superior people, he is able to compare the custom to that of the savages who "stick brass nails, wire, buttons, and entrails of beasts all over them to give them importance" (1:37). The denouement of exposure comes, however, when he views his uncle lying unadorned in bed with the wig on a nearby table. The puzzled Young Henry does not know to whom he should pay his respects, his bareheaded uncle or the wig alone.

In the latter half of *Nature and Art*, the disjunction between word and meaning is played out in the encounter between the sexes to demonstrate the devastating effect duplicity has on the uninformed and inexperienced. The tone of this section is decidedly more serious; gone are the humourous revelations of social absurdities. Hannah Primrose is unaware, until it is too late, that there is a harsh discrepancy between action and intention. The drama of seduction was alien to her, and she had "frequently been deceived from the appearance of circumstances" (1:99). She understood William's vows of affection to be literal indications of love rather than signs of the physical attraction that constituted his feelings for Hannah. Unschooled in language, and deprived of the "natural" upbringing of Young Henry's sort, Hannah is at a disadvantage. She becomes William's victim because she does not have knowledge or even the skills of inquiry. The harsh literalness of Hannah's existence is manifest in her desperate act of attempted infanticide when she finds herself deserted by the self-serving William. The baby itself becomes a symbol that bears the same confusion as words. Because he is found in the woods by Henry and Rebecca, they are presumed to be the child's parents. The longer the baby's true parentage remains unknown, the more hurt arises from assumptions made on insufficient evidence.

Deception and secrecy, enemies of the enlightened knowledge espoused by the Jacobins, are presented in *Nature and Art* as key to the maneuvers of great men – particularly in the legal domain. William, who is now a student of law, and his father, who is a magistrate, learn to live by deceit. For a young man schooled in falsehood, the law is a most appropriate profession, and William thrives in it. At a young age, he is appointed to a judgeship and in that capacity unknowingly sentences the victim of his crime, Hannah Primrose, to death. In this poignant scene, the grave irony of Inchbald's social criticism is that the guilty man, empowered by law, passes judgment on his own victim whom desertion has forced into a life of crime. The courtroom is not a site of enlightenment or reason, and the process of legal debate is not one that provides truth. Legal discourse has no immunity from the manipulation of language. The Dean, aware of his son's guilt in fathering an illegitimate child, implicates himself, as well, when he chooses to act against his better judgment and hushes up his son's affair with Hannah Primrose. "When men submit to act in contradiction to their principles", we are told, "nothing is so precious as a secret. In their estimation, to have their conduct *known* is the essential mischief – while it is hid, they fancy the sin but half committed; and to the moiety of a crime, they reconcile their feelings, till, in progression, the whole, when disclosed, appears trivial" (1:100).

Secrecy is presented as a policy of state. The dichotomy between word and meaning corresponds to the gap between what the nation is told about its prosperity and the daily reality of many who struggle to find food and lodging. As Dean, the magistrate is responsible for the welfare of the poor in his district. He is fully aware of their situation and even reprimands his wife's dissatisfaction with dinner by elaborating on the plight of the needy. Yet the Dean writes and publishes a pamphlet on the prosperity of Britain in which he ignores those who have no access to the British "fruits of the earth, the beasts of the field, the birds of the air, and the fishes of the sea", those who know not "peace, ease, plenty: and all ranks, liberty" (1:57–58). It is Young Henry, of course, who reminds the Dean that such wealth is known only by the privileged few. And it is Young Henry who reminds the reader that the practice of denial and deception by the government is a common one.

The question of what to do about poverty pervades Inchbald's novel. Young Henry poses his idealistic answer when he simply observes that if Britain is such a fruitful nation, there should be an abundance of resources, and no one need go without basic sustenance. In the context of this innocent observation, Inchbald attempts to address the prickly notion of benevolence. Whereas generosity is represented as one of our social responsibilities – Henry and Rebecca are virtuous in their care of the abandoned baby, even when it costs them their reputations – the dependence created by charity is often dangerous. The relationship between the elder Henry and his brother William is one of patron and recipient. Henry plays the fiddle in hopes of persuading a wealthy client to find a position for his brother. After some time, he is successful and convinces a man to provide William with a living of five hundred pounds a year upon the incumbent's death. Before long, William receives "the gift" (1:12). He is ordained and then later promoted to Dean. But the dependence established by these acts of patronage drives a wedge of resentment between the two brothers and causes a separation from which they never recover. As Marcel Mauss has argued, the gift brings obligation with it. A "present" can act as a contract which obliges reciprocation. This "polite fiction" may be, in actuality, "economic self-interest" and a means of rendering another inferior, particularly if a gift goes unreciprocated. "Charity is still wounding for him who has accepted it".[76] Moreover, the patron gleans a form of proprietorship over the recipient. In *Nature and Art*, the narrator explains,

As the painter views with delight and wonder the finished picture, expressive testimony of his taste and genius: as the physician beholds with pride and gladness the recovering invalid, whom his art has snatched from the jaws of death: as the father gazes with rapture on his first child, the creature to whom he has given life – so did Henry survey with transporting glory, his brother, drest for the first time in his canonicals, to preach at his parish church. He viewed him from head to foot – smiled – viewed again – pulled one side of his gown a little this way, one end of his band a little that way – then stole behind him, pretending to place the curls of his hair, but in reality, to indulge, and to conceal, tears of fraternal pride and joy. (1:13)

The parental pride in one's creation may seem selfless, but it breeds severe resentment in the recipient because it robs him of his self-ownership. William chafes with the pressure of obligation and the feelings of inadequacy that result from being dependent on another.

'I am eldest brother', he [William] thought to himself, 'and a man of literature; and yet am I obliged to my younger, an illiterate man'. – Here he suppressed every thought that could be a reproach to that brother. But there remained an object of his former contempt, now become even detestable to him – ungrateful man! the very agent of his elevation was now so odious to him, that he could not cast his eyes upon the friendly violin, without instant emotions of disgust (1:14)

Young Henry, himself the recipient of his uncle's good will, explains in his Socratic way, the burden of obligation to the wealthy Lady Bendham when she declares that the poor should be beholden to herself and Lord Bendham because they provided the village with a gift of one hundred pounds last Christmas. Young Henry calls this act of generosity "prudent", but not benevolent, because obligation is a great hardship. To Lord Bendham, he argues that the affliction of the poor was "that what the poor receive to keep them from perishing, should pass under the name of *gifts* and *bounty*. Health, strength, and the will to earn a moderate subsistence, ought to be every man's security from obligation.... if my lord would only be so good as to speak a few words for the poor as a senator, he might possibly for the future keep his hundred pounds, and yet they never want it" (1:73). Young Henry speaks here in his most radical voice because he is promoting political action rather than charity as a solution to social problems.

   The character of Young Henry provides something of a model for the new citizen in his courageous confrontation of artifice, his emotional responsibility, and his call to political action. His pursuit of inquiry offers at least a beginning to the quest for a discernible truth that was advocated by Godwin. Finally living a life of *elected* simplicity, Henry, Young Henry, and Rebecca decide to live "upon their *own* exertions alone; on no light promises of pretended friends, and on no sanguine hopes of certain success" (2:108). Their livelihood they will derive from "their own industry" and labour to protect themselves "from patronage and from control" (2:108). This fervent independence attempts to instill a sense of integrity and contentment in the new citizen, who is urged to relinquish idolatry of wealth and enjoy good labour and reflection. While the conclusion of *Nature and Art* undoubtedly takes a step back from the proposal of radical political action suggested by Young Henry, the powerful independent self it celebrates is in itself a politicized image. Inchbald revised *Nature and Art* between her completion of the manuscript in 1794 and its actual publication in 1796. The intervening years were fraught with political pressures – not the least of which were the Treason Trials of 1794 – and it is possible that Inchbald tempered the radicalism of her text for very practical reasons.[77] Nonetheless, her criticisms of the nation's ineffective attempts to deal with poverty, such as the magistrates' charities, resonate through the novel, and they are not forgotten in the image of pastoral contentment at the end of the text.

Robert Bage, *Hermsprong; or, Man As He Is Not*

The image of the fierce individualist, with which Inchbald leaves us, is taken up by Robert Bage in *Hermsprong; or, Man As He Is Not*. Published in 1796, *Hermsprong* celebrates the new citizen in the figure of a man who has it all: landed wealth, commercial success, love, respect, and political power. He links the old world with the new, the gentry with the merchant middle class, and the independent radical with the responsible member of the community. In many ways, Hermsprong is a Young Henry grown to adulthood. He is the "noble savage", the outsider who offers frank analyses of the social fabric and proposes change. Yet Hermsprong is also a more philosophically developed character than Young Henry, particularly in his embodiment of a maturing theory of individual, inalienable rights. In his economic independence and powerful wielding of his birthright (the foundation of inalienable rights), Hermsprong is perhaps the most definitive English Jacobin figure of citizenship.

In the course of the novel, we find out that the man we thought was entirely "self-made" is actually of noble birth, and consequently Bage's radicalism may strike us at first as tempered, as less adventurous perhaps than that of Holcroft's in *Anna St Ives*. Indeed, Hermsprong's marriage to the more conventional Caroline Campinet, rather than to the courageously transgressive Maria Fluart, seems an unfortunate concession to tradition. The compromises Hermsprong represents, however, constitute a considerable threat to the status quo because they most accurately describe the qualities of those who were to benefit from the transition to a body politic invested with limited political authority: men of property. As a man of landed wealth *and* commercial success, Hermsprong denotes the figure who successfully negotiates the transition to a capitalist economy and a civil society based on the contract. His name "Hermsprong", sprung from the Greek god Hermes, frees him from the limitations of inheritance (he is not dependent solely upon his title) and points to his role as not only a messenger but also the bearer and overseer of property.[78]

Bage works in the tradition of sentimentalism by describing "man as he is not" but has the potential to be. As in Holcroft's narrative vision, humanity in *Hermsprong* seems to be full of possibility, and the benefits of the individual are in concert with those of the community. The image is so ideal that it has sometimes incited critics to mock the protagonist "Imagine Sir Charles Grandison brought up on a diet of the *Contrat Social*", Oliver Elton writes in an early critique, "and we shall have some conception of the hero of Robert Bage's novel, *Hermsprong; or Man as He is Not* (1796) – a title that is only too accurate".[79] Still, the figure of the authoritative and immensely effective Hermsprong makes a crucial contribution to the corpus of the Jacobin novel by confirming the powerful place of the individual in relation to the law and by acknowledging that this relationship to civil authority is determined by property. Hermsprong presents himself as the alternative to the aging, ineffectual, and corrupt aristocracy, and he heroically pursues his individual right of property, which protects him from attempts to circumvent his self-determination.

Bage narrativizes the expression of self-determination through what Michael McKeon refers to as an "assimilationist" plot structure. The protagonist's progressive movement to a status of respect, virtue, and wisdom, which seems to be of his own volition and by his own talent and merit, is ultimately subverted by the convention of revealed noble parentage.[80] Hermsprong, whom we know only as a man born of English and French parents, raised in America, and well-traveled throughout Europe, turns out to be not just a mysterious outsider but the rightful lost heir to the Grondale estate. Whereas this literary maneuver is something of a disappointment to radicalism, it allows Hermsprong to claim success on every level, not the least important of which is economic. Hermsprong enters the scene as an enigma and maintains his personal obscurity until it is advantageous to reveal it. In the meantime, he falls in love with Caroline Campinet, the daughter of the corrupt Lord Grondale (current owner of the Grondale estate), and banters with his female counterpart Maria Fluart, a frank, outspoken, and independent young woman. Hermsprong's dialogues with a number of characters are the vehicle by which he espouses the rights of man, preaches about self-determination and the need to educate women, and refuses to acquiesce in the traditional economic maneuvers of marriage or the demands of filial obedience for the sake of obedience. In a coup d'état at the end of the novel, Hermsprong triumphs by continuing to enjoy the profits of his sound business sense (he is involved in a partnership), laying claim to his estate, and marrying his distant cousin Caroline Campinet.

The mechanism Bage uses to distinguish the new citizen is to demonstrate his powerful position in relation to the law and contrast it with the situation of those who remain subject to legal restrictions. What emerges is the necessity of self-determination to enjoy civil liberties and of property to acquire independence. Hermsprong's liberty is a function of his ability to exercise ownership rights; he experiences extraordinary freedom because of his numerous connections to property. He has acquired wealth through inheritance as well as commerce, and because he declares the rights of man, he also claims a fundamental ownership of the self that allows him a far-reaching autonomy. Hermsprong's family property is extensive. His father's money is the result of trade, while his mother's fortune is real property (in France) that he sells to make further investments in England, Italy, and America. In accord with the practice of primogeniture, he eventually inherits Lord Grondale's estate.

But it is Hermsprong's particular embodiment of the combined force of inherited wealth and commerce that proves to be such a force. Commerce gains in respectability in *Hermsprong*. It becomes a viable alternative to the machinations of the corrupt aristocracy and the abuses of the control of property through familial inheritance. Hermsprong's father turned to business when he was exiled from his family and could no longer rely on familial income. He conducted his fur trade among the American Indians and was successful because his presence was welcomed by the native people. He lived among them, learned their language, religion, and philosophy, and in that way "gratif[ied] his ardent desire to know man" – an empowering interest Hermsprong shares.[81] Commerce, ironically, bridges the gap between the European and the uncivilized worlds and sees one of its most successful manifestations in the midst of a people living "in a state of nature". While the recollection of the past that is implied in depictions of the noble savage usually operates as "a polemic against modernity", here it supplies the setting for an endorsement of economic development. In his support of commerce, Hermsprong does not eliminate the role of inherited wealth. He instead provides an assimilation of economic systems, a smooth transition in which the past is incorporated rather than rejected outright. Hermsprong corrects abuses to integrate the "new man" of commerce with the stable landowner *and* the proponent of individual rights. Hermsprong's peaceful conversion exemplifies an adjustment to the historical situation that reflects Burke's warning that a state "without means of some change is without the means of its conservation".[82] It reflects the kind of quiet revolution that was occurring throughout the evolution of the contract as the social bond.

Hermsprong's strength of self is central to his ability to acquire, maintain, and responsibly use property and to represent transition. The self he presents is complex, yet it is distinguished by integrity and self-understanding. To Lord Grondale's question "Who are you, sir?" Hermsprong simply replies, "I am a man, Sir" (20). Hermsprong first appears as the primitive "other". In that role, he is a romantic figure of innate power and human potential. His interests are the interests of the state, and he is untroubled by divisions between the individual and the community. Because the primitive figure, as Chris Tennant argues, seems to "always have had the right to self-determination", he/she embodies hope for those in search of political agency.[83] Hermsprong frequently provides the service of inspiring others to discover their own distinct identities. He brings his message specifically to Gregory Glen, who is the narrator and, significantly, the "son of nobody": a man unable to inherit because of his status as illegitimate.[84] To Glen, Hermsprong speaks as an unequivocal supporter of individual rights when he proclaims,

> I see not the difficulty of man's becoming a judge, tolerably just, of the temper of his mind, as well as of the temperature of his body; and learning the lesson, conceived so hard to be learned, of thinking himself what he is. – I have energies, and I feel them; as a man, I have rights, and will support them; and, in acting according to principles I believe to be just, I have not yet learned to fear. (98)

Inspired by Hermsprong's proclamation, Gregory Glen responds,

> I wish the world, that is the original thinkers in it, would meet together in some bar, it need not be very large, and determine what

is to be thought of such pretensions. Is this the stuff of which the pride of our people of rank and fashion is made? That it is pride of some sort, I have no doubt; for I, Gregory Glen, the son of nobody, felt myself raised, exalted by it. I almost began to think myself a man. But it is a word of bad augury. Kings like it not; parsons preach it down; and justices of the peace send out their warrants to apprehend it. (99)

Hermsprong's message incorporates a significant bravado in terms of "the law". Hermsprong declares himself "a judge" in regard to his own life, thereby justifying his self-governance and the right to act "according to principles [he] believe[s] to be just". He is persuasive enough to make Gregory Glen begin to feel a new-found strength and sense of self. He is also provocative enough to cause Glen to cringe under the threat that the rights of man posed to "people of rank". Social, political, and economic constructs were undoubtedly challenged by the idea that the populace could begin to claim inalienable rights to self-determination and pave the way to voting privileges. A powerful sense of personal identity meant a weakening of the family structure and the political prerogative associated with familial status.

Glen's final observation about justices of the peace sending out warrants to apprehend "it" is a reference to the censoring of Paine's *The Rights of Man*. Paine's essay plays a central role in Bage's novel as the manifesto by which Hermsprong speaks and acts. The publication and dissemination of *The Rights of Man* was fraught with political tension that is worthy of Gregory Glen's concern that the powerful sense of self within the concept of inalienable rights is a "bad augury". Paine was charged by the Attorney General with seditious libel on 21 May 1792, and his trial was set for December of that year. Paine's counsel, Thomas Erskine, argued that Paine did not encourage "destruction of property rights or disobedience to law", and that the real issue was liberty of the press. But the court ruled that "[f]reedom of the press and of opinion were not absolutes. They were relative to the times". Given just how dangerous the times were, Paine was found guilty and was forbidden to return to England.[85]

Hermsprong's advocacy of such a controversial document lends the novel most of its radical dialogue, notably in the form of discourse that places the individual in a position of power and independence from tradition. As the "new man" of "a freeborn mind" (73), unburdened by prejudices and Burkean prescriptiveness, Hermsprong speaks prophetically. In a direct reference to Burke and his reliance on the authority of antiquity, Hermsprong exclaims that "[i]n vain would the reasoners of the polished country say, every thing is due to the authors of our existence". In defiance of one of the foundations of British conservatism – that each generation is indebted to the past – Hermsprong proclaims, "Merely for existence, I should have answered, I owe nothing" (217). His position paves the way for reform and invites the kind of generational recreation of government that was advanced by Paine. In fact, the evidence used against Hermsprong in the charge of French espionage is the accusation that he has read Paine's *Rights of Man*, and that he has no clear parentage in which to submerge his individual identity.

Hermsprong's role as "new man" and social critic is enabled by his status as a "noble savage". As an outsider, he may claim a privileged vision and discretionary ability. Yet the primitive is not a "civil being"; therefore, as an ideal of citizenship, it is inadequate, and Hermsprong must show his ability and authority to function as a leader in society. He must confront civil authority and at the same time demonstrate his ability to be the model for the social being of modernity. It is a difficult balance to maintain, but Hermsprong has the strength of property in numerous forms on his side. Once we discover that Hermsprong is actually a member of the gentry and heir to Lord Grondale's fortune, our perception of his transgression changes. His is no longer the external threat of a foreigner with vague familial ties infiltrating British society; it is an internal threat from a member of a propertied, and therefore powerful, well-known family. Hermsprong functions adeptly within civil society, and in the end we see that civil authority works to protect his interests.

The civil authority that supports Hermsprong is shown to be responsive to truth and virtue; however, truth and virtue are revealed to be characteristics of the individual rather than of a particular class or the law itself. Hermsprong's brand of radicalism is both an assimilation of economies and a revolution in the concept of humanity. The required compromises are primarily points at which individuals are called on to respond to social duties, often in the form of reciprocity. When a group of miners rebel against rising costs, Hermsprong steps in and preaches loyalty and restraint to the riotous mob. In a voice that echoes Burke, Hermsprong tells them that "there is no possible *equality* of *property* which can last a *day*", and in what seems to be a reference to the French Revolution, he adds that even "[i]f you were capable of desiring it, ... you must wade through such scenes of guilt and horror to obtain it as you would tremble to think of" (225).[86] The verbal abuse of King George by one of the miners stirs an uncharacteristic violence in Hermsprong, and he passionately warns, "[B]ut so to revile your *King* is to weaken the *concord* that ought to subsist betwixt him and all his subjects, and overthrow all *civil* order" (226). While Hermsprong acts as a mediator by containing and dissipating tension, he continues to imply the power of the individual. It is Hermsprong, rather than representatives of the law, who quells the disturbance and keeps the peace. It is his call to social responsibility, not based on prescription or sensibility but on the reasonableness of social order, that is to the benefit of all.

Although Hermsprong confronts and frequently oversteps the boundaries of law, the civil system of justice – what Adam Smith calls "the main pillar that upholds the whole edifice" of society – ultimately works in Hermsprong's favour.[87] When he decides to reveal his identity as Sir Charles Campinet and lay claim to his inheritance, the law recognizes his status and restores what is rightfully his. In the battle of "*law* versus *truth*", both win. Hermsprong's experience in the courtroom is distinguished by the law's recognition of truth – an event that does not necessarily reaffirm the law's ability to realize truth through legal debate, but that negates the necessity of a legal contest Lord Grondale and his lawyer, Mr. Corrow, are willing to "overlook little improprieties", and attempt to manipulate the law to their own advantage (220). Their plan is to imprison Hermsprong, charge him with "rioting", seduction of the affections, and disrespectful behaviour toward a nobleman, and then secure his movement to another kingdom. But their misuse of the law is unsuccessful. The legal system rises to the occasion and acknowledges truth when expressed by a man endowed with individual rights (and plenty of property). By simply telling his story, Hermsprong is "honoured with the approbation of far the major part of the court", and the senior justice announces that "it [is] not the wish of the bench to give him [Sir Charles] any further trouble" (228). Further legal argument becomes unnecessary because Hermsprong is not giving a deposition but merely asking for a "remitter", defined as "restoration to rights or privileges" (263). As a result, "Sir Charles, having nobody to go to law with but himself, is under the necessity of not going to law at all" (248). Hermsprong's careful manipulation of his identity and control of his financial interests have allowed him to make the law respond to his truth.

Hermsprong's position of strength in relation to civil authority predominates in the novel; however, the contrasting fate of women is a resonating subtext that reminds the reader of the limitations of the rights of man as they were being conceived within contract theory.

Ownership of the self as property works for Hermsprong, who has control of his identity, can manipulate it for his own gain, and is able to maintain and reaffirm it through marriage. Identity does not require a familial context for Hermsprong (though he benefits from it in the end), as it does for Caroline Campinet, whose self is at least partially absorbed by the property in which she is included, and whose identity is inextricably linked to her position as a daughter and a wife. When Caroline is first introduced, she is characterized by passivity. She is described as a social introvert, raised by a similarly reclusive maternal aunt. The first news we receive of Caroline is her supposed death. Although she is able to reflect on superior subjects such as "the operations of the human mind, the right or wrong of human actions", she is excluded from much of civil society, which renders her observations less sagacious and influential than Hermsprong's. She absorbs the tensions of assimilation, ultimately represented by her marriage; however, her compromises are not an elected yielding to forms of authority that are malleable in her hands and that will ultimately work to her advantage, as is the case for Hermsprong. Caroline is also embroiled in the economy of the family, although her familial connections are unsupportive and hinder her advancement. She is the only surviving daughter of Lord Grondale from his first marriage, yet he regards her as a "guest" (112). She is in a tenuous position as an unwelcome heir.

Faithfully, Caroline attempts to fulfill her social responsibility as a daughter, but the harsh treatment she receives at the hand of her father makes it impossible for her to reconcile her individual desires with familial duties. She anticipates, and tries to engage in, the reciprocity between parent and child that Wollstonecraft presents as the relationship preferable to the more common one of parental tyranny, but she faces an unequal exchange.[88] The structure of her family is analogous to a monarchy, and it proves to be inadequate to the needs of the individual as evidenced by its failure to reconcile personal needs with social duty. Caroline gains access to wealth through marriage to Hermsprong, but she has no legal right to property. More important, she cannot claim the proprietorship of the self, which would yield her the protection of the law. When the individual woman encounters a civil contract such as marriage, she experiences a loss of rights, unlike Hermsprong, whose liberties are reaffirmed.

Caroline's troubles, like Anna St Ives', are those of the paradigmatic eighteenth-century heroine based on Richardson's Clarissa. She wrestles with filial obedience, faces a forced marriage and imprisonment, and is threatened with disinheritance and rape to secure a marriage to which she will not willingly submit. But it is the conception of Caroline as property of another that is foregrounded as the culpable force behind her demise. When Caroline encounters the law, it is as the subject of a property dispute. Among other accusations of entitlement violations, Lord Grondale charges Hermsprong with seduction of the affections. The seduction is regarded as a "private wrong" enacted against Grondale, not Caroline, which means it is a violation of his individual property rights.[89] Furthermore, what might first be considered a personal encroachment is immediately read as a political transgression. Hermsprong's charge of seduction is easily translated into accusations of "public wrongs" such as French espionage and rioting.[90]

The marriage of Caroline and Hermsprong concludes the novel and serves as an apparent resolution to the misuse of property and privilege. Through this act, Caroline seems to be releasing herself from the oppression of an undue filial obedience and exercising her will when she consents to a civil contract. Moreover, the political economy of this marriage is clearly meant to be based on reciprocity and equal exchange – an arrangement that corresponds to the preferred commercial form of trade rather than a reliance on inherited wealth. The marriage to Hermsprong, however, does not provide Caroline with the right of property or a distinct legal identity. Hermsprong secures the Grondale estate for Caroline through marriage, but it remains under his control. The marriage also proves to be a means of securing the Campinet wealth and keeping it within the family; in the tradition of endogamy, economic power has been concentrated and secured, much as Burke argued it should be for the security of the nation.[91]

While Caroline exemplifies the traditional place of women within the "old" society, Maria Fluart entertains the possibilities of a "new woman" whose freedoms should correspond to those of Hermsprong, the "new man". Maria's ability to experience more liberty than Caroline is attributable in part to the weakness of her family connections. At the death of her parents, she was left under the guardianship of Mr. Sumelin and Mrs. Merrick and therefore escaped the worst pressures of filial obedience. Through the course of the novel, she never marries and thus never faces the financial and legal dependency matrimony imposes on women. As a proponent of individual rights, Maria is aware of the inevitable losses she would face if she did marry. At the very least, she would lose to her husband her income of twenty thousand pounds. In the end, she remains unwilling "to buy herself a master" (247), averse to engage in an economic

exchange that guarantees her loss, and disinclined to make a purchase that involves relinquishing an unsanctioned property in
herself. For women, marriage is not "a barter of life for life, ... a
mutual and total alienation of person between a man and a woman",
as Marc Shell describes it in comparison to the Judaeo-Christian lex
talionis of a life for a life.[92] It is not an equal or free exchange.
Hermsprong maintains his legal identity and property, including self-
governance, in marriage and only stands to gain more wealth,
whereas his wife does not. A "child of commerce" like Hermsprong,
Maria is acutely aware of the inequality of exchange and the parallel
between the sacrifice of individual will to a husband and the transferal of rights to a political sovereign.[93]

Like Hermsprong, Maria is a "philosophic" character and functions
in a prophetic role. She warns Caroline that "[u]nder the name of
father, or brother, or guardian, or husband, they are always protecting
us from our liberty" (191). Maria is also characterized by her activity as
much as Caroline is by her passivity. At the attempted forced marriage
of Caroline to Sir Philip Chestrum – a manifestation of Caroline's submission of her will – Maria devises a scheme of hidden identity that
rivals Hermsprong's revelation in the courtroom. She substitutes
herself for Caroline as the bride and then in the midst of the ceremony
unveils herself and her symbolic substitution of the female advocate of
individual rights for the submissive daughter victimized by her father.
The groom Sir Philip, in a state of shock, knocks over a girondole – an
image used metaphorically by Maria to refer to artificial feminine sentimentality as opposed to the true content of reason represented by "a
simple candle" (107). The metamorphosis of a woman is witnessed by
the prominent characters in the novel and in civil society. The reverend "lifted up his eyes and hands toward heaven in pious wonder",
the lawyer "stared – a vacant stare", Sir Philip "bore all the marks of
fatuity", and finally "fire began to flash from the terrific eyes of Lord
Grondale" (210). Only Mrs. Stone and Caroline's maid, with apparent
sympathy and delight, are driven to laughter. Sir Philip tries to pick up
the fragments of the girandole to restore what was broken – but to no
avail. Maria also offers to marry him, but he refuses because the goods
in this exchange have been altered, and he would no longer be acquiring that which he intended to purchase.

As triumphant as Maria's scheme seems to be, there are significant
distinctions between her revelation of identity and Hermsprong's
that betray the limitations of what she has accomplished. First,
Hermsprong's disclosure leads to his acquisition of a title and an estate,

while Maria's only confirms her inability to marry if she wishes to keep her property. Hermsprong sees a restoration of his rights, whereas Maria reconfirms the inability of women to acquire such liberties given their confinement to the domestic sphere. Second, Hermsprong's revelation takes place in a courtroom and receives the approval of secular law; Maria's unveiling takes place in the family home, obtains only the approval of the women present, and the law is called in to restore control. It is clear that while Hermsprong's proclamation of rights coalesces with his role in civil society – and places him at its center – Maria's attempt to claim her liberties only serves to exile her. An attempt is made to imprison Maria for her transgression of authority and for her violation of the transaction of marriage. Maria simply refuses to be imprisoned and, acting with a confidence based on her assertion of self-ownership (an inalienable natural right that implies protection from arbitrary imprisonment), produces a pistol. In the face of an attempt to violate her individual rights, Maria takes the law into her own hands and responds with a defiant expression of self-defense. She dares anyone to stop her and "walk[s] on to the hall-door, which she opened herself unimpeded". She rebukes, rejects and abandons the terms of the aristocracy and "[a]t the door of the garden leading into the village" she is "received by Hermsprong and Glen" (215). It is a grand act of defiance, but it leaves Maria with the status of an "outlaw" – far different from the leadership role that Hermsprong derives from his confrontation with the law.

In Bage's novel, then, we see the development of a theory of inalienable rights embodied in the individual who is allowed to realize his potential. Hermsprong acts as a mediator, a revealer of truth, a prophet of the rights of man, and a model for the citizen who will reap the benefits of a capitalist economy and a democratic government. His successes are an encouragement to the new citizen and usher in hope, even at a time when the French Revolution has turned terrifyingly violent, government pressures on radicals in Britain was intensifying, and the morale of reformers was crumbling. Yet even within Bage's celebration of the new man is the recognition that the rights of man were not being extended to the financially dependent, such as women. Law and other forms of civil society are supportive of a propertied man with strong familial and economic ties – the sort of person civil society has traditionally supported.

4
Acquiring Political Agency

In the framework of the eighteenth-century family and society at large, women could not claim the legally protected civil and economic independence that was necessary to self-governance in the public domain. Also excluded from consideration were others who could not claim the right of property, such as servants and beggars. While the gradual conversion to a market economy and the rise of commerce demanded that the concept of ownership be closely aligned with the development of the self, women and servants continued to be seen only in relation to domestic roles. At the same time, beggars, who were reliant on the charity of others, were situated outside the family, at the periphery of society. All were considered "part of their masters", dependents who would speak and act on the wishes of fathers and husbands or acquiesce to the desires of financial supporters. Because of their lack of economic autonomy, their identities were absorbed in that of others. Consequently, one sees in the novels of the English Jacobins a pervasive concern with exploring definitions of property and the boundaries of the self. In contrast to the sanguine novels envisaging the new citizen, William Godwin introduces the problem of exclusion in *Caleb Williams* and thereby changes the course of the English Jacobin novel. Mary Hays and Mary Wollstonecraft, in their respective novels *Memoirs of Emma Courtney* and *The Wrongs of Woman: or, Maria*, respond in kind and focus on the restrictions that deny women the "rights of man".

The problem of exclusion for the unpropertied is recorded in the place of women in formal patriarchalism, as well as in contractarianism. In both instances, women found themselves deprived of the benefits of subjecthood or citizenship. The requirement of obedience by force of nature, which was at the heart of the analogy between father and king in formal patriarchalism, persisted in the domestic lives of women in the social contract. Instilling a profound sense of dutifulness by securing loyalty and submissiveness in the home was an important component of Sir Robert Filmer's widely read treatise on absolute government, *Patriarcha*, because obedience was seen to be a potent force in reaffirming monarchy and stemming the tide of political instability.[1] Enforcing obedience, however, was also a crucial element in continuing to control property within the family, restricting access to wealth, and eliminating women and other dependents as agents in the manipulation of economic resources in the social contract. The popularity of Filmer's *Patriarcha* was ultimately short-lived,[2] but the image of the patriarchal family, according to S.D. Amussen, was a ubiquitous force that "defined the ideals of the gender system" in the community at large and "provided a model for all relations between women and men".[3]

Locke's response to Filmer seems to have ensured ongoing interest in *Patriarcha*. In *Two Treatises of Government*, Locke attacks the notion of absolute political authority by countering Filmer's literal claim that the king is the father of his people. While Filmer admits that "all kings be not the natural parents of their subjects", he insists that they are "the next heirs to those progenitors who were at first the natural parents of the whole people, and in their right succeed to the exercise of supreme jurisdiction".[4] He also deems the categories of "family" and "state" inseparable and writes of the sovereign's relation to his subjects "as if they were all one extended kinship system".[5] According to Filmer, "[i]f we compare the natural duties of a father with those of a king, we find them to be all one, without any difference at all but only in the latitude or extent of them ... all the duties of a king are summed up in an universal fatherly care of his people".[6] Locke dismantles Filmer's scheme with a rationalist argument against Adam's dominion over his own species and the succession of political governance through the "ancient fathers", Noah, Abraham, and Nimrod, who had "regal authority" by right of fatherhood.[7] In reference to God's granting "Dominion over every Living thing that moveth on the Earth", Locke contends that "whatever God gave by the words of this Grant, I *Gen.* 28. it was not to *Adam* in particular, exclusive of all other Men: whatever *Dominion* he had thereby, it was not a *Private Dominion*, but a Dominion in common with the rest of Mankind". With a literalness of his own, Locke argues that the proof lies in "the Plural Number" in God's statement. "God blessed *them*", Locke writes, and "'tis certain *Them* can by no means signifie *Adam* alone".[8] His reading then works as evidence on behalf of the contract, which, according to Locke, is the origin and end of government.

Locke's *Two Treatises* is notable for its detailed and thorough rebuttal of Filmer's literal patriarchalism, but it is also important because it offers a clear and salient indication of the direction liberal individualism was to take, including the place of women and other dependents within that tradition. Despite the attention Filmer's *Patriarcha* received in 1679–81, by the time Filmer wrote his essay (*c.*1620–42), and certainly by the time it was republished in 1679, kinship as a principle of social organization was already in decline, the state as a distinct institution was emerging with formidable power, and the family was withdrawing into a private realm.[9] Locke's insistence that "the power of a *magistrate* over a subject may be distinguished from that of a *father* over his children, a *master* over his servant, a *husband* over his wife, and a *lord* over his slave" served to solidify intellectually the movement toward the conceptualization of political power as a consenting contract and the supremacy of law in civil society.[10] One of the fundamental principles that emerges out of Locke's exchange with Filmer is the political nature of the family, especially in regard to property. While Filmer declares the family political because at its origin was a hierarchical system of governance that required obedience by all others,[11] Locke tries to disassociate conjugal rule from political power and break down the stalwart form of economic control: inheritance. Even if one could determine the correct lineage deriving from Adam, Locke argues, "the knowledge of which is the Eldest Line of *Adam's* Posterity, being so long since utterly lost, that in the Races of Mankind and Families of the World, there remains not to one above another, the least pretence to be the Eldest House, and to have the Right of Inheritance".[12] Furthermore, Locke brings history to bear on Filmer's interpretation of the succession of power. "*Heir*, indeed, in *England*", Locke explains "signifies the Eldest Son, who is by the Law of *England* to have all his Fathers Land", but there is no "*Heir of the World*" or universal natural law that renders us born into subjection to an absolute monarch or necessitates the practice of primogeniture.[13]

Locke's redefinition of political authority, particularly his insistence on the separation of family and state, appears to take an important step toward an equality of gender and status because it seems to give women the opportunity to expand their identities beyond that of daughters and wives and because it implies an extension of political agency beyond familial wealth. Equality of birth is one of the central axioms Locke maintains in his *Two Treatises*. The ambivalence Locke expresses regarding the extension of rights to women, however, is indicative of the precarious position women held in the social contract. When Locke observes that God gave dominion to Adam *and* Eve, he also claims that "if it be said that *Eve* was subjected to *Adam*, it seems she was not so subjected to him, as to hinder her *Dominion* over the Creatures, or *Property* in them".[14] Yet Locke does not entirely dismiss the usefulness and validity of Eve's submission to Adam and therefore of a wife to her husband. In reference to Genesis 3:16, where God punishes Adam and Eve for their disobedience and subjects Eve to the will of her husband, Locke writes:

> God, in this Text, gives not, that I see, any Authority to *Adam* over *Eve*, or to Men over their Wives, but only foretels what should be the Womans Lot, how by his Providence he would order it so, that she should be subject to her husband, as we see that generally the Laws of Mankind and customs of Nations have ordered it so; and there is, I grant a Foundation in Nature for it.[15]

Locke gives women an opportunity to reach past the confines of Eve's subjection. His equivocation on the subject of women's obedience to paternal authority seems to leave open the possibility of independence, but it renders women responsible for their own development. A woman may "contract with her Husband" to "exempt" her from submission or simply "endeavor to avoid it".[16] Locke, however, is more interested in isolating the issue of a woman's obedience to her husband from the question of the rightful form of political authority than he is concerned that women attain citizenship. To remind us of Eve's role in the creation story is not to persuade us of women's worth, it is to weaken Filmer's argument for monarchy – an argument that is dependent on Adam's singular dominion.

Similarly, Algernon Sidney's republican response to Filmer, *Discourses Concerning Government*, focuses on opposing monarchy and virtually ignores the impact of democracy on women. The purpose of breaking down the patriarchal analogy of father and king was to distance proponents of the contract from their image as mere rebellious sons; it was not to dismantle the patriarchal family. Although Sidney disputes paternal power in government, he argues that "every Man should be chief of his own Family, and have a Power over his Children".[17] When Sidney does address the rights of women, it is to bolster his argument against the inheritance of political power. The folly of a woman ruling a country is further evidence that one cannot or should not accept the absolute governance of a king or queen simply because he or she is deemed heir to the throne. Despite Sidney's support of a separation of family and state, women's subordinate role in the home continues to be the rationale behind his notion that women are inadequately equipped for public life. "That Law of Nature", Sidney writes, "which should advance them [women] to the Government of Men, would overthrow its own work, and make those to be the heads of Nations, which cannot be the heads of private Families; for, as the Apostle says, 'The Woman is not the head of the Man, but the Man is the head of the Woman'".[18] Hence, the patriarchal family remains intact.

The mandate of independence, espoused by Sidney and other contract theorists, is most effective in prohibiting women from participating in civil society beyond their domestic roles. "Liberty", Sidney writes, "solely consists in an independency upon the Will of another, and by the name of Slave we understand a man, who can neither dispose of his Person nor Goods, but enjoys all at the will of his Master". When Sidney explains further that there is no freedom in being dependent on the benevolence of a monarch, he inadvertently points to the predicament that women face when their inability to own property is enforced by law. "There is no such thing in nature as a Slave", Sidney observes, "if those men or Nations are not Slaves, who have no other title to what they enjoy, than the grace of the Prince, which he may revoke whensoever he pleaseth".[19] Largely unable to claim title to land and other forms of wealth and being at the mercy of a benefactor's goodwill, women, by Sidney's definition, are slaves. In contrast, the "multitude", which is to enjoy the rights of contract, is composed of "Freemen, who think it for their convenience to join together, and to establish such Laws and Rules as they oblige themselves to observe".[20] What a mistake it would be, Sidney continues, if "a Woman that is seldom able to govern her self, should come to govern so great a People".[21] Several chapters of Sidney's *Discourses* are devoted to proving that no one, not even a monarch, is above the law and that dominion over a nation can be justified only by the judicial system. By rendering women subject to the law but not instrumental in its design or approval, Sidney denies them the most comprehensive and fundamental of rights in the new commonwealth – that of being an agent of legislation.

Rousseau also places women in a definitively subordinate position in the private sphere. Women are excluded from the body politic, not only because they are considered incapable of holding public office, but also because they pose a threat to the social contract. In his

Discourse on Political Economy, Rousseau addresses Filmer briefly and outlines the distinction between the family and the state; however, as in Sidney's essay, the family remains a patriarchal institution in which women are unequivocally secondary to men. Rousseau is adamant that the functions of the magistrate are different from those of the father, and that public economy differs from private economy. The magistrate has transitory authority bestowed on him by law, while the father has static and absolute power. Rousseau describes the state as a "great family" in which "members are all naturally equal, political authority, being purely arbitrary in the way it is established, can be founded only upon agreements, and the magistrate can command others only by virtue of the laws", whereas the responsibilities of the father in the nuclear family are "dictated to him by natural feelings", and "all property rights belong to him or emanate from him".[22] The authorities of husband and wife are not equal in the domestic setting, and the husband may "oversee" his wife's behaviour because of the need to be certain of patrimony.

Although Rousseau's *Social Contract* provides some of the key components of contract theory, particularly in his advocacy of political equality, he spends little time on the role of women in the commonwealth. Where he does elaborate on the contributions of women is in *Émile*, published in 1762, the same year as *The Social Contract*. In Book V of *Émile*, when Rousseau discusses "Sophy" (or the ideal woman), he focuses on the differences between the sexes: "men and women are and ought to be unlike in constitution and in temperament".[23] Civically recognized authority belongs to men, while women must rely on subversive tactics to maintain their status as helpmeets rather than slaves. By her "beauty", "wiles", and "wit", a woman may take advantage of a man and control him through his own strength. But this power is never sanctioned by law. As a model for contemporary society, Rousseau cites the place of women in ancient civilizations: in the home. "When the Greek women married," Rousseau writes, "they disappeared from public life; within the four walls of their home they devoted themselves to the care of their household and family. This is the mode of life prescribed for women alike by nature and reason".[24]

According to Rousseau, nature and reason also decree that women "be at the mercy of man's judgment", and that girls be taught restraint because their lives will always require obedience.[25] "They must be trained to bear the yoke from the first, so that they may not feel it, to master their own caprices and to submit themselves to the will of others", Rousseau writes.[26] Girls need not be educated as boys are because their role is to charm and please. But they must be scrupulous in their deportment because their misconduct could eventually destroy the family, "the bonds of nature", and the security of the nation. When a woman bears an illegitimate child, Rousseau warns, "her crime is not infidelity but treason".[27] While Rousseau supports the separation of family and state, he links the private and the public in his accusation of treason for an act of personal intimacy. Because clarity of proper ownership is essential to the management of property, a woman's sexual behaviour is a concern of the community. A woman's conduct, in spite of its context of intimacy, is, according to Rousseau, "controlled by public opinion", and any threat to that role is a threat to the social contract.[28]

Locke's ambivalence about the role of women in a society organized by contract, and Sidney's and Rousseau's views on the subordination of the female sex were issues with which English Jacobin writers had to contend when they endorsed republicanism. Patriarchy, Carole Pateman observes, did not vanish with Sir Robert Filmer. It continued to inform modern society when the "social contract" became a "sexual contract", when patriarchy "ceased to be paternal" and women were "subordinated to man *as men*", rather than as fathers. When the *fraternité* replaced the family as the image of government, it continued the policy of excluding women.[29] Moreover, patriarchy as it persisted in the social contract had an impact on anyone who fell into the category of the unpropertied and the status of a dependent, such as servants and beggars. The Jacobins then had to address the fact that while contract theory was a means to expanding the body politic not everyone was considered a free agent qualified to enter into a binding agreement. Thus, they went in pursuit of agency that would bolster "the 'individual' as owner" – "the fulcrum on which modern patriarchy turns."[30]

William Godwin, *Things As They Are; or the Adventures of Caleb Williams*

In *Things As They Are; or, the Adventures of Caleb Williams*, William Godwin applies the patriarchal paradigm of exclusion for women, to all dependents. The protagonist Caleb is manifest at different times in the novel as a servant, a beggar, and a wife, and in each role he suffers from his debilitating condition of vulnerability. In addition, the relationships in the text – the Hawkinses and Barnabas Tyrrel, Emily

Melvile and Tyrrel, Caleb Williams and Mr Falkland – are pre-dominantly feudal ones, and they all result in the destruction of the parties involved. As the stories of these characters unfold, Godwin con-structs evidence that the feudal relationship – a patriarchal and per-verted form of "contract" – marks contemporary society and it could easily persist into any reconstructions of the body politic. Moreover, each of these relationships is characterized by claims of ownership and struggles to gain independence that ultimately lead to confrontations with the law. Once they encounter the forces of legal institutions, the Hawkinses, Emily, and Caleb find that protection by the law and against the law is determined by proprietorship. Because they are eco-nomic, social, and political dependents, because they cannot assert a total self governance, the law cannot (will not) work to their advan-tage, and they are all rendered victims rather than proprietors in society.

In *Caleb Williams*, Godwin turned his focus to the law in all its manifestations, from positive law to individual conscience and private judgment. At the appearance of the novel, there was a great deal of interest in Godwin's representation of British law. William Enfield in *The Monthly Review* observed Godwin's "peculiar opinions" on juridical institutions, which he summed up as the thesis that "law itself, in its origin and essence, is unjust".[31] *The British Critic* was outraged by "the evil use which may be made of considerable talents" and incensed by Godwin's "odious" portrayal of his country's laws.[32] Most of the responses were either surprise or con-tempt at Godwin's general distaste for legal orchestrations in society, but a letter to *The British Critic* took Godwin to task for very specific misrepresentations of the law in the story of the Hawkinses and the trials of Falkland. The Hawkinses were a father and son evicted for voting against the wishes of their landlord, persecuted under the Black Act, and eventually hanged for the murder of a local landowner. The correspondent to *The British Critic* found numerous discrepancies between Godwin's narrative and his own reading of the law, such as the unlikelihood that a landlord would coerce a tenant into voting according to his direction, and that a mere tres-passer could be charged with a capital offense. He also notes that Mr Falkland, who is charged with murder, could not be tried twice for the same crime, as occurs in the first edition of the novel.

Godwin is indeed openly critical of law in *Caleb Williams*. In the course of telling the Hawkinses' tale, the narrator interjects comment-ary on why the legal system is an inadequate means of obtaining justice.[33] Reviewers critical of Godwin's legal analysis were responding to remarks such as the following:

> Wealth and despotism easily know how to engage those laws, which were perhaps at first intended (witless and miserable precaution!) for the safeguards of the poor, as the coadjutors of their oppression.... Hawkins had hitherto carefully avoided, notwithstanding the injuries he had suffered, attempting to right himself by a legal process, being of opinion that law was better adapted for a weapon of tyranny in the hands of the rich, than for a shield to protect the humbler part of the community against their usurpations. (40)

When Hawkins does try to reach a fair settlement through the courts, he faces a web of legal intricacies, and "by affidavits, motions, pleas, demurrers, flaws and appeals" the dispute is perpetuated "from term to term and from court to court". It all becomes "a question of the longest purse" (41).

Godwin's written response to *The British Critic* counters some of the specific criticisms of legal inaccuracies. He insists that in practice one can be tried twice for the same charge and cites accounts from the *Newgate Calendar* and *Lives of the Convicts*. Nonetheless, in the second edition (published in 1796), Godwin transforms the first trial of Falkland in Volume 1 into a hearing or "examination", which allows for the subsequent trial in Volume 3. In addition, Godwin professes that he was more concerned with the systemic issues of law than its details and that these very disputes only serve to exemplify the equivocal spirit of law. The object of exposure and censure in *Caleb Williams* was "the administration of justice and equity, with its consequences, as it exists in the world at large, and in Great Britain in particular".[34] Godwin's clarifications, however, did nothing to silence his critics; the magnitude of his critique only exacerbated their ire. To condemn the British legal system and its assumptions about justice and equity was transgressive enough, but to do it in "the form of a novel, to make it circulate among the ignorant, the credulous, and unwary" was the ultimate error.[35]

Although Godwin addresses the law in its expansive and multiple manifestations, he does in fact expose particular legislation that reflects an oppressive or at least a questionably restrictive ideology. One such mandate was The Waltham Black Act (9 George I c.22). Instituted in 1723, the Black Act was first seen as a piece of emergency legislation intended for a period of three years, yet it remained in effect for the next century. It was not repealed until 1823.[36] The act presumably responded to the increased activities of groups of armed men with blackened faces who were poaching wildlife and hustling forest warrens in Waltham Chase, Hampshire (hence, the "Waltham" Black Act).[37] Under the Black Act, it was a capital offence to appear in a forest "armed with swords, fire-arms, or other offensive weapons, and having his or their faces blacked, or being otherwise disguised".[38] The act first reads as an extreme measure to contain poaching that had run wild, but its impact was far-reaching, and before long it was being invoked in cases of trespassing, cutting down a young tree, being armed without a blackened face, or being disguised but not carrying a weapon. Furthermore, prosecution was made convenient. The defendant could be tried in any county in England, and if the accused refused to surrender himself, he could be "sentenced to death without further trial".[39]

The instance of trespassing in *Caleb Williams* exemplifies the extent to which the Black Act was easily exploited. In a campaign of harassment, the landowner Barnabas Tyrrel barricades a broad path that is the Hawkinses' only access to a road leading to the market town. Since the path crosses the land of one of his tenants, which is adjacent to the Hawkinses' farm, Tyrrel believes himself justified under the ordinances protecting private property. The younger Hawkins, who is indignant at this obvious act of persecution, "went in the middle of the night and removed all the obstructions that had been placed in the way of the old path, broke the padlocks that had been fixed, and threw open the gates" (41). Having been observed, he is immediately caught, jailed, and tried for burglary. In the second edition, Godwin recasts the details of young Hawkins' violations into activities more clearly punishable under the Black Act. Young Hawkins had unfortunately "buttoned the cape of his great coat over his face as soon as he perceived himself to be observed; and he was furnished with a wrenching-iron for the purpose of breaking the padlocks" (288 n.237). In addition, according to the prosecuting attorney, the field in question was a feeding site of hares. Disguised, armed, and on private property containing wildlife, Hawkins is charged with a felony punishable by death.

Godwin's demonstration of the malleability of the Black Act is cited by E.P. Thompson as exemplifying one kind of abuse that could be (and was) incurred.[40] Godwin's story is also mentioned by Thompson because it points to the growing concern for the definition and protection of private property in the seventeenth and eighteenth centuries. Thompson argues that "the Blacks", whose operations provoked the passage of the act, were not quite "social bandits, and they [were] not quite agrarian rebels, but they share[d] something of both characters". He claims that they were "armed foresters, enforcing the definition of rights to which the 'country people' had become habituated", and they were "resisting the private emparkments which encroached upon their tillage, their firing and their grazing".[41] The Black Act offered extensive protection of private property and, through its retribution of death, placed human life in a subordinate position to the preservation of deer, fish, cattle, trees, barns, and out-houses. It suggested the growing authority of property in the eyes of the law "until justice itself was seen as no more than the outworks and defences of property and of its attendant status".[42] The passage of the Black Act, Thompson contends, may have been an instance of the government pacifying its greatest supporters (the most propertied), but it likewise indicated "a prior consensus as to the values of property in the minds of those who drafted it". The Black Act also pointed to a recent trend in criminal enforcement when it employed "terror" to assert its authority.[43]

Terror as a tool of the law is at work throughout *Caleb Williams*, and it is interwoven with multiple disputes over property. At the heart of the representation of property in *Caleb Williams* is the controversy about ownership of other persons and the extent of control over others' behaviour. For example, the source of trouble for the Hawkinses is a battle over agency. The elder Hawkins balks at being forced to vote according to his landlord's wishes and suffers eviction because of his gesture of independence. When Tyrrel allows him to rent a piece of his land, Tyrrel decides that he wants Young Hawkins in his service. The elder Hawkins resists, and the conflict that follows leads to the barricaded path and the charge of Young Hawkins under the Black Act. Within the context of the debate over natural and civil rights, the narrator's description of events is surely meant to be contentious. Tyrrel wants to take the boy "into his family" and "make him whipper-in to his hounds" (37). The father resists, and Tyrrel gives vent to his expectations of dominion. "I made you what you are", Tyrrel declares, "and, if I please, can make you more helpless and miserable than you were when I found you. Have a care!" (38). In his possessiveness, Tyrrel violates the crucial maxim of contractarian thought that was articulated by Paine: "Man has no property in man".[44] Tyrrel also reverts back to behaviour reminiscent of feudal arrangements of power and treats the Hawkinses as if they had the medieval status of the "villein", which referred to "unfree peasants". Although villeins had some rights in the twelfth century, such as protection under criminal law, they were in numerous ways subject to the will of the lord of the manor. The landowner could seize the property of villeins, exercise corporal punishment over them, and prohibit them from escaping their tenancy.[45] Much as the medieval concept of liberty as inheritable property was retrieved by Burke, Tyrrel's expectations of control over his tenants indicate that the spirit of villeinage (unfree status) lived on even after its elimination as a formal rank in the thirteenth century.

Meanwhile, Hawkins declares his and his son's autonomy. Of himself, he says, "Though I am a plain working man, your honour, do you see? yet I am a man still. No; I have got a lease of my farm, and I shall not quit it o'thaten" (39). For his son, he pleads, "[w]e have all of us lived in a creditable way; and I cannot bear to think that this poor lad of mine should go to service. For my part, I do not see any good that comes of servants. God forgive me, if I am unjust! At present he is sober and industrious, and, without being pert or surly, knows what is due to him" (38). It is important to note that part of Hawkins' strength comes from the fact that he now owns the lease to his property, and this ownership provides him with the ability to resist. Nevertheless, the stance he takes against Tyrrel is a brave one, and his assumption that his son is "owed" better opportunities than servitude points to the notion, also advanced by Paine, that the individual is a proprietor in society. At the very least, Hawkins' belief that his son's expectations of advancement are legitimate elevates the individual to a figure who has broken through the limitations of status and proven himself to be capable of advancement.

The events in Volume I of *Caleb Williams* are often neglected or regarded as troublesome to the aesthetic unity of the novel.[46] A closer look, however, reveals that there are a number of parallels between the first and the last two volumes. The alliance between Barnabas Tyrrel and the Hawkinses offers numerous foreshadowings of the relationship between Falkland and Caleb Williams that is developed through the course of the novel. Tyrrel's forced exile from society is also a hint of future events for both Falkland and Caleb; all of these characters suffer social ostracism at some point in the narrative, although Caleb's is the most profound. Finally, the fate of Emily Melvile, a young cousin of Tyrrel who dies as a victim of his extreme possessiveness, is analogous to Caleb's demise. The "economy" of her situation is mirrored in Caleb's financial dependency on Falkland, and together Caleb and Emily figure a conflation of gender and status concerns in the novel. Caleb's circumstances as a servant are significantly analogous to those of women subject to the control of fathers, elder brothers, or husbands.

While the dilemmas of Volume I are to some extent the common stock of novels with an added Jacobin twist to elucidate the politics of social relations, they establish the paradigm of conflict for the more complex encounters between Caleb and Falkland.

In the story of the Hawkinses, Falkland himself unwittingly predicts his own future conduct when he advises Tyrrel on his behaviour in the entanglement over the Young Hawkins. Tyrrel continues to lay claim to his authority in the situation – that is, his right as a landlord to demand the services of Young Hawkins. "Is not the man my tenant? Is not my estate my own? What signifies calling it mine, if I am not to have the direction of it?" he asks (43). "I took up Hawkins when every body forsook him, and made a man of him", he claims (44). Falkland's response is that of a sober, benevolent man not yet faced with crises of his own. He urges reason, kindness, and forgiveness and even seems to have some understanding of class disadvantages. But his comments are sprinkled with remarks that establish him as a Burkean figure. He bases his interference in Tyrrel's affairs on a chivalric code between landowners. Thus, Falkland says to Tyrrel, "If I see you pursuing a wrong mode of conduct, it is my business to set you right and save your honour" (43). His sense of benevolence is likewise grounded in a policy of *noblesse oblige*. To Tyrrel, he explains, "I believe that distinction to be a good thing, and necessary to the peace of mankind. But, however ne-cessary it may be, we must acknowledge that it puts some hardship upon the lower orders of society.... We that are rich, Mr Tyrrel, must do every thing in our power to lighten the yoke of these unfortunate people" (43).

Particularly in the context of the Hawkinses' story, and in contrast to Tyrrel, Falkland seems to speak as a reasonable man. His calm, however, is deceptive, and his politics are equally misleading. In the next few moments of this scene, passions escalate, and the dangerous forces of unwieldy emotion begin to show the potential breadth of their influence. In the expanded scene in the second edition, Falkland's admonitions to Tyrrel anticipate his impending confrontations with Caleb. In utter frustration, Falkand lashes out:

> I am ashamed of you! Almighty God! to hear you talk gives one a loathing for the institutions and regulations of society, and would induce one to fly in the very face of man! But, no! society casts you out; man abominates you. No wealth, no rank, can buy out your stain. You will live deserted in the midst of your species; you will go into crowded societies, and no one will deign so much as to salute

you. They will fly from your glance, as they would from the gaze of a basilisk. Where do you expect to find the hearts of flint, that shall sympathize with yours? You have the stamp of misery, incessant, undivided, unpitied misery! (288 n.244)

Falkland's emotional outburst at first appears to shatter Tyrrel's complacency and self-righteousness and instill some sense of guilt. On the surface, it seems that the unleashing of such passion has a positive effect; however, the eventual outcome of the encounter between Tyrrel and Falkland is in itself a signal that warring passions will come to no good. As Pamela Clemit argues, *Caleb Williams* is a novel about the importance of rationality as much as it is one about the lethal outcome of uncontrolled desires, appetites, and obsessions.[47] As a result of this episode, Tyrrel begins to think about revenge – "[v]engeance was his nightly dream, and the uppermost of his waking thoughts" – and Falkland, further exasperated by another scene of tyranny, is soon driven to murder (288–289 n.4).

Another story in Volume I that is an important precursor to Caleb's tale is that of Emily Melvile. The dynamics of her relationship with Barnabas Tyrrel are later duplicated in the economic and emotional alliance between Caleb and his "Master" Falkland. In many ways, Emily and Caleb are alike, and the similarities between them contribute to the overall structural unity of the novel as well as to its articulation of political possibilities. The conflation of a male servant and an unpropertied woman points to the contingency of agency on the right of property, the function of emotion in the operation of tyranny, and the necessity of self-governance that is recognized by the law for confrontations with the law. Without an acknowledgment of property in the self, one could not obtain status. Correspondingly, as the legal historian J.H. Baker observes, "status could profoundly affect property rights and contractual capacity, not to mention access to the common-law system itself".[48] Emily and Caleb are both "orphans"; therefore they enter adulthood without stable familial connections and without status.[49] In Burke's construction of rights, they are at a severe disadvantage. They are also in serious danger, and their respective fates illustrate just how perilous existence can be without a guarantee of self preservation.

Emily and Caleb are innocent figures when young; they are inexperienced and ingenuous until they are confronted with the actions of men who are fearful of losing their authority and all of its attendant privileges. Emily comes to know the evils of the world only too late: "Conscious herself that she would not hurt a worm, she could not conceive that any one would harbour cruelty and rancour against her" (52). Caleb's natural and boyish curiosity leads him directly into his fatal confrontation with Falkland. Emily and Caleb also suffer from excessive imagination and a romantic temperament. Emily falls in love with Falkland, and she begins to behave obsessively – to Tyrrel, quite annoyingly. Emily's thoughts of Falkland and his kindnesses "made her heart palpitate, and gave birth to the wildest chimeras in her deluded imagination" (49). Caleb is driven by his "ungovernable suspicion, arising from the mysteriousness of the circumstances, and the delight which a young and unfledged mind receives from ideas that give scope to all that imagination can picture of terrible or sublime" (111). Caleb eventually discovers that he too loves Falkland, and his devotion to his master impedes his ability to fight for his personal liberties. Both are swept away by Falkland's part in a "political romance". He seems to fit the image of the paternal landowner looking after his subordinates, and for Emily he becomes the conventional romantic hero. He saves her from a fire and an attempted rape and then pays her "debt" to her guardian in a final effort (which ultimately fails) to save her life. Emily's circumstances never allow for the moment of enlightenment or the crucial exercise of reason that would reveal Falkland's darker side. Caleb likewise remains deluded until the end, but his activities divulge to the reader the dangers of succumbing to the fictions of a sovereign's good will.

Emily's story also serves as a vehicle to disclose the typical distresses of women who are the objects of ownership in a society dominated by property. The laws governing married women's property first come under attack in the account of Emily's parents. Emily was born into poverty because her father spent her mother's modest fortune and because the portion of her mother's estate that should have reverted to Emily was used "to swell the property of the male representative" (46). These actions were sanctioned by the law, and they left Emily without a place in a family, without a clear status. She was taken in by the Tyrrels, but she was not received as a member of their family, and she was not even accorded the position of a domestic. Her state of formal non-existence left her especially vulnerable to abuses of authority, and her survival came to depend on placating her guardian, who had fallen in love with her but wished neither to give her a proper status as his wife nor to see her happily married to another. She becomes a typical female character whose sufferings in the domestic realm contradict its image as a site of personal and national security.

As the story continues, Emily evolves into a Clarissa-like figure. She falls in love with Falkland, and when her guardian Tyrrel disapproves, he tries to force her into a marriage with the brutish labourer Grimes. At Emily's insistent refusal to acquiesce in his design, Tyrrel locks her in an apartment and plans to have her abducted and raped. The plan fails because of Falkland's intervention, but Tyrrel soon has her arrested for "debt", and, unable to endure further trauma, Emily falls sick and dies. After Richardson, and certainly by the 1790s, Emily's fate is not an unusual one in the plot of a novel. The Godwinian mark, however, is the identification of property in a political context as the culprit behind the machinations that destroy Emily and the critique of emotions that are complicitous in the perpetuation of unequal social relations. Emily's encounters with Tyrrel become, like the Hawkinses', a battle of wills. She tries to assert her independence, and Tyrrel, through application to the laws of ownership, tries to claim Emily as his possession and thereby justify his control of her actions.

The language of possession appears throughout the scene in which Emily defies Tyrrel's assertion of power over her. "Do you think I will let any body else chuse a husband for me?" she asks, and continues: "I am right to have a will of my own in such a thing as this". But Tyrrel counters by asserting that he will reduce her to her true status, which is really none at all, and he derides her overactive fancy. "You must be taken down, miss", he cries, "[y]ou must be taught the difference between high flown notions and realities" (54). Tyrrel's contemptuous recasting of status conflict as a matter of emotion and imagination was a device frequently used in the Anti-Jacobin movement. It was an attempt to detract from the political importance of the situation and displace the actual issue at hand. Despite Tyrrel's efforts at distraction, when the narrator tells us that Tyrrel was "accustomed to talk of women as made for the recreation of the men, and to exclaim against the ill-judged weakness of people who taught them to imagine they were entitled to judge for themselves", the reader is forced to consider the questions of self-governance and private judgment (57). The language of possession becomes most intensified, however, when Tyrrel feels that he is losing control. When Emily demands to know by what "right" he keeps her captive, he invokes the authority of "the right of possession". "This house is mine", he argues, "and you are in my power". He presents his guardianship in terms of money – "I will make you a bill for clothing and lodging" – and threatens her with the legal action to which he eventually resorts. "Do you not know", he asks, "that every creditor has a right to stop his runaway debtor?" (62). At the failure of his scheme to have Emily abducted and raped, Tyrrel carries out his final threat and has Emily arrested "for a debt contracted for board and necessaries for the fourteen last years" (71). She is ultimately reduced to an object of economic exchange and in the process loses even the remotest sense of self, autonomy, or agency she might once have imagined she could claim. Falkland's mediation and effort to obtain her liberty by paying her debt is ineffective because he cannot procure it for her – she must claim it for herself. Emily's liberty cannot be so easily had. In the final confrontation between Emily, Falkland, and Tyrrel, it becomes clear that only her ability to assert her individual rights, the property in herself and her own self-governance, would enable her to enjoy liberty and simply preserve her life. Emily has no natural or civil liberties and therefore no juridical protection against the manipulations of positive law by others.

Godwin's philosophical writings on law are well known for their indignant criticisms of legal systems. In *Political Justice*, Godwin provocatively calls law "an institution of the most pernicious tendency" and a lawyer one who can "scarcely fail to be a dishonest man".[50] In an early chapter of *Political Justice* on the "Influence of Political Institutions Exemplified", Godwin explains his assessment of how the law works in society, and he provides the philosophical basis for his fictionalized presentation of positive law, including the Black Act in *Caleb Williams*. He reiterates his conclusion that "legislation is in almost every country grossly the favourer of the rich against the poor". He cites for condemnation the game-laws, "by which the industrious rustic is forbidden to destroy the animal that preys upon the hopes of his future subsistence, or to supply himself with the food that unsought thrusts itself in his path".[51] He denounces the disparity of revenue from the land tax (which had been reduced) and the tax on consumption (which had been increased). This contrast, Godwin argues, is an example of the government shifting financial burdens from the rich to the poor. In addition, he portrays the morass of legal procedures in a manner that anticipates Dickens' *Bleak House*. Like Holcroft, he remarks on the "glorious uncertainty of the law" that lends itself to "the multiplied appeals from court to court, the enormous fees of counsel, attornies, secretaries, clerks, the drawing of briefs, bills, replications and rejoinders".[52] Law may have been intended as the means by which the citizenry knows what to expect and how to behave, but it is "a labyrinth without end" and a "mass of contradictions that cannot be extricated".[53] In fact, ambiguity is, according to Godwin, a principle upon which the legal institution was founded.

Confusion is the basis of legal argument, whereas clarity is what is sought in justice.

With a plethora of evidence that Montesquieu's maxim "[l]aw in general is human reason" does not inform the practice of positive law in Great Britain, Godwin offers a proposal to replace law with reason.[54] "Legislation, as it has been usually understood", Godwin explains, "is not an affair of human competence. Reason is the only legislator, and her decrees are irrevocable and uniform". In addition, society does not make laws but can only interpret that which is declared by "the nature of things" and "the propriety of [that] which irresistibly flows from the circumstances of the case" (95). Ideally, positive law would become extinct over time, and reason would gradually fill the void. The manifestation of legislation by reason in society would be the recognition of "private judgment", which Godwin describes as the basis of justice: "To a rational being there can be but one rule of conduct, justice, and one mode of ascertaining that rule, the exercise of his understanding". There is, Godwin argues, a "moral arithmetic" to each case that must be understood and followed before an act can be considered "just". What is better for twenty is simply more just than what is better for only one. Morality for society at large, according to Godwin in *Political Justice*, "requires that we should be attentive only to the tendency which belongs to any action by the necessary and unalterable laws of existence".[55] Moreover, it is our *social obligation* to be rational beings, ascertain what is just and equitable, and conduct ourselves appropriately. "If there be any truth more unquestionable than the rest", Godwin concludes, "it is, that every man is bound by the exertion of his faculties in the discovery of right, and to the carrying into effect all the right with which he is acquainted".[56]

Godwin's exceptional adherence to a belief in the ability of human reason to discern justice is often disregarded in analysis of *Caleb Williams*. Because Godwin makes fascinating observations about the workings of the human mind and heart, it is easy to forget that *Caleb Williams*, like Wollstonecraft's *Wrongs of Woman*, Smith's *Young Philosopher,* and Edgeworth's *Castle Rackrent*, is about "things as they are", and not as they should be. Investigation and inquiry are crucial to bringing about change, and Godwin's narrative is a form of investigation that Godwin hoped would reveal the insidious workings of government in our private/public lives. In *Political Justice*, Godwin cites Sidney, Locke, Paine, Rousseau, and Helvétius as writers who have placed liberty in "the security of our persons, and the security of our property". Furthermore, they agree that 'these objects could not be effected but by the impartial administration of general laws". Where Godwin diverges from contractarians is in his assessment of government's influence on private lives. Government is, for Godwin, "the most powerful engine for promoting individual good", and of course equally powerfully in promoting evil.[57] That the personal is utterly political is a proposition that Godwin explores throughout *Caleb Williams*. The relationship between Caleb and his master Falkland involves an acknowledgment of status and the economic exchange of labour, but it is fused with emotion in Caleb's love for Falkland, rather than with reason. Each irrational facet of their association supports the other. Falkland's basis for his claim to Caleb's life is his ownership of Caleb as a servant. Caleb's love is to a great extent born of his admiration for Falkland's place as "one of the most enlightened and accomplished men in England" (109). Their relationship is corrupted on many levels, and it epitomizes the kind of unequal social relations that have helped to perpetuate the Burkean world and must therefore be eliminated if widespread reform is to be realized.

Like many of his fellow English Jacobin authors, Godwin is at odds with the family in *Caleb Williams*. To counter Burke's notion of inheritable rights, it was necessary to show the damage done in domestic settings and to reaffirm their politicization. Emily Melvile's situation is one powerful instance of familial abuse, but the story of Caleb Williams is even more riveting and profoundly disturbing because it so thoroughly de-privatizes the kind of tyranny at work between Emily and her cousin Barnabas Tyrrel. Caleb is a servant whose master Falkland claims him, in totality, as a possession. Falkland, whom some critics have argued is the principal character in *Caleb Williams*,[58] is a powerful paternal figure whose obsession with "honor" renders him a despot. In Volume I, Falkland appears as one might expect (and perhaps hope) if one wanted to believe in the good will and virtue of the landed classes. He seems honest, compassionate, and benevolent. He is a magistrate one might wish to trust as a reasonable mediator in legal disputes. But we are given indications, early on, that this Burkean ideal is fallible and not to be revered.

In the first volume, we are introduced to a Mr Clare who held an "intellectual ascendancy" in the community and was the only one who could effectively subdue Tyrrel and mediate local controversies. While Mr Clare was resident in the neighbourhood, Collins reports, Tyrrel's behaviour had improved. "Such was the felicity of Mr Clare's manners that, even while he corrected, he conciliated, and excited no angry emotions in those whose actions were most curbed by the appre-

hension of his displeasure" (34). As it turns out, Falkland is a poor substitute for Mr Clare's sobering balance, and it is precisely because
Falkland cannot claim an "intellectual ascendancy" and becomes
obsessed with honour that he does not measure up. Mr Clare's death is
the passing of one who would have "governed by reason and justice"
(32). On his death-bed, Mr Clare warns Falkland of the very weaknesses
in him that will soon wreak havoc and lead to the loss of lives:

> Falkland, I have been thinking about you. I do not know any one
> whose future usefulness I contemplate with greater hope. Take care
> of yourself. Do not let the world be defrauded of the benefit of your
> virtues. I am well acquainted with your weakness as well as your
> strength. You have an impetuosity and an impatience of imagined
> dishonour, that, if once set wrong, may make you as eminently mis-
> chievous, as you will otherwise be useful. Would to God you would
> think seriously of exterminating this error! (32)

Mr Clare is the English Jacobin spokesperson in *Caleb Williams*. His reference to Falkland's deficiency as an "error" is one sign that he serves
as the voice of Godwin and other Jacobins such as Holcroft. Mr Clare is
also a poet and in that capacity fulfills the expectations of a poet as a
"prophet" and a "legislator" that Shelley later outlined in his *Defence of
Poetry*.[59] He is admired by society both for his gift of art and for his reasonableness. He is distinguished by a "perpetual suavity of manners, a
comprehensiveness of mind, that regarded the errors of others without
a particle of resentment, and made it impossible for anyone to be his
enemy". He is a natural judge. "He pointed out to men their mistakes
with frankness and unreserve: his remonstrances produced astonish-
ment and conviction, but without uneasiness in the party to whom
they were addressed: they felt the instrument that was employed to
correct their irregularities, but it never mangled what it was intended
to heal" (23–24). At Mr Clare's death, the Jacobin image of the ideal,
rational citizen disappears from the novel, and we are left with the tor-
tured, tumultuous, impassioned world of Caleb and Falkland.

Falkland is, as Mr Clare recognizes, an ambitious man obsessed with
honour and reputation. He has for some time been driven by his pride
and "the rhapsodies of visionary honour" (9). Like Caleb, but in the
manner of the privileged, Falkland has been raised on romance. He is
enamored of "the sentiments of birth and honour" and has "drunk ...
deeply of the fountain of chivalry" (11). Gary Kelly identifies Falkland
as a fictionalized version of Lucius Gray, second Viscount Falkland

(1610?–1643), a man who also seems to have had "a fatal chivalric code of honour".[60] Pamela Clemit likens Falkland to Richardson's Sir Charles Grandison, but she considers the comparison to be a means of showing that "ostensibly unaccountable features of character are in fact only too explicable in terms of political corruption".[61] Indeed, Falkland's behaviour is quite politically explicable in that it voices Burke's backward-looking vision in the revolution debates, demonstrates the fatal consequences of his ideas when put into government policy and everyday village activities, and reveals the crucial role of sensibility in Burke's design (as well as his reversion to feudal norms). Falkland often echoes Burke's *Reflections*, and he falls victim to emotion in the same way that Burke does in his essay. Moreover, Falkland's passion at first seems deeply buried, but it soon rears its head. Falkland's rage, particularly when he feels his position of authority threatened, is a political warning, in gothic proportions, of what is just below the surface in the discourse of chivalry and honour. Likewise, Burke's concern for the decay of chivalry not only epitomizes Falkland's sense of loss over the decline of aristocratic privilege but also defines the basis of Caleb's character in relation to the *ancien regime*. "But the age of chivalry is gone", Burke writes. "That of sophisters, oeconomists, and calculators, has succeeded; and the glory of Europe is extinguished for ever. Never, never more, shall we behold that generous loyalty to rank and sex, that proud submission, that dignified obedience, that subordination of the heart, which kept alive, even in servitude itself, the spirit of an exalted freedom".[62] As a servant, beggar, and "wife", Caleb represents those who are loyal, submissive, obedient, and/or subservient, but certainly not free. The "spirit of exalted freedom" lives neither in those in control, such as Falkland, nor in those in service, such as Caleb.

Caleb's roles as a servant and a beggar are evident in the text itself, but his role as "a wife" can be inferred from Godwin's preface to *Fleetwood* (1832), where he compares the relationship between Falkland and Caleb to that of Bluebeard and his wife. Even without Godwin's analogy, however, the parallel to Emily Melvile's story and the gender-defined arrangement of authority and subordination that is implied in the absolute possession of Caleb by Falkland are grounds for discussing Caleb as a kind of spouse. In the same way that Montesquieu observes that "the nature of honor" is "to aspire to preferments and titles", the arrangement between Caleb and Falkland is absolutely dependent on inequality.[63] The symbolic gendering of "Caleb as wife", on one level, simply reinforces the hierarchy of the sexes. On another level, it reaffirms the result of Godwin's investigation into the factors of gender and status as they impinge on the "rights of man": property is the pivotal determinant of one's interaction with the law. As a financially liable servant or utterly deprived beggar, Caleb has no hope of enfranchisement; as a "wife", his economic and emotional dependencies render him a victim of civil authority. Subsequently, the legal system fails to provide him with the protection it offers to the propertied. Without the guarantee of an inalienable right of autonomy, Caleb is devastatingly vulnerable. He is hunted like a beast, and he is denied the basic legal assurances of one who owns his civil liberties: the rights to due process of law and protection from arbitrary arrest, trial, and imprisonment.

In Caleb's story, Godwin presents an argument about the political urgency of recognizing an inalienable right of property that, in Lockean terms, begins with finding and claiming property in oneself. In *Political Justice*, Godwin echoes Locke on property, when he writes that "[i]n the same manner as my property, I hold my person as a trust in behalf of mankind". But Godwin places far more emphasis on the utility of ownership and the social obligations attached to property than does his contractarian predecessor. Out of a sense of both justice and duty, Godwin explains, "I am bound to employ my talents, my understanding, my strength and my time for the production of the greatest quantity of general good".[64] Moreover, Godwin argues for the necessity of a radical redistribution of property. "[T]he established system of property", he asserts, has produced "the spirit of oppression, the spirit of servility, and the spirit of fraud"; the only remedy is for society to seek "the justice of an equal distribution of property" that is based on a rational assessment of need.[65] In *Caleb Williams*, Falkland's and Caleb's relationship as master and servant exemplifies an arrangement of false dependence that is a result of "the established system of property". The dynamics between the two protagonists is also an illustration of Godwin's response to Burke that "[i]ndeed 'the age of chivalry is' not 'gone!' The feudal spirit still survives, that reduced the great mass of mankind to the rank of slaves and cattle for the service of a few".[66] Falkland's concept of justice relies on compassion and paternal benevolence rather than on social and economic equality. His code of "honour" and "virtue" turns a blind eye to the cruelty of his tyranny over Caleb, and his "love of fame" distorts his view of the world.[67] Falkland's and Caleb's relationship casts them both into a state of delusion – a state that is the very antithesis of the rational one that, Godwin insists, is absolutely necessary to justice.

When Caleb learns, through his uncontrolled curiosity, that Falkland is the true murderer of Barnabas Tyrrel and he allowed two innocent men to be hanged for the crime, Caleb disturbs the balance of power. Consequently, Falkland begins to lay claim to his possession of Caleb. Caleb's curiosity, it is important to note, is a deviant form of inquiry that Godwin and Holcroft alike deplored in contrast to intellectual inquiry. So it is no surprise that this less than virtuous means of discovering information should lead to the dramatic confrontation, chase, and tragic ending that it does. At his moment of confession to Caleb, Falkland assesses Caleb's situation in terms of property (and the story of Faust). "Do you know what it is you have done?" he asks. "To gratify a foolishly inquisitive humour you have sold yourself.... It is a dear bargain you have made" (123). Before long, Caleb realizes he is Falkland's prisoner, and that Falkland "undertook to prescribe to every article of [his] conduct" (129). He recognizes "the supernatural power Mr Falkland seemed to possess of bringing back by the most irresistible means the object of his persecution within the sphere of his authority" (145). At a hearing over which Mr Forester, Falkland's elder half brother, presides, Falkland betrays the politics of his harassment of Caleb. He charges Caleb with robbery, but it is not the stealing of wealth that concerns him; it is Caleb's theft of his honour and his facade, and Caleb's withdrawal of loyalty, that are at issue. Caleb's attempt to gain independence is, finally, the most severe threat. The trial only demonstrates the inability of legal systems and the structure of positive law to miss the "truth". Circumstantial evidence is easy to find, but it has no relation to actual events; it is lost in the maneuvers of interpretation.

Caleb's flight from the persecutions of his oppressor is a series of encounters with the corruptions of law. He witnesses trials that are theatrical farces, he experiences the deplorable conditions of jails, he meets up with a gang of outlaws, and he becomes an outlaw himself. But Caleb also cooperates in the process that leads to his exile and loss of self. As Caroline says to Maria in Bage's *Hermsprong*, "it is a sight of every day, ... that women, wives at least, continue to love their tyrants".[68] At the very moment Falkland claims possession and control, Caleb responds with love and articulates the depth of his attachment to his master. Caleb's sense of himself is deceptively glorified and reinforced when he considers the elevation of his once humble character to a level of importance. He derives a false sense of power from contributing to the well-being of Falkland, a man of status. These "ennobling" emotions, Caleb admits, "attached me to my master more eagerly than ever" (109). Caleb foolishly thinks that Falkland, like the law he represents as a magistrate, is a "generous protector". Because Caleb, as Alex Gold so insightfully points out, is always deluded by love, he does not see that Falkland and the legal system, in their compassionate benevolence, are bent on destroying the autonomous individual and denying the already disenfranchised the right of property.[69] The protective relationship between women and the law, as purported by Blackstone, is shown in the relationship between Falkland and Caleb to be a dangerously misleading one. For Caleb and Falkland, paternal protection leads to the destruction of the individual.

Godwin's concern for the development of the individual and the right of private judgment is embodied in the struggle between Caleb's attempt to claim justice for himself – "I stood acquitted at the bar of my own conscience" (272) – and the comprehensive extent of Caleb's tragedy: the loss of identity and eventually of a sense of self-preservation, which is the "first law", according to Rousseau, of common liberty.[70] Caleb's life as a fugitive devolves into a life of disguises, and he is prevented from "acquiring a character of integrity" (259). In the manuscript ending of *Caleb Williams*, Caleb's victimization by Falkland and his acute inward withdrawal are unmistakable when he declares himself one of the "living dead". Caleb concludes, "it is wisest to be quiet .... True happiness lies in being like a stone ... a GRAVE-STONE! – an obelisk to tell you, HERE LIES WHAT WAS ONCE A MAN!" (340). The published version likewise ends with self-loathing. Though he has finally heard Falkland's confession to murder, Caleb receives no sense of accomplishment or justice. He relinquishes his pursuit of truth and simply declares, "I have now no character that I wish to vindicate" (277). Through Caleb's loss of self, Godwin articulates the English Jacobin concern for the fate of those who are automatically disenfranchised when rights are considered inheritable property and those who are threatened with confinement to a distinct private domain and exclusion from the contract that informs government.

At the opening of the novel, Caleb tells his readers that the story he is about to unfold is his personal memoir. At the end of his tale, Caleb explains why he chose narrative as a means to pursue justice. After several attempts to free himself from the relentless scrutiny of Falkland, Caleb decides to go into "voluntary banishment" and sail to Holland (265). But while waiting for a ship, he returns to an inn only to see Jones, the man who has been tracking him for Falkland, enter his room.[71] Jones reminds Caleb, "[y]ou are a prisoner at present" and "all your life will remain so" (265). As such, Caleb cannot leave the country; he must remain in England, Scotland or Wales so that he will never be out of Falkland's reach (265). Caleb's reaction to Jones' warnings is one that carries the reader back to garden scene in Volume 2 when Caleb realizes that Falkland is the murderer of Barnabus Tyrrel. In both instances, a form of knowledge overwhelms Caleb physically, emotionally, and intellectually. "The intelligence thus conveyed to me", Caleb explains, "occasioned an instantaneous revolution in both my intellectual and animal system". "[M]y blood", he continues, "has been in a perpetual ferment. My thoughts wander from one idea of horror to another with incredible rapidity.... I sometimes fear that I shall be wholly deserted of my reason" (266). But in the earlier garden scene, the "instantaneous revolution" was characterized by "a kind of rapture" and it was followed by "the most soul-ravishing calm" because it is at that point that Caleb realizes "it was possible to love a murderer" (117). By the end of his story, those transporting emotions have disintegrated and Caleb is now likening Falkland to Caligula and himself to the victim of the most "dark, mysterious, unfeeling, unrelenting tyrant!" (266).

Still, Caleb's "revolution" continues, and at the very moment he succumbs to the command in the middle of the page to "Tremble!", he turns the emotional directive around and considers the possibility that the tyrant himself might give way to fear. Thinking of Falkland, he asks, "What should make thee inaccessible to my fury?" And then he announces his weapon of defense – not a knife or a sword, but a tale. "No, I will use no daggers! I will unfold a tale – ! I will show thee for what thou art to the world, and all the men that live shall confess my truth!" (266). Caleb embraces narrative as the most effective method of achieving justice. "I will tell a tale – ! The justice of the country shall hear me! The elements of nature in universal uproar shall not interrupt me! I will speak with a voice more fearful than thunder!... With this engine, this little pen I defeat all his machinations; I stab him in the very point he was most solicitous to defend" (267). He asks Collins to preserve his papers, in hope that "they will one day find their way to the public" (267). Finally, Caleb returns to the image of the chest, the Pandora's box that unleashed the turmoil that ultimately consumes both Falkland and Caleb. He speculates that the secret contents of the chest might include, again, not a dagger or "some murderous instrument" but rather a "faithful narrative", one that might tell the truth about Falkland's involvement in Tyrrel's death. Since Caleb assumes that Falkland's narrative will never be revealed, he suggests that his story "may amply, severely perhaps supply its place" (267–68).

The significance and power of narrative emerges at the end of *Caleb Williams* in this scene of resolve. Much of the dispute between Falkland and Caleb has been about the manipulation of stories and the interpretation of events, the control of information and efforts to discover secrets. Mark Philp has linked *Caleb Williams* to the tensions resulting from the pursuit and persecution of British radicals in 1793 – a pursuit and persecution that made extensive use of spies (such as Jones) and culminated in the Edinburgh and London treason trials.[72] Indeed, at the heart of the fear of British radicalism and of the trials themselves was the authority and influence of narrative and the interpretation of language and intention.[73] The complexity of the conflicts surrounding narrative and the law is ultimately represented in the crisis Caleb faces when he tries to tell his story in court. Once in the confines of a trial, confronting officers of the law, Caleb is unable to convey "the truth" and assert his narrative. He gives way to his love of, and loyalty to, Falkland and yields to the process of self-annihilation that has been underway in the last two volumes of the novel. Narratives of silenced truths – narratives of women, servants and beggars – cannot survive in the gothic trappings of the law; they must find an external venue, such as that of the novel. While Caleb loses himself, unprotected by the law and/or the right of property, all that remains is his memoir; however, that memoir carries with it a mode of authority that seems to be the only one within reach of those excluded from political participation in a constitutional monarchy or a reconstructed social contract.

Mary Hays, *Memoirs of Emma Courtney*

Mary Hays' quest for agency focuses on women. By tracing the development and consequences of Emma Courtney's excessive ardour for Mr Augustus Harley, in *Memoirs of Emma Courtney*, Hays reveals the pitfalls awaiting those who eschew the discerning the ways of reason. While Hays acknowledges the important role emotion plays in molding character, determining the nature of attachments, and affecting the outcome of events, she also warns that the deluding power of unbridled feeling is dangerous. Emma and the recipients of her affection are destroyed by false hopes and obsessive behaviour. In addition, Hays treats passion as deserving of a comprehensive investigation, but she is also careful to observe that political dialogue, legal discourse, and epistemological inquiry are all firmly rooted in rationalism – as evidenced by the formal rhetorical structures of her letters to the *Monthly Magazine*, in 1796, on the materialism of Helvétius and Godwin, the human capacity for learning, and the education of women.[74] Strongly influenced by her upbringing in the Dissenting tradition,[75] Hays regarded the pursuit of knowledge as a natural right which must be extended to women if they are to function as responsible parents and enjoy full citizenship.[76] Only if women could show themselves capable of emotional balance and cognitive maturation could they be considered active members of civil society and worthy participants in a contract. In *Memoirs of Emma Courtney*, Hays narrativizes the urgency not only of proper education but also of the natural right to question, investigate, reason, and attain knowledge in the quest to gain agency.

Although Hays's treatment of passion and reason in *Emma Courtney* is energetic and sweeping, it is also marked by some ambivalence. In its early readership, the novel received swift condemnation for what seemed to be an indulgence in, and endorsement of, emotion because Hays spends so much time on the subject. The *Critical Review* remarked in 1796 that the protagonist's "passion, not love at *first sight*, but even *before* first sight, ... will perhaps, to some readers, appear to favour of extravagance".[77] Still, as Gary Kelly suggests, by foregrounding sensibility, Hays elevates the feminine culture of intuitiveness, sympathy, and compassion to the level of virtue. Moreover, she merges these qualities with the Dissenting doctrine of spiritual egalitarianism and presents sensibility as a powerful source of radical activism. She draws a connection between feminist politics and aesthetics, Kelly argues, "by implying that women may not be disabled from sublime experience by 'retirement' in domestic life but rather empowered subjectively and thus artistically".[78] Hays emphasizes passion partly because the self-reflexive sentimentalism of *Emma Courtney* attempts an in-depth critical reevaluation of sensibility. Whereas rationality remains, in the text, a vague and unexplored ideal, Hays gives credence to the function of passion and finds a crucial place for it in her analysis of human motivation. In one of her letters defending Helvétius in the *Monthly Magazine*, Hays argues that "the true method of generating talents is to rouse attention by a lively interest, by a forcible address to the passions, the springs of human action. Our attainments will be in an exact proportion to our excitement".[79] The fictional Emma likewise explains that passion has a central function in the development of individual talent: "Sensation", comments Emma, "generates interest, interest passion, passion forces attention, attention supplies the powers, and affords the means of attaining its end: in proportion to the degree of interest, will be that of attention and power. Thus are talents produced" (8). Additionally, in the preface to *Emma Courtney*, Hays declares her novel to be "a useful fiction" because, like Godwin's *Caleb Williams* and Radcliffe's *The Italian*, it traces how "the consequences of one strong, indulged, passion, or prejudice, afford materials, by which the philosopher may calculate the powers of the human mind, and learn the springs which set it in motion" (3). The key to benefiting from one's emotions, according to Hays, is to channel the power of feeling in the direction of personal stability and social good.

Still, while Hays acknowledges the significance of passion as a source of energy, she also embraces a steady and measured reason. In her preface, Hays explains that Emma's fate, as a result of her indulgence in emotion and imagination, is "calculated to operate as a *warning*, rather than as an example" (4). Freedom of thought and speech, the ability to doubt, examine, and ascertain truth are, she writes, "the virtue and the characteristics of a rational being" (3), and a rational being is the "hero" of contract theory. Locke insists that a covenant is an agreement among reasoning individuals in a state of nature.[80] Sidney considers reason to be man's "own Nature" and that which governs the necessary restraints on liberty.[81] Blackstone lists mental soundness as one of the qualities necessary for consent in a contract, and Paine also contends that the "nation" which precedes government is comprised of rational participants.[82] Emma Courtney, however, lacks access to free thought and speech because she is "enslaved by passion", liable to errors that are "the offspring of sensibility", and is victimized by laws and social customs that restrict her access to the pursuit of knowledge (4). Thus, she is something less than rational. The political urgency that drives *Emma Courtney* is the certainty that, as long as Emma or any woman is seen as deficient in reasoning powers, she will be regarded as an incomplete person and therefore unworthy of citizenship. Reason, Genevieve Lloyd notes in her study of rationality and gender, has long been a factor in our definition of what it is to be human. It is assimilated "not just into our criteria of truth, but also into our understanding of what it is to be a person at all, of the requirements that must be met to be a good person, and of the proper relations between our status as knowers and the rest of our lives".[83] Acquiring agency means cultivating a rational mind.

Emma Courtney's candor and determination are at times enviable and would seem proper raw material for the fashioning of a keen, discriminating intelligence. But Emma's admirable energy is focused on a reluctant lover, and her relentless quest for Augustus's affection soon becomes tiresome and embarrassing when her repetitious vows of love and demands for truth seem to fall on deaf ears. The breakdown in communication that plagues relationships throughout the novel culminates in Augustus's suppression of the truth and his refusal to explain his reticence. Augustus responds evasively to Emma's repeated attempts to discuss love, presumably because he is secretly married and must keep this fact concealed to qualify for an inheritance that requires him to remain single. Despite the practical motives behind his furtive behaviour, Emma suffers an overwhelming and debilitating frustration because Augustus withholds information that would allow her to see her situation more clearly, analyze it, and free herself from the snares of passion. By hoarding knowledge, Augustus keeps Emma from learning the truth, and this maneuver enables him to continue to enjoy her love but not reveal his own for as long as he desires. At the end of the novel, we find out that in spite of his silence Augustus is unhappily married and has loved Emma all along.

Access to knowledge and clarity of communication are pivotal in the process of empowerment and governance of the self. Emma explains this point to young Augustus (son of the elder Augustus Harley), for whom she writes her memoirs. To warn him away from the same trap of passion in which she was caught, Emma insists (echoing Godwin) that morals can be the subject of scientific study. In fact, she asserts that they must be investigated, and she promises to lift "the veil" (9) that shrouds the story of his birth so that he may benefit from information in ways that she did not. Ambiguity, confusion, and mystery lead to a paralysis of mind and social existence, and those who perpetuate uncertainty continue to control (or rather tyrannize) the situation. Although Augustus Harley remains "an undifferentiated Object" throughout the novel, he maintains remarkable command of his relationship with Emma.[84] Despite an overt focus on language in the text, largely in the form of letter-writing, Hays shows that silence and secrecy are equally if not more effective. But, as Emma warns Augustus, his silence only elicits conjecture and obscures the truth (105–7).

Hays's emphasis on the freedom of inquiry places her in the tradition of both religious radicalism (her particular affiliation was the Unitarian faith) and English Jacobinism. Mary Hays was raised in a middle-class family of Rational Dissenters in Southwark. As an adult, she met such leading Nonconformists as Dr Joseph Priestley, Theophilus Lindsey, and John Disney, and she continued to correspond and converse with other reformers including the poet George Dyer, the Baptist minister Rev. Robert Robinson, and the Cambridge mathematician William Frend.[85] Her first publication was a small pamphlet entitled "Cursory Remarks on an Enquiry into the Expediency and Propriety of Public or Social Worship" (1792), in which she argues against Gilbert Wakefield's suggestion that devotion be an exclusively private matter.[86] Hays also moved within the Jacobin circle of intellectuals. She became a rather close friend of William Godwin and Mary Wollstonecraft and wrote Godwin lengthy and effusive letters about her love for William Frend. A large part of these letters comprises, almost verbatim, the text of Emma Courtney's epistles to Augustus Harley.[87] Hays reintroduced Godwin and Wollstonecraft in January of 1796 – a meeting which was to begin the affair that led to Wollstonecraft's pregnancy and their subsequent marriage – and she proved to be a loyal and steady friend, staying at Wollstonecraft's bedside as she lay dying.[88]

The influence of Hays's radical associations is evident in nearly all of her writing. In her essays, which Katharine Rogers cites as especially valuable for their particularization of abstract philosophy and plain directness of tone, Hays's emphasis is consistently on the crucial impact of education, social conditioning, and the influence of external forces over inborn talents.[89] While not necessarily embracing Locke's *tabula rasa*, she affirms the equality of all human beings at birth in fundamental capacities for perception and comprehension. Responding to criticisms lodged against philosophical inquiry, she writes, "That man is the creature of sensation, affords a simple and solid basis for enquiries, which it has been a fashion to ridicule under the abstruse and undefinable term metaphysics".[90] Yet, she continues, "bodily as well as mental powers are principally attributable to education and habits, and are equally the result of the circumstances in which the being may have been placed".[91] In the spirit of the English reform movement, Hays emphatically refers to intellectual pursuits as a "liberty" that, she also observes, has long been denied to women.[92] Like Thomas Paine, who considers "rights of the mind" among the natural liberties he discusses in his essay *Rights of Man*,[93] Hays supports the freedom to inquire and pursue truth in her *Letters and Essays, Moral and Miscellaneous* (1793).[94] In the spirit of the Kantian definition of "enlightenment" – daring to know (*sapere aude*)[95] – Hays claims that "of all bondage, mental bondage is surely the most fatal" (19). She reveres the "emancipated mind" and celebrates it as a force that surpasses and should overpower and supersede existing forms and conditions of civil society, especially law. "I again earnestly repeat the wish", she writes, "that the wisdom of the legislature may keep pace with the national light" (16). To Burke and the legal theorists Coke, Hale, and Blackstone, Hays's devaluation of the predominating role of law in society is a radical act. Common law theorists shared a faith in the superior authority of law and emphasized the legal foundations and structures of society over and above individual or collective thought, no matter how enlightened.[96] While Blackstone acknowledges "absolute rights of the person" – the right to personal security, liberty, and property – he insists that one forfeits part of one's natural liberty when entering into civil society.[97] One has the absolute right to the security of one's very existence, but that right may be breached by laws of capital punishment; one has the right to the enjoyment of private property "without any control or diminution, save only by the laws of the land".[98]

Hays relies heavily on the materialism of Helvétius and Godwin for her defense of women and education. She bases her argument on Helvétius's contention in his *Treatise on Man* that "the understanding, the virtue and genius of man" are "the product of instruction", and that people will eventually learn that "they have in their own hands the instrument of their greatness and their felicity, and that to be happy and powerful nothing more is requisite than to perfect the science of education".[99] Furthermore the importance of coming to an understanding about knowledge and humanity is essential to the operations of government. Assumptions made about human thought processes and capacities for learning are directly linked to the legislation that shapes the modern citizen. "The science of man", Helvétius writes, "makes a part of the science of government. (1) The minister should connect it with that of public affairs. (2) It is then that he will establish just laws".[100] From Godwin, Hays borrows the premise put forward in *Political Justice* that individuals are determined by external circumstances. If it is true that one's socio-political destiny is not determined at birth, then women may argue that feminine "weaknesses" are not bred in the bone but are the result of a biased, inadequate education and a socially constructed emotional and financial dependence. In *Emma Courtney*, Emma's unhappiness illustrates Helvétius's assertion that one's well-being is a function of one's opportunity for learning and access to knowledge. Emma is continually stifled in her development as a human being by the willful miscommunications among the envious Morton women, Augustus Harley's silences, and Mr Montague's own passionate excesses that distort reality. Only Mr Francis (purportedly based on Godwin) provides unencumbered honesty, and only he offers Emma advice and information she can trust.

The damage done by intellectual neglect or inappropriate education is a theme Hays explores in *Emma Courtney* as well as in her *Letters and Essays* and a later treatise, published anonymously but attributed to Hays, an *Appeal to the Men of Great Britain in Behalf of Women* (1798).[101] Women, she contends in *Letters and Essays*, are unprepared to operate in the public sphere because they have had "neither system, test or subscription imposed upon them" (12). They have "no claims to expect either pension or place" in society, and they have not been trained in the analytical reasoning that would prepare them for citizenship. Women, furthermore, are caught in a social contradiction that exacerbates their confusion and prohibits their advancement. "It is a melancholy truth", Hays writes in her *Appeal*, "that the whole system raised and supported by the men, tends to, nay I must be honest enough to say hangs upon, degrading the understandings, and corrupting the hearts of women; and yet! they are unreasonable enough to expect, discrimination in the one, and purity in the other" (59). Emma echoes Hays's outrage in one of the most openly provocative political scenes in *Emma Courtney*. After a fiery dinner discussion about slavery, Emma retreats to the parlour with the other female guests, and there she confronts them with their complicity in domestic servitude. Emma tries to convince Mrs Melmoth that "to be treated like *ideots* was no real compliment, and that the men who condescend to flatter our foibles, despised the weak beings they helped to form" (113). But all of the women to whom Emma speaks are so entrenched in the sort of female training that denies rationality and cultivates romantic delusions that they cannot muster the reason it would take to understand Emma's point.

Emma Courtney, like all the characters of Hays's novel, is a product of her environment. As an adult, Emma reflects back on her education and assesses it as the source of her "sexual character". "I am neither a philosopher, nor a heroine – but a *woman, to whom education has given a sexual character....* I have neither the talents for a legislator, nor for a reformer of the world. I have still many female foibles, and shrinking delicacies that unfit me for rising to arduous heights. Ambition cannot stimulate me, and to accumulate wealth, I am still less fitted" (117). As a child, Emma fed her imagination with romances from the circulating library. Her guardian aunt, Mrs Melmoth, was a kindly but fanciful thinker, enamoured of illusory fiction. Stories eventually become Emma's passion and, all too frequently, her escape. But Emma also embodies the potential of an intelligent woman who has received proper instruction. When Emma's biological father insists she read those subjects usually reserved for men – history, science, and the classics – a new world of the intellect opens up to her. She realizes, quite importantly, that this is the domain of public thought and discussion. After reading her first classical text, her mind is "pervaded with republican ardour", her sentiments are "elevated by a high-toned philosophy", and her heart "glows with the virtues of patriotism" (22). When she is introduced to philosophical debate at the dinner discussions of her father and his friends, she notices profound changes in her mental processes: "my mind began to be emancipated, doubts had been suggested to it, I reasoned freely, endeavored to arrange and methodize my opinions, and to trace them fearlessly through all their consequences: while from exercising my thoughts with freedom, I seemed to acquire new strength and dignity of character" (25). Broad education, public intellectual exchange, and the consistent exercise of judgement are all forms of learning that contribute to fortifying the self and become a form of property that enhances Emma's existence.

What soon brings an end to Emma's enjoyment of "free thinking", however, are the material realities of dependence that afflict women by arresting the development of a distinct identity. When Emma's guardian aunt and her biological father die, she is left with only a small fortune in both financial and intellectual terms. She realizes that although her education taught her to deliberate, it did not provide her with a profession, nor was it sufficient to equip her with an enduring independence of mind. As her susceptibility to Rousseau's *La Nouvelle Héloïse* has foreshadowed, Emma sinks back into the mire of emotion and instability. The story of her excessive behaviour then affords us an opportunity to see the workings of passion so that we may discover the value of feeling and its place in the process of human thought and action without falling prey to its distorting seductiveness.

In her analysis of the politics of emotion and the effect of passion on human behaviour, Hays often focuses on the hardships specific to women. When Emma speaks so frequently of her need to admire, esteem, and love, we are reminded of recent feminist theory that foregrounds the importance of relationship in feminine moral systems.[102] But Emma is also terrified of dependence, and we see from her own example how vulnerable a woman is when she is unable to secure financial autonomy. It is, however, more than monetary independence that Emma seeks. She wants a place in the public sphere and freedom from an increasingly isolated private domain. Emma comments:

> While men pursue interest, honour, pleasure, as accords with their several dispositions, women, who have too much delicacy, sense,

and spirit, to degrade themselves by the vilest of all interchanges, remain insulated beings, and must be content tamely to look on, without taking any part in the great, though often absurd and tragical, drama of life. Hence the eccentricities of conduct, with which women of superior minds have been accused – the struggles, the despairing though generous struggles, of an ardent spirit, denied a scope for its exertions! The strong feelings, and strong energies, which properly directed, in a field sufficiently wide, might – ah! what might they not have aided? forced back, and pent up, ravage and destroy the mind which gave them birth! (85–86).

Hays was well aware that women were being left out of political and economic developments, and that they were not to be legislators of the world.[103] Emma reiterates the dilemma women face when excluded from civil society and points to the destruction that results when rights of the mind are denied.

"[P]assions", Emma often reminds us, is "another name for powers" (86). Indeed, in this decade of revolution, emotion was a formidable force. Yet because we are all products of our environment, and women have received deficient instruction in how best to use this power, they have misdirected it, often turned it inward, and rendered themselves the odd beings Emma describes. The insulation that was meant to provide safety, social stability and the security of the family has worked against women. The private sphere that was intended to offer protection has only been a source of repression for energies that if given free rein would be capable of revolution, or at least reform. Moreover, because women are denied the social and economic means of defining a distinct propertied self, they indulge in the sort of distortions Emma does in imagining an ideal lover. Emma Courtney engages in a Pygmalion-like construction of a lover because she is desperate for challenge and activity. Influenced by that most dangerous of texts, Rousseau's *La Nouvelle Héloïse*, which affects her with an overwhelming sensibility, Emma describes her immersion into a sea of feeling from which she only occasionally surfaces. "With what transport, with what enthusiasm, did I peruse this dangerous, enchanting work! – the pleasure I experienced approached the limits of pain – it was tumult – and all the ardour of my character was excited" (25). The "love" for Augustus that Emma begins to create is, according to Janet Todd, "an extension of self, a fantasy of self-love" that occurs because the "needs of the self" go unmet in Emma Courtney.[104]

Emma's personhood is further diminished when her self-deceptions and obsessive behaviour undermine her activities within the text and her authority in the mind of the reader. Her reliability as a spokesperson for women is problematic because as readers we are forced to vacillate between feeling suspicious of Emma's thoughts – since she is deceived by passion – and feeling sympathetic when she delineates the reasons why she and other women and men are the victims of extravagant imaginations and emotions. For example, when Emma criticizes those who "bend implicitly, to custom and prescription" in addition to others for whom "the deviation of a solitary individual from *rules* sanctioned by usage, by prejudice, by expediency, would be regarded as romantic" (79), we must ask whether she is presenting a cogent argument against Burkean prescription or she is defending her own romantic immersions? When Emma argues that "the Being who gave to the mind its reason, gave also to the heart its sensibility" (81), are we to agree and then value emotion, particularly as a part of a chain that produces talent? Or are we to remember that these words are spoken by a woman overpowered by love? Undoubtedly, one of the lessons we are to glean from this confusion is the necessity of clarity and rational thought. While passion may be a component of power, it becomes dissipated or misdirected and destructive unless it is guided by education and opportunity.

A form of authority Emma does claim at the opening of her text is that she is qualified to analyze sensibility. Despite recognition that immoderate feeling is primarily associated with the feminine domain, Emma assumes that uncontrolled sentimentality is a potentially universal affliction when she instructs young Augustus Harley in the perils of an obsessive romantic love. She presumes that the experiences of a woman in love would be of value to a young man – that he too is susceptible to the seductions of passion. In addition, Mr Montague, the man Emma later marries, is as victimized by the excesses of his emotions as is Emma. He cannot control his passions and is eventually driven to suicide. Hays extends the role of sentiment, which has been diminished in its affiliation with the feminine, to both sexes and resurrects it in the novel as a subject worthy of philosophical inquiry.[105]

In Hays's assessment of the motives for human action, which begin with sensation, passion lends itself to the construction of a far more powerful self than one sees in a Burkean critique of talent. Personal ability, according to Burke, is a danger to national security because it is a threat to accumulated wealth. With a provocative use of war-like images, Burke describes property as a "sluggish, inert and timid" entity, and ability as a "vigorous and active principle"; therefore, property is in constant danger of "invasions" by ability, and it must be kept "in great masses of accumulation, or it is not rightly protected. The characteristic essence of property, formed out of the combined principles of its acquisition and conservation, is to be *unequal*".[106] Hays and her fellow Jacobins, however, saw their time of social upheaval as an opportunity to decentralize wealth. The empiricism that is at the core of Hays's emphasis on circumstances rationalized subjectivity and rendered it, as Gary Kelly argues, "implicitly democratized and posited as uniquely individual and authentic", thereby strengthening the role of the individual and "justifying a wide range of political, social, economic, and cultural programmes".[107] The notion of universality that fed the fires of natural law and natural rights in the 1790s was supported by the literature that not only espoused the critical ideal of common predicaments and shared solutions but also advocated an increased recognition of individual will.

The story of Emma Courtney culminates in the destruction of several individuals who have impeded the flow of accurate information and/or succumbed to their own uncontrolled emotions. Themselves unable, or prohibiting others, to exercise the natural "rights of the mind", they are trapped in a prison of gothic conditions, literally represented by thunderstorms and wild carriage rides. The return to a cohesive family structure for protection is adamantly rejected in Hays's novel. Emma's own negligent family illustrates the Godwinian view that familial bonds are "the mere chimeras of prejudice", unless they are sanctioned by reason, or habits of affection (28). The rule of primogeniture is shown to be destructive and is overridden by Augustus Harley when he distributes the fortune he inherits as the eldest son among his younger brothers and sisters. As a solution to her indulgences in passion, Emma tries to put together a family with Mr Montague, but it crumbles because it is a mere shell, void of the strength an honest love would provide. What Hays does offer as a remedy to the predicament of women is an organic and arguably "feminine" conceptualization of rationality. In the new society brought about by reform, Mr Francis professes that "reason will fall softly, and almost imperceptibly, like a gentle shower of dews, fructifying the soil, and preparing it for future harvests" (50). The challenge Hays presents to women is to embrace this nurturing form of rationalism and cultivate their own reason so that they may be instrumental in reform. Evidenced by Emma's demise, neither delusionary love nor the fabrication of an empty familial structure can replace the need for an independent mind.

Mary Wollstonecraft, *The Wrongs of Woman: or, Maria*

Mary Wollstonecraft's *The Wrongs of Woman: or, Maria*, an unfinished novel published posthumously in 1798 by William Godwin, also urges women to cultivate reason. In fact, Wollstonecraft borrowed fictional devices from Hays to reinforce the need for rationalism. Henry Darnford is a constructed ideal akin to Augustus Harley, Jemima experiences the same elevation of mind that Emma does when exposed to analytical discourse at the dinner table, and Maria is also misled by the dangerous romanticism of Rousseau's *La Nouvelle Héloïse*. But the emphasis of Wollstonecraft's novel is much more decidedly on the specific laws that prohibit women from ownership and from participating fully in the public sphere. While Hays focused on the independent mind, Wollstonecraft made the more sweeping connection between liberty and property that is at the foundation of *a priori* theories of rights. In *Wrongs of Woman*, Wollstonecraft argues that without an inalienable claim to ownership of the self, recognized by civil society, women were not only excluded from the processes of justice but unable to "own" – that is, direct the management of – property. Without property, women and other economic dependents were excluded from the franchise and additional means of directive participation in the public sector. Focusing on juridical agency, Wollstonecraft tries to extricate women from this dilemma.

In *A Vindication of the Rights of Woman*, Mary Wollstonecraft notes her intention to write a second, companion volume because, she explains, "[m]any subjects ... which I have cursorily alluded to, call for particular investigation, especially the laws relative to women, and the consideration of their peculiar duties".[108] Although this intended volume never appeared, Wollstonecraft did conduct a legal inquiry in *Wrongs of Woman*. The legal term "wrongs", in the novel's title, highlights the theme of law and casts secular law as the transgressor of women's rights. The narrative itself investigates the numerous civil restrictions on the acquisition and control of property, rights of inheritance, legal status, and legislation governing marriage and the family. The recent focus on sensibility by critics of Wollstonecraft has led to accusations of complicity with masculine concepts of authority, a failure to rise above sentimentalism, or, conversely, a reluctance to embrace and legitimize the feminine domain of intuitiveness, compassion, and moral virtue. Mary Poovey, for example, claims that "perceptive, intelligent writers like Mary Wollstonecraft continued to envision social change and personal fulfillment primarily in terms of individual effort, and therefore they did not focus on the systemic constraints exercised by such legal and political institutions as marriage".[109] It is, however, the very system of English law, particularly as it affects women in relation to marriage and the family, that Wollstonecraft comprehensively attacked. She exposed it as the chief civil force that defines, isolates, and persecutes the female sex. And she does so cognizant of Locke's re-definition of political power that focuses on juridical privileges: "*Political power*, then, I take to be a *right* of making laws ... and of employing the force of the community, in the execution of such laws".[110] The tendency to read *Wrongs of Woman* as a sentimental novel and to concentrate on the ambivalence in Wollstonecraft's personal attitude toward the power of emotion has often overshadowed the political radicalism from which Wollstonecraft did not "retreat" (as Poovey argues) but explored and ultimately championed in all its complexity.

Mary Wollstonecraft insisted on considering women as civil beings, even while they were victimized and/or ostracized by society. Fully aware, by the mid-1790s, that women were being left out of political developments in France as well as in England, Wollstonecraft pushed even harder for a basic assumption of sexual equality that would ensure rights. If women continued to be seen as "benefactresses" of English law (as Blackstone deemed the female sex), women would remain susceptible to violations of all kinds because benevolence does not provide a guarantee of authority that supersedes the law. As passive and dependent recipients, women were far more easily sequestered to the private sector where their confinement was enforced by a legal system that rarely acknowledged their distinct existence. In keeping with the now famous passage from Blackstone that explains a wife's loss of legal identity, women were forced to relinquish their property and their identity when they married. Blackstone writes,

By marriage, the husband and wife are one person in law: that is, the very being or legal existence of the woman is suspended during the marriage, or at least is incorporated and consolidated into that of the husband: under whose wing, protection, and *cover*, she performs everything; and is therefore called in our law-french a *feme-covert*, *foemin viro co-operta*; is said to be *covert-baron*, or under the protection and influence of her husband, her *baron*, or lord; and her condition during her marriage is called her *coverture*. Upon this principle, of a union of person in husband and wife, depend almost all the legal rights, duties, and disabilities, that either of them acquire by the marriage.[111]

In the state of *coverture*, a woman's property became that of her husband, unless it was protected in a trust, and she became his property, such that he could claim damages if she were abducted or beaten.[112] Yet, perhaps the most critical distinction that emerges in Blackstone's explanation is that because a woman has no legal identity in a marriage, "a Man cannot grant any thing to his wife, or enter into covenant with her: for the grant would be to suppose her separate existence; and to covenant with her, would be only to covenant with himself".[113] A wife's inability to participate in a contract within marriage reflected her incapacity to enter into a covenant in civil society. As a *baron*, a married man immediately assumed proprietorship and a socio-economic status, whereas a married woman lost access to ownership and self-governance when she was defined by a merely biological referent such as *feme*. Wollstonecraft, therefore, made a bold presumption, through elucidating the "wrongs" women suffer, that women could indeed claim the civil and natural "rights of man". Moreover, she made a case that women (and the unpropertied in general) were urgently in need of inalienable liberties because they were the most vulnerable members of the community.

Legislative events in revolutionary France surely fueled Wollstonecraft's campaign to find a secure place for women in civil society. Wollstonecraft travelled to Paris in December of 1792 to look for literary opportunities and to observe conditions of the revolution. She wrote a social history of France, largely derived from articles in the *Analytical Review*, entitled *An Historical and Moral View of the Origin and Progress of the French Revolution; and the Effect It Has Produced in Europe* (1794).[114] Under the Old Regime, the French legal system reflected many of the principles associated with English law. The financial and contractual obligations of marriage were under the jurisdiction of civil charters,[115] primogeniture was encouraged as a means to concentrate wealth, and custom was integrated into the more formal framework of jurisprudence. In marriage, a woman became part of a *communauté* (partnership) of which her husband was the head.[116] Although laws governing property in marriage varied somewhat from region to region, the influence of Roman law from the sixteenth century on saw that a wife relinquished her assets to the husband unless they were protected by a marriage contract for that specific purpose.[117] Montesquieu outlines the patrilineal design of the family in *The Spirit of the Laws*:

> It is almost everywhere a custom for the wife to pass into the family of the husband.... This law, which fixes the family in a succession of

persons of the same sex, greatly contributes, independently of the first motives, to the propagation of the human species. The family is a kind of property: a man who has children of a sex which does not perpetuate it is never satisfied if he has not those who can render it perpetual".[118]

As in England, the husband's obligation to the wife, in exchange for her property, was that of protection. Under the Intermediate Law of the revolution, women saw some beneficial developments. In 1791 they were no longer prohibited from inheriting property, in 1792 divorce laws were relaxed and in 1793 they were granted a right to communal property.[119] But French women were not to enjoy full rights of citizenship even in revolutionary France. In the closely watched developments in France during the 1790s, Wollstonecraft and the other English Jacobins were disappointed to see restrictions on the franchise even amidst the crusade for the rights of man. The *Déclaration des droits de l'homme et du citoyen* (adopted in 1789) and the constitution (ratified in 1791), gave the vote to those declared "active citizens": men over the age of twenty five who could claim a stable residence for at least one year and pay the equivalent of three days labour in tax.[120] The Constituent Assembly rejected calls for universal suffrage and excluded economically dependent persons – servants, bankrupts, women, and the very poor – from political participation in the new France.[121]

English law was an especially appropriate target for late eighteenth-century feminists not only because legislative policy had a direct impact on women's lives but also because the doctrine of prescription and the understanding of authority inherent in established charters permeated conservative rhetoric. In *Vindication of the Rights of Men* and in *Wrongs of Woman*, Wollstonecraft carefully scrutinizes Burke's thoughts on law. In Burke's defense of the ancient constitution and in his reliance on the paradigmatic process of inheritance to justify civil processes, Wollstonecraft recognizes a desire to conserve an arrangement of property acquisition and transmission benefitting the already propertied. In *Wrongs of Woman*, she foregrounds the crucial lack of autonomy for women within familial structures as well as for others on the periphery of the family, such as domestic staff. She maintains that Burke's conceptualization of liberty as inheritable property means that those excluded by ownership laws will inevitably suffer a restriction of rights and remain disempowered. Consequently, laws and customs that regulate inheritance and restrict ownership by women bear the brunt of Wollstonecraft's criticism. In contrast to Bage's *Hermsprong* or

Holcroft's *Anna St Ives*, Wollstonecraft's novel recognizes no beneficial compromises with authority or models of individual empowerment that demonstrate human potential. Nor does Wollstonecraft make available a heroic advocate of natural rights ready to intervene and protect women from the law. The civil contract of marriage that works to Hermsprong's advantage is unequivocally a "bastille" for women – a public institution in which a woman's liberty, as well as her legal identity, is negated. At the same time, the life of a woman who is single and unpropertied is the life of a slave; she is subject to the will of society but denied full membership in the community.

To provide graphic evidence of the material consequences of property laws for women, and to forge what Susan Snaider Lanser calls a feminine "communal voice" that crosses class boundaries, Wollstonecraft juxtaposes the fates of Maria, a married woman of property, and of Jemima, an unpropertied female domestic.[122] Wollstonecraft insists that women be "read" in a civil social context; hence the stories of Jemima and Maria remind us that women are gravely affected by socio-political policy but are prevented from influencing it. While Wollstonecraft did promote the egalitarian family, she did not propose it as the "basis of good government", as Anne K. Mellor has argued.[123] The family was the vehicle through which property was carefully controlled and transferred, and it was instrumental in the exclusion of women from the economy. Wollstonecraft presents the family as a monolithic structure, particularly in the stories of Jemima and Maria, and argues that such a corrupt institution must be destroyed. While Wollstonecraft shows that relationships like those between Jemima and Maria, and Maria and Henry, are crucial to development of the self, she also contends that the propertied individual remains a necessary prerequisite to political agency.

Jemima's narrative records the absolute dehumanization of a person, who is not only deprived of ownership rights but also thrust into the state of becoming the raw material from which others reap wealth. Regarded by the community as "a creature of another species" (111), Jemima sees herself as "a slave, a bastard, a common property" (112) all conditions of extreme vulnerability, unprotected by rights or Paine's adage that "man has no property in man".[124] Jemima's state of being common property is the result of having no familial status in a Burkean world (the environment of *Wrongs of Woman*). Born an illegitimate child, Jemima is immediately placed outside of the family and the law. Typical of seductions and pregnancies of the period, Jemima's mother is seduced by a fellow servant with promises of marriage soon forgotten. While she is left to bear the social and economic consequences of an illegitimate birth, her father "after a slight reproof" (107) is allowed to remain in his place of employment.[125] In one of the many examples Wollstonecraft gives of women turning toward acts of self-negation under the pressure of social censoring, Jemima's mother begins to starve herself and, nine days after giving birth to Jemima, dies. Initially cast beyond the confines of civil society, Jemima must live the rest of her life on the fringe. She is raised by a wet nurse who lives in poverty, then kept as a "slave" in her father's house. She works exclusively within the domestic sphere, and she functions in various roles as a pseudo family member – she is a mistress rather than a wife, a nursemaid rather than a mother. As such, Jemima has no chance of obtaining property in any form. Furthermore, Jemima's work is not an independent exchange of labour for wage because Jemima is not free to sell the property in her labour. When she is brought into her father's house, it is not as a gesture of affection or even an act of parental obligation but as a means to save money. In an attempt to reduce the poor rate funds spent on the maintenance of illegitimate children, legislation was enacted in 1733 to hold the father financially responsible for his illegitimate child.[126] Since he is legally bound to "provide for" his daughter, Jemima's father turns that duty into a profitable financial arrangement by sentencing her to servitude; he thereby both stays within the law and eliminates the need for a potential wage earner.

Jemima's worth is determined by her value as an economic commodity, whether in providing sexual pleasure, rearing children, or doing laundry. In addition, Jemima is evaluated in terms of her potential as an economic threat. In one place of "employment", Jemima is raped by her master, forced into becoming his mistress and eventually impregnated. When the liaison is discovered by her master's wife, it is Jemima who suffers the wife's anger and abuse because her pregnancy is an economic threat to the family. An illegitimate birth meant not only another child to support financially, but possibly another party to consider in the bequest of property. After having been largely excluded from inheritance under Puritan pressures in the early seventeenth century, illegitimate children had begun to reappear in wills in the early eighteenth century.[127] A precedent was set, as well, by the Convention of revolutionary France when it passed legislation in November of 1793 that guaranteed illegitimate children equal rights of inheritance.[128] Jemima also poses a familial economic threat when in another situation of domestic employment her master dies suddenly. His heir immediately intervenes to collect his property in fear that

Jemima, as the man's mistress, would attempt to lay some claim to the property or would simply steal it.

Jemima's life as a commodity follows a logical course toward prostitution as a means of subsistence. Prostitution itself becomes the epitome of a misuse of property, a loss of the self, and the inability to claim one's sexuality and labour as one's own.[129] Like her mother's fate, Jemima's profile fits a historical one. She is an example of the young domestic servant, sexually exploited and abandoned because of an illegitimate pregnancy, and driven to prostitution out of economic dependence.[130] Yet even as a prostitute, Jemima finds that the property she might have in her body is subject to the pervasive tyranny of civil authority. Jemima explains that watchmen extort tithes from prostitutes to ensure their "liberty" on the streets (113). If sexuality is power, as Catharine MacKinnon suggests, then Jemima's libidinous potential must be controlled.[131] Indeed, her sexuality is regarded as a threat in each of her encounters, but law continues to provide means of counteracting and diffusing that power primarily by preventing her from obtaining any form of property, that is, ownership of her self, her sexuality, and her work.

In a scene reminiscent of Emma Courtney's introduction to reasoned discourse, Jemima experiences a new sense of pride when she learns to read and is exposed to the powers of the mind. While in domestic service for a learned and liberal gentleman, Jemima is finally given a position at a "family" table and is allowed to join in the conversations of a group of literary men. In addition, when her master is in need of "untutored remarks" on a piece of writing, he often solicits her opinions. Although Jemima's participation is largely passive in these encounters, she has a first taste here of the natural right to exercise the intellect, and this is enough to provide her with a sense of having "acquired new principles" that stir the hope of "returning to the respectable part of society" (114). She begins the process of the broad and liberal education that, according to Wollstonecraft, is necessary preparation if women are going to contribute to "the progress of knowledge and virtue" and participate in the campaign for the rights of humanity.[132] Yet new principles and the beginnings of an education (though essential components of personal and public fulfillment) are not enough when encountering civil society; Jemima also needs money. Jemima will obtain the respect or mere toleration of humanity only through financial independence. Even the thievery that had been a constant part of Jemima's life was committed with an apparent understanding on her part of the importance of property, even beyond survival. She realized that property would never be given to her, nor would she ever have legitimate access to it.

The tale of the poor we find in Jemima reaches its final crescendo when physical deprivation leads one of the oppressed to turn on other victims. Driven by starvation, Jemima, by her own admission, begins to behave like an animal and commits what she realizes is her most inhumane act, the destruction of another woman. Devoid of the rights of humanity, denied the opportunity to engage in the exchange of labour for a wage sufficient to survive, refused property of any sort, Jemima is compelled to fight for a place in the house of a tradesman, and like a "wolf" she convinces this man to turn out his pregnant mistress (117). Jemima places this young girl in the same desperate position in which she once found herself, and the young girl drowns herself in a watering trough. The cycle of the unpropertied woman continues. Now driven to self-loathing, Jemima experiences an estrangement from civil society that seems complete. "I began to consider the rich and poor as natural enemies, and became a thief from principle. I could not now cease to reason, but I hated mankind. I despised myself ..." (118). She becomes one of the "idle poor", then one of the "labouring poor", first dependent on charity, then on the workhouse. Finally, she ends up working as a housekeeper in an asylum and finds herself in the site of ultimate confinement for women because the association with madness reinforces their condition as irrational beings unqualified to participate in the public sector.

The portrait of Jemima in *Wrongs of Woman* seems to be derived from a passage that appears in Wollstonecraft's *Vindication of the Rights of Men*. While the unrelenting tragedies of Jemima, as a fictional character, may be too overwhelming to elicit sympathy in the reader, her excessive condition and the charged tone of her story suggest the high pitch of emotion that permeates the discourse of rights. As Virginia Sapiro notes in her analysis of Wollstonecraft's political writing, "the Revolution controversy was truly a debate, a conversation in raised (written) voices".[133] In reference to Burke's notorious *Reflections* passage in support of the royal family in revolutionary France, Wollstonecraft matches Burke's pathos in the following excerpt from *Vindication*:

I have turned impatiently to the poor, to look for man undebauched by riches or power – but, alas! what did I see? a being scarcely above the brutes, over which he tyrannized; a broken spirit, worn-out body, and all those gross vices which the example of the rich, rudely copied, could produce.... Man preys on man; and you mourn for the idle tapestry that decorated a gothic pile, and the dronish bell that summoned the fat priest to prayer. You mourn for the empty pageant of a name, when slavery flaps her wing, and the sick heart returns to die in lonely wilds, far from the abodes of men.[134]

Jemima's weighty synoptic tragedies are just that – the collective demise of the poor and the estranged who are saturated with a destructive energy that has made the truly gothic events of the French Revolution possible. As one of the few lower-class characters of central importance in the English Jacobin text, Jemima reminds us that the contest over rights is a grittily economic one, and at the heart of the debate is a material (as opposed to abstractly theoretical) concern with the redistribution of wealth. Were Jemima able to claim individual liberties, the restrictive social construction of womanhood would be turned upside down and she could become a participant in the public economy. But her inability to "own" her labour or property prevents her from participating in the growing market economy or affecting public policy in any way.

When Jemima's tale is juxtaposed with Maria's, "demon property" and the legal forces that "systematize oppression" come into clearer relief (88). Encoded in Maria's story is the imperative that one must lay claim to the right of property and ownership of the self before real possession is possible. Maria has wealth that should provide her with liberty; instead, it leads to her imprisonment. She is held captive in a madhouse because of an attempt by her uncle to circumvent the law that renders a married woman's property her husband's. He leaves the largest part of his fortune to Maria's daughter and appoints Maria guardian. Though the transferal of property to a trust was one of the primary means of protecting the fortune of a married woman, it did not secure her from legal suits and other attempts at gaining possession of her wealth.[135] Indeed, Maria confronts these very threats from her elder brother and husband – those most frequently entitled by law to property through inheritance. Her brother simply "vents his rage", but her husband has her abducted and imprisoned in the madhouse for her refusal to surrender her property to him. The property meant to free Maria from her husband's tyranny only serves to bind her more firmly (and legally) to his arbitrary power. Maria escapes to Italy with her baby and her uncle's money, but Maria's flight is an illegal act because a woman has, in the eyes of the law, no right to her children. Like wives, children were the property of the husband, and if a woman deserted her husband, she was certainly entitled to nothing. Furthermore, it was perfectly legal for a husband to force his wife to return, regardless of her reasons for leaving.[136]

Wollstonecraft's illustrations of female disadvantage in confrontations with civil authority culminate in the juridical scene toward the "end" of her unfinished novel. While the courtroom in *Hermsprong* is the site of a revelation of truth and a restoration of rights, the courtroom in *Wrongs of Woman* reveals the vulnerability of those who do not enjoy the inalienable right of property, and whose position in the public sphere is precarious at best. Maria's defense of her lover, Darnford, against seduction charges is a defense of her "self", and it challenges a legal system that does not authorize her distinct identity. One of the few breaches of sexual morality to fall under a jurisdiction outside of the ecclesiastical courts, seduction assumes that a wife is the property of her husband.[137] As it is a breach of property rights (in addition to marital rights), seduction is a criminal violation. When Maria tries to defend Darnford, she pleads for a form of legal autonomy by arguing that the affair was voluntary, but her argument is futile because it presumes a proprietorship of the self to which she has no legal right. "I voluntarily gave myself", she argues, but that self is not hers to give. In the anonymous eighteenth-century text *Laws Respecting Women* (1777), the author explains that although an "abduction" may be done "with the consent of the wife, ... the law always supposes compulsion and force to have been used, because the wife is not supposed to possess a power of consent". In addition, because a woman is the property of her husband, "by writ of ravishment or action of trespass", the husband is compensated "not the possession of his wife, but damages for taking her away".[138] Frustrated in her attempts to work within the civil legal system, Maria attempts to distinguish "laws of moral purity" from "the will of [her] husband" sanctioned by positive law. This attempt, however, only leads her to a willing unlawfulness. Maria's final appeal in her courtroom treatise is to step outside the law, reaffirm a dichotomy between morality and the legal system and act according to her own sense of justice by declaring Darnford free of the charge of seduction.

Maria's exile from the law is both self-imposed and legally enforced. Although she chooses to love outside the law in her affair with Darnford, in numerously legislated ways she is debarred from activities in the public sphere. Maria is unable to bear witness in court to her husband's harassment. Because husband and wife are considered one person in the law, a wife is rarely allowed to testify against her husband.[139] As "no one is allowed to be a witness in his own cause", it is also true, Blackstone writes, that "no one is bound to accuse himself". Hence, a woman testify-ing against her husband (and vice versa) could easily be construed as a person testifying against herself.[140] In defiance of the restrictions that enforce her silence, Maria attempts to bear witness against her husband, defend her actions and assert her own legal identity by having her treatise read in court. Writing was for Wollstonecraft and other late eighteenth-century women, Gary Kelly contends, a means of participating in the public life from which they were otherwise banished. Yet Wollstonecraft steps even further into an unfamiliar realm when she engages in the political and legal rhetoric usually defined as male.[141]

The option of divorce holds little relief for Maria and her efforts to free herself from her husband's pursuit. If Maria were to consider breaking her marriage contract as a legal release from her oppressive condition, she would only receive a "separation from bed and board" (*a mensa et thoro*). While adultery by either husband or wife was considered sufficient reason for dissolving a marriage, divorces *a vinculo matrimonii* (absolute divorce) were solely obtainable by an act of parliament, an expensive process usually accessible only to the very wealthy. "Between 1670 and 1799", Lawrence Stone reports, "there were only one hundred and thirty-one such Acts, virtually all instituted by husbands, and only seventeen passed before 1750".[142] In cases of divorce *a mensa et thoro* alimony is usually required; however, if a wife elopes and lives with her adulterer, she receives no alimony.[143] Divorce for Maria, then, is a final loss of the prop-erty she has already shown is essential (albeit troublesome) to independ-ence. According to Blackstone, the private sphere (where the civil contract of marriage places women) should be a secure and sheltered place. In Wollstonecraft's representation, however, women are "impris-oned" in a space defined by the interaction of the private and the public but devoid of protective natural or civil rights.

Jemima and Maria are both condemned to a family structure that has irretrievably broken down; they each live an isolated life within an ostensibly benevolent social unit yet without the boundaries and rights of the self that comprise an individual recognized by the state. As in many of the English Jacobin novels, Wollstonecraft exposes the family as a tyrannical institution and reveals the romance that often leads women into the trap of economic dependence. The relationship Jemima and Maria develop attests to the fact that the concept of prop-erty is at the source of their common trouble. Denied the "rights of man", Maria and Jemima are both delivered into the legal "wrongs of woman". In a study of Blackstone's *Commentaries*, Teresa Michals points to a state of civil existence (in common law) somewhere between individual autonomy and material for trade: "a third option [was] a collection of persons who were also property, the objects of a personal dominion that did not involve commercial exchange". Slaves and wives fit into this category, and their liberty according to Blackstone consists in "protection", not in an equality of rights.[144]

The gothic setting Wollstonecraft chooses for *Wrongs of Woman* has been seen as a component of a feminist version of the picaresque because it serves as the site of psychological exploration for women.[145] It has also been regarded as a "socially imposed metaphor" used to elicit criticism of emotional excess.[146] Yet, given the emphasis in Burke's *Reflections* on architecture and the stability of structures, as well as Blackstone's comparison of the common law to "an old Gothic castle, erected in the days of chivalry, but fitted up for a modern inhabitant", the eery, decrepit prison of the madhouse could, in one of its many symbolic functions, refer to the institution of British law that "protects" women through confinement and denial of rights.[147] In her *Vindication of the Rights of Men*, Wollstonecraft makes direct reference to the British system of justice as a gothic castle. Responding to Burke, she also addresses Blackstone who looks back to the constitution of the Goths as a foundation for British liberty.

> But, in settling a constitution that involved the happiness of millions, that stretch beyond the computation of science, it was, perhaps, necessary for the Assembly to have a higher model in view than the imagined virtues of their forefathers; and wise to deduce their respect for justice. Why was it a duty to repair an ancient castle, built in barbarous ages, of Gothic materials? Why were the legislators obliged to rake amongst heterogeneous ruins; to rebuild old walls, whose foundations could scarcely be explored, when a simple structure might be raised on the foundation of experience, the only valuable inheritance our forefathers could bequeath?[148]

Wollstonecraft's pursuit of authority, like that of other radical women novelists, is not without fundamental ambivalence toward the figure of the autonomous individual. Yet women continued to be seen as indistinct entities at a time when the self-governing individual with clear boundaries is being posited as the model of citizenship in contract theory. For Wollstonecraft the female territory of relationships is a site of ambivalence that corresponds to the paradoxical place of women "within" the public sphere. Romance can be sustaining, but more importantly it can also be delusionary and dangerous. Again like Emma Courtney, Maria's victimization begins with a state of heightened emotion and an overactive imagination. Her desire for romance leads her to believe she is in love with the deceptive libertine George Venables, and it keeps her unaware of his avaricious designs until after the marriage. While in the madhouse, she discovers Rousseau's *La Nouvelle Héloïse* and Henry Darnford at the same time. Their relationship seems to offer the liberating breath of fresh air one craves in the claustrophobic atmosphere of the novel that has been observed by Eleanor Ty.[149] But their freedom, which is an illusion, is private, and it does not respond to the systemic inequalities that continue to render women prisoners in a domestic realm. In addition, as Claudia Johnson notes, Darnford exemplifies "republican manhood" with its roots in libertinism; while Darnford may provide another instance of "the disastrousness of heterosocial relations", as Johnson contends, he also embodies the limitations of the promises of republicanism for women.[150] Regardless of the romance Maria has found, she and other women continue to be victims of political policy, but confined to silent, passive roles in the operations of civic institutions. Much like Emma Courtney, Maria is a character whose authority of perspective is not always reliable. While she gives voice to the sufferings of her sex, she is in constant danger of the passion that will distort her reasoning mind. Faced with the image of the economically independent individual as the paradigm of the new citizen, women had to maneuver their way through a minefield of legal restrictions prohibiting their participation in civil society as well as the traps of romance and sentimentalism that provided an enticing but fatal escape.

The encounter of women with the law that we witness in *Wrongs of Woman* foreshadows the position women acquired in civil society. While Wollstonecraft's contribution to movements away from Filmerian patriarchalism is largely undisputed, her insights into the direction that contract theory seemed to be moving have been less frequently acknowledged. Wollstonecraft represents the domestic sphere as neither safe nor distinguished by virtue but as a disenfranchised state of material poverty and social, economic, political, and emotional vulnerability. In Seyla Benhabib's terms, Wollstonecraft struggled against the "*privatization* of women's experience" and the view of the self as "a *disembedded* and *disembodied* being".[151] She attempted to expose the "social meaning" imposed on women, particularly by the legal system, and presumed that because the category of woman is socially constructed, it is subject to change.[152]

5
Bestowing the Mantle

Two late English Jacobin novels, Charlotte Smith's *The Young Philosopher* and Maria Edgeworth's *Castle Rackrent* consider the situation of reform at the end of a decade marked by soaring hopes and sobering disillusionment. The pervasive running, hiding, wandering, and searching of Smith's novel is matched by the chaos and lawlessness of Edgeworth's text, as both authors struggle for a stabilizing center and a legacy to pass on to the next generation of enlightened individuals. *The Young Philosopher* investigates not so much the rationale for radical change as the frustrations of reformers who have attempted to respond to the exclusions from political advancements and have accepted the sacrifices that accompany the promotion of change. Making way for the "young philosophers", Smith's characters assess the state of radicalism at the end of the century, candidly revealing its confusion and uncertainty. Edgeworth's characters are for the most part not reformers but those responsible for creating the turmoil in contemporary society. The world of Castle Rackrent is devoid of integrity, and thus it is in search of moral agency. The bestowing of the mantle on the next generation is done not with the expectation of an imminent New Jerusalem but with an acknowledgment of ongoing turbulence in a fallen world.

The image of a fallen world was one of the consequences of opposition that had been brewing for much of the 1790s. As British radicalism gained momentum during the 1790s, Prime Minister William Pitt the Younger and his administration began taking measures to stem the tide of popular rebellion.[1] A network of spies and informers was created to infiltrate radical societies, such as the London Corresponding Society (LCS) and the Society for Constitutional Information (SCI). Habeas corpus was suspended, radical leaders were rounded up, imprisoned and charged with high treason, and a Committee of Secrecy was formed to review documents seized during the arrests. Thomas Hardy, secretary of the LCS, and Daniel Adams, former secretary of the SCI, were among the first to be arrested on 12 May 1794. In the weeks that followed, more than thirty members of radical societies were also served arrest warrants, examined by the privy council, and imprisoned.[2] The London trials for high treason were held in the autumn of 1794, and they ended in acquittals; those still awaiting trial were soon released.

Despite the favourable outcome for reformers, the fears generated by the treason trials in London (and in Edinburgh a year earlier) reverberated through the decade. Additionally, passage of the Treason and Sedition Act of 1795 and the Combination Acts of 1799 and 1800 continued to put obstacles in the way of those who persisted in their struggle for parliamentary reform and a transformation of the body politic.[3] The Treason and Sedition Act modified the law of treason to bring under its jurisdiction "any who 'compassed or devised' the death, bodily harm, imprisonment or deposition of the King, who exerted pressure on him to change his measures or counsels, who plotted to assist foreign invaders, or to intimidate or overawe both houses or either house of Parliament, whether such intention was expressed, as hitherto, by overt act, or by speech or writing".[4] The Combination Acts targeted "unlawful combinations", specifically including the United Englishmen, United Britons, and the London Corresponding Society.[5] It prohibited new societies requiring oaths that were forbidden by the Unlawful Oaths Act of 1797 and those operating under a veil of secrecy. This legislation was intended to suppress the activities of radical societies and to enable prosecution of those thought to endanger the welfare and stability of the nation.[6]

Because of the aforementioned measures in Britain, as well as the violent turns taken by revolutionary France and the tyrannical forces unleashed in Napolean's reign, popular radicalism suffered what E.P. Thompson describes as a "lost coherence" at the end of the eighteenth century. The reform movement was not "extinguished", he argues, rather it was rendered "inarticulate by censorship and intimidation. It lost its press, it lost its organised expression, it lost its own sense of direction".[7] At first, in the face of persecution, the impulse of activists was "to press further the process of radicalization", but in time reform movements had to reassess their priorities and their methods of promoting change.[8] Some radical societies dissolved, other re-grouped, and still others continued on in defiance of attempts to repress them. This "lost coherence" in reform movements and the need to reconsider direction are reflected in the sense of loss and confusion that over-whelms both Smith's and Edgeworth's novels.

Charlotte Smith, *The Young Philosopher*

Given the title of Charlotte Smith's 1798 novel, *The Young Philosopher*, one might expect to find in the narrative a particularly refined portrait of the new legal subject. The focus of Smith's novel, however, is less on the development of George Delmont, the novel's budding English *philosophe*, and more on the activities of an array of competing fam-ilies: the Glenmorrises, Delmonts, De Verdons, and Winslows.[9] Rather than investigate the extraction of the individual from familial con-straints, as so many of her fellow authors had done, Smith represents the liberated individual re-immersed in the family structure and then examines how that reconstructed family fares in a persistently corrupt world. Following a difficult period for reformers, *The Young Philosopher* offers a sober reflection on the repercussions of radicalism and a candid assessment of the current state of affairs. Of radicalism, Smith's is a tol-erant and circumspect view. It admits to a degree of disillusionment, particularly with the violence of the French Revolution, and it allows for differences among reformers and their means of political expres-sion. On the current state of affairs, however, the report Smith proffers is rather bleak. When the new family, comprised of "free-thinkers" (Smith's term for reformers), encounters the institutions of civil society, it enters into a struggle that results not in political reform but in eventual social and national displacement. To live by their convic-tions, the new family must live in exile.

Like that of other English Jacobin novelists, Smith's critique of the social contract is embedded in the tableau of institutionalized domestic maneuverings that implicate the law, economics, familial customs, and emotional attachments. The ingredients of the investigation are nearly the same as those we see in *Caleb Williams* and *Wrongs of Woman*: tyrannical patriarchs and matriarchs, corrupt magistrates, abusive laws, and disenfranchised victims. In addition, the primary culprit in the novel continues to be Wollstonecraft's "iron hand of property" and its determining role in the relationship between the individual and juridical institutions. However, Smith's text does at times depart significantly from other English Jacobin novels. Although her novel clearly nods toward Godwin, particularly in the figure of Mr Armitage, it takes a few decisive steps back from Godwin's glaring analysis of human identity. First, Smith privileges the reconfigured family over the self-contained individual as the representative figure of the new commonwealth, and she reintroduces the sentimental as the relational adherent within the family. Smith's conclusion sees the dissipation of the traditional (and hence, oppressive) household, but it leaves intact the family unit that is bound and sustained by affection, sympathy and loyalty. Second, Smith begins to question the function of property and to cast doubt on the significance of citizenship. The most striking yet potentially troubling feature of *The Young Philosopher* is that the final vision of the family's place in the future – exile in America – is drawn as a pastoral and political ideal that renounces national identity.

The emphasis on the family rather than the individual in *The Young Philosopher* is underscored by the autobiographical components in the text. While Smith's novel is certainly a fiction of political intent, admittedly, much of the thematic content bears an autobiographical source. Early reviews of her novel cite her reliance on personal experience and her indulgence in public lamentations as faults of her work. *The Anti-Jacobin Review and Magazine* complains that Smith's "desire of obtruding on the public her own private history has given a sameness to her tales".[10] Similarly, though perhaps more sympathetically, *The Critical Review* regrets the "personal satire" of the legal profession to which Smith yields because it appears that she writes "under the influence of resentment".[11] Smith's depiction of the legal system as a thoroughly depraved institution does indeed seem to be influenced by her own intricate and prolonged involvement in legal matters. As one of the executors to her father-in-law's will, described by her sister as "a most voluminous document!", Smith spent an inordinate amount of time enmeshed in legal entanglements.[12] Richard Smith died in 1776, and the settlements were not completed until 1813, seven years after Charlotte Smith's death.[13] As evidenced by her letters, she was very much ensconced in legal wrangling during the years that she was writing *The Young Philosopher*.[14] Moreover, the themes of imprisonment, exile, and loss that inform the novel are all substantiated by experiences in her married life that was by all accounts an unhappy one. Her husband Benjamin was imprisoned for debt in 1783, and she spent much of the seven months of his incarceration with him in the King's Bench Prison.[15] Due to additional financial difficulties in 1784, Smith's husband was forced to flee to France, and she followed him there with their numerous children in tow, to live in a dreary, secluded chateau.[16] Lastly, the debilitating effect of a lost child that dominates much of the second half of the novel was something Smith knew first hand, having seen the deaths of five of her twelve children. Like the character of Laura Glenmorris, Smith apparently fell into a similar state of distracted wandering at the death of her twenty-one year old daughter, Anna.

The plot of *The Young Philosopher* is also driven by familial concerns – by the conflicts within and between a series of families, each of which represents a place on a broad spectrum of political sympathies and social development. The Glenmorrises are the jacobinical reformers, the Delmonts are a divided family in transition, the De Verdons maintain the bastions of tradition, and the Winslows are a caricature of social climbers. All are themselves proof that the domestic is political and abusive familial maneuverings are forms of social, legal, and economic "tyranny and injustice".[17] The novel begins with the collision of these four families, precipitated by the conventional carriage accident in which a young woman "possessing above fifty thousand pounds" is saved by a handsome and virile young man (I:1). The meeting sets in motion the machinations of courtship and fortune-hunting. How each family conducts itself in these "domestic matters" indicates its political positioning, largely because in the process each family reveals its relationship to property. While the De Verdons try to maintain the concentration of their wealth and the Winslows are in a greedy search for more, George Delmont wishes only to farm his little bit of land. As the narrative shifts its focus to the Glenmorrises (their story preoccupies the novel), property is the source of trouble between the Delmont brothers and the force behind Laura Glenmorris' legal entanglements, Medora's abduction, and Mr Glenmorris' imprisonment. The conclusion, though ambivalent, requires a settlement of property, but more important than distribution is the decision each family makes about its relationship to land, wealth, and self-determination.

At the end of the novel, when the plot approaches a resolution, the "state of the family" is the "state of the nation", and all is in flux. The traditional family is dissipating, and a new one is struggling to emerge. The Glenmorrises, who represent the forces of change as well as the consequences of radicalism, are of the first generation to espouse jacobinical principles and to strike out on their own as a young married couple. Their union is a product of filial disobedience, disinheritance, and defiance of familial traditions. Most striking about the Glenmorrises, however, is the tainting of their commitment to radicalism with suffering and sacrifice. To follow their hearts and minds, they have had to forgo certain pleasures and conveniences, as well as endure very specific hardships such as expulsion and dispossession, abduction and captivity, and relentless embroilments with the law. They depict the politically progressive family under attack.

The threat of exclusion permeates Smith's novel, as it does so many other English Jacobin texts, but Smith takes it a step further into the state of exile. The conclusion to *The Young Philosopher* tries to leave the reader with an ideological vision, a lucid assessment of the past and a confident, propitious direction for the future; however, that vision is marred by the implications of exile for the pursuit of rights. The ideal envisaged for the family is the emigration of the Glenmorrises and the young Delmonts to America, where, according to Glenmorris, the "great book of nature is open" to those who wish to engage in "noble study" and examine "human nature unadulterated by inhuman prejudice" (IV:392). Thus, one might anticipate in Glenmorris' plan a simple transferal of citizenship, from Britain to America, based on ideological grounds. Yet even as Glenmorris seems to embrace America, as a nation, he rejects outright the restrictions and exclusive identifications of nationalism. He boldly asserts that "wherever a thinking man enjoys the most uninterrupted domestic felicity, and sees his species the most content, *that* is his country" (IV:395). Glenmorris' hopes and visions are buoyed by an ingenuous belief in the availability of intellectual freedom, and he leaves us with a final image of an autonomous and self-determining family that is indeed "a state" of its own. Still, when Glenmorris abandons national identity, and thereby renounces civil law, he does not provide a philosophical foundation for exile, such as Godwin's notion of private judgment or Paine's articulation of natural rights, that shores up civil liberties. We do not know what will sustain or guarantee the assumed freedoms for the Glenmorrises and the Delmonts.

Smith's study of exile is developed through the confrontation of reformers with the combined authorities of the family and the law. With a personal history that is coloured by varying degrees of isolation, Mr Glenmorris is the first character to embody the state of exile. His Scottish origins deem him an "outsider" from the start, and his status as an orphan leaves him in the familial fringes. As he develops into "a scholar, a poet" and "a young man of extraordinary, though somewhat eccentric genius", he finds himself unable to fit in to the everyday world of business, in particular, the drudgery of a mercantile house (II:6–7). His clandestine courtship with Laura de Verdon renders him a forbidden suitor, and his eventual marriage to her decisively alienates him from his relations. Newly married, he is abducted from his estate in Scotland by a party of international "buccaniers" and held for ransom (II:235). His captivity and eventual journey home involve protracted meanderings that bring him to France, America, Jamaica, and Ireland before arriving in Scotland. Once he returns home, the accumulated trouble resulting from claims to his lairdship, causes the Glenmorrises to remove themselves to Switzerland, and finally to America.

This medley of banishments is underscored by Glenmorris' distance from narrative events as they unfold in the novel. While his wife and daughter pursue their claim to family property, Glenmorris is confined to America because of his political views and his debt. He is described as a man who "to obtain a perfect freedom of speaking, writing, and acting ... has become an alien from his country, and has sought in another hemisphere the liberty which he could not exercise in his native island" (I:230). His involvement in his wife's legal affairs, and the trouble that thereby ensues, is limited to letter-writing; however, even this epistolary effort of support proves futile. His letters from America are delayed because the ship carrying them is detained by business complications and bad weather. Moreover, when he re-enters the narrative, in the fourth volume, he is first seen with his daughter, Medora, who has been missing. Yet, as the details emerge, we discover that he did not knowingly rescue, or even find, her. He merely happens upon her by chance when he enters a carriage in which she is riding. For most of the narrative, then, Glenmorris is absent and his return to the plot is hardly heroic.

Glenmorris' situation, however, is crucial to the text as it introduces and develops a central conflict in the novel that confounds the theme of exile: the simultaneous pull of attachment and independence, involvement and exclusion. His state of displacement is neither "pure" nor productive. It is an unsatisfactory condition, and the complications that result cast doubt on the efficacy of the Glenmorrises' resolution to emigrate to America. Given the turmoil that occasions exile within the novel, one must wonder about the future of the family that chooses expatriation as the solution to its trouble. As described by his wife, Glenmorris' position hovers between estrangement and inextricability. "[T]here is hardly any case", she admits, "wherein it is possible for a man, however determined he may be, to shake off the fetters which are for the most part wantonly imposed, so entirely to emancipate himself, as not to be dragged back in some instance to the forms of society" (I:232). Glenmorris is indeed "dragged back" at the end of the narrative, and the purpose of his return is, arguably, to elucidate an irresolvable predicament of principled exile and social connection. There is no simple extraction of the individual, endowed with rights, from society and the family in Smith's novel. The forces of attachment relentlessly complicate the lives of reformers.

Despite Glenmorris' significance to the ubiquitous theme of exile, his wife, Laura, is the character who takes us on the central journey of the narrative, from rebellion against her fate as the younger daughter in a traditional family of the gentry, through her physical and emotional breakdown, and finally to her decision that exile is the only solution to her predicament. The family into which Laura Glenmorris is born – the De Verdons – is a typical union of fortune (on her father's side), and pedigree (on her mother's). As a young woman, she falls in love with Glenmorris, who holds the last remains of a Scottish lairdship and is a distant relation of Laura's mother, Lady Mary. Together they form an idealized couple. Glenmorris "appeared rather like an hero, such as Homer or Virgil describes, than a mere mortal of the present day", while Laura is a devotee of nature and pastoral simplicity who fancies herself "a wood nymph or a shepherdess" (IV:196; II:4–7). Their daughter, Medora, is a "child of nature" (I:244), who is raised at least in part according to the assumptions of Locke and the dictates of Rousseau. According to her mother, "a girl of Medora's age has no mind; it remains to be formed – Her character must be a mere rudiment – One cannot say what it will be" (I:244).

The influences of Locke, Rousseau, Wollstonecraft, and early Edgeworth on education and the formation of the intellect are clearly at work in the formation of the new family in *The Young Philosopher*. And, as in other Jacobin texts, these philosophical foundations work to justify broad political change. For example, Locke's notion of a child entering the world with a mind like "white Paper", and furnished with ideas only "by degrees", is akin to and bolsters Paine's proposition that it is the right of each generation to act free of prescription and to create government anew.[18] The dangers of interpretation and artifice, such as we see in Delmont's construction of Medora, haunt Smith's narrative and force the reader to consider the political consequences of obscurity and falsification. Ignoring the "real" or simply retreating from it in fear or frustration impedes the forces of change by distracting and misdirecting vast resources of energy and commitment. Smith gives us an early warning of the effects of distortion when, in her preface to *The Young Philosopher*, she announces as one of her intentions, to expose the "unhappiness" derived from "too acute sensibility, too hastily indulged" (I:vii). In terms of the plot, she refers to Laura Glenmorris' breakdown at the loss of her daughter. Yet one is also reminded by this caution of Smith's dissatisfaction with the excessive passions – that is, violence – of the French Revolution. Moreover, Laura Glenmorris' wanderings, as the result of "too acute sensibility, too hastily indulged" replicate the ramblings of political radicalism at the end of the century, and her break down mirrors the dissolution of organized movements as disillusionment began to spread among reformers.

Through the education of the young philosopher, George Delmont (who will eventually marry into the Glenmorris family), as well as the trials and tribulations of Laura Glenmorris, Smith enacts the struggle to strike a balance between acute sensibility and rational control. This is quite a familiar tension in the English Jacobin novel, but Smith approaches it with perhaps more prevarication than we have seen in other texts. A keen sensibility is a political necessity; it is essential to eliciting compassion for the poor and the dispossessed and imagining new possibilities for society. Yet reform requires seeing the world clearly, with an unadulterated eye, and recognizing "things as they are" to envisage how they might be. Mrs Delmont, George's mother, is a progressive woman who raises her son in the same manner that Medora is educated, according to the principles of Rousseau. She sees it as her responsibility to "strip from the gaudy pictures that are daubed with vermilion and leaf gold, to excite emulative ambition in childhood, their paint and their gilding" in hopes that her son would grow to be "the benefactor instead of the successful destroyer of his fellow men" (I:87). Mrs Delmont's understanding of her duty is a direct offspring of Rousseau's child-rearing instructions in *Émile*. Throughout his essay, Rousseau directs parents to steer their children away from "gilded surface[s]" and toward the "phenomenon of nature". He even discourages figurative language when introducing a child to the world. "Never tell a child", he counsels, "what he cannot understand: no descriptions, no eloquence, no figures of speech, no poetry". Furthermore, "never substitute the symbol for the thing signified, unless it is impossible to show the thing itself" because the child will be distracted by the signifier.[19]

In *The Young Philosopher*, clarity of thought and directness in speech are not only educational devices. They separate the enlightened from the deceived and those attempting to claim inalienable rights from those trying to inhibit them. The promotion of representational "simplicity" also reinforces the idea that the truth of the individual's just relation to civil society need only be revealed, not adorned, not artificially imposed. Despotism works through a method of representation that privileges what Mrs Delmont calls "the dazzling and false medium of prejudice, communicated from one generation to another" (I:87). Mrs Delmont's observation certainly evokes Burke and his insistence that each generation be obliged to those previous, as well as his concern that in the reconfiguration of society, "[a]ll the decent drapery of life is to be rudely torn off". Burke feared the loss of protective veils; he worried that "[a]ll the pleasing illusions, which made power gentle, and obedience liberal, ... and which, by a bland assimilation, incorporated into politics the sentiments which beautify and soften private society, are to be dissolved by this new conquering empire of light and reason".[20] Softening the sharp edges of political ramifications with sentiment was exactly what reformers did not want to do. It was to their advantage, practically and rhetorically, to strip away the beautification of repressive policies. In addition, one of Burke's arguments against the validity of natural rights was that such a pure entity could not exist. Rights, he insists "undergo such a variety of refractions and reflections, that it becomes absurd to talk of them as if they continued in the simplicity of their original direction".[21] Indeed, the notion of individual, inalienable rights demands the conciseness, the clean lines, of an imperative, and boasts of an epistemological simplicity.

Smith continues to explore the quantitative facets of "dazzling and false mediums" in *The Young Philosopher*. While shunning such excesses, she draws a particularly important connection between the distortions of "vermilion and leaf gold" and the concentration of wealth, one of Burke's tenets for national security. In gaudiness is the aesthetically garish (and, arguably, ineffective) accumulation of resources and an allurement based on false premises. The removal of excesses to establish an aesthetic and conceptual simplicity corresponds with a broader and flatter distribution of wealth, based on necessity. George Delmont is the character who most succinctly represents the potential of an alternative attitude toward property. Because he has been raised as an "enquirer", he has no voracious appetite for wealth. Mary Cardonnel as well, through her generosity (she pays Glenmorris' debt), offers an example of wealth responding to need. Rather than worry about the invasion of property by "ability", as Burke does, Smith entertains a view of property similar to that of Wollstonecraft when she refers to property as fluid.[22]

Concerns with property also inform Smith's explorations of sensibility in *The Young Philosopher*. Mrs Glenmorris' story is a tale of romantic inclinations and gothic terror; however, it serves as a purposeful philosophical tool, as well – a contrived device to illustrate the horrific effect of familial domination in a traditional patriarchal family and the consequences of exile. The gothic apparatus is used, primarily, to depict the ancient families in the novel: the De Verdons and the extended Glenmorris clan. The De Verdons represent familial control of status and property and remind the reader of the role of inheritance in the political and legislative process. Lord Daventry, their proper son-in-law, holds "a seat among the hereditary legislators of his country", and thereby reinforces and perpetuates the politics of inheritance (II:29). The principal family seat of Laura's mother, Lady Mary, is Sandthwaite Castle. The surrounding countryside is described as "wild and gloomy", and from its "Gothic windows" there is "a view of the Irish Channel, and an immense extent of land, covered only at times by the tide, which took off the bold grandeur of a sea view, and left only ideas of sterility, danger, and desolation, in its place" (II:31). As in other English Jacobin novels, the gothic scene is a site of imprisonment, a setting for the denial of agency. Involved in forbidden love, Laura is sequestered in a particularly old, run-down part of the castle and forbidden contact with Glenmorris.

Sandthwaite Castle is also a repository for "relics of ancient chivalry", both literal and metaphoric (II:36). Lady Mary, the family matriarch, is the keeper of these relics, and she is the subject of pointed irony that seeks to conflate the reverence for the ancient and eminent with gothic machinery. For example, the origin of "illustrious blood" that she claims for her family is an illegitimate union that in the context of late eighteenth-century Britain would have been associated with a Jacobin libertinism. Furthermore, Lady Mary reads her supposed family history in old parchments, helmets, and armour that she finds rummaging about the castle. She forms a narrative out of these bits, but it is a narrative that is easily transformed into a fairy tale and is eventually indistinguishable from a ghost story. The servants, who imagine the lofty ancient ancestor Geoffrey Plantagenet involved in "nocturnal mysteries", turn his story into a tale that involves hidden money, heathen gods, and fairies. This ancient ancestor, revered by Lady Mary, generates not only her family but also a narrative epidemic. Similar to the creeping popularity of the gothic novel in the 1790s, stories of the supernatural invade and proliferate, like an "infection", and debilitate all who hear and believe them (II:44). Smith turns this situation around, however, through using it as the means by which Laura escapes her confinement and runs off with Glenmorris. To liberate themselves, they use the equipment of superstition. Glenmorris dresses in the coat of armour that was thought to have belonged to

Geoffrey Plantagenet, frightens the servants on watch about the house, and secures their flight.

The ability to make profitable use of fear, superstition, and chivalric excesses is a mark of earlier English Jacobin optimism. In Smith's novel, however, the confidence that one can turn repressive institutions in on themselves soon gives way to an acknowledged struggle with a significant opposition. The victory of this first escape, and the humour associated with the proliferation of ghost tales, succumbs to the relentlessness of a series of persecutions. As Mrs Glenmorris' story continues, the gothic framework is more firmly enmeshed in the narrative and becomes a force that must be understood. One must be able to distinguish the fairy tale – that which is purely fiction – from the representation of "things as they are". Laura Glenmorris' narrative illustrates the ease with which the romantic is transformed into the gothic. After her escape with Glenmorris, Laura's "girlish imagination" takes flight and "delight[s] itself with the prospect of the wild romantic solitude which love only was to embellish" (II:77). Laura's description of the Glenmorris house, which goes on at length, is an embodiment of the sublime. The "stone fortress" was built on "an almost perpendicular rock". The mountains to the west bore "summits crowned with eternal snow" and "[f]rom between two rocks of fantastic form started a mountain torrent" (II:78). The setting not only reflects, and emerges from, Laura's state of mind, but it also invites the series of terrors that are to come. Her vulnerability and the proximity of threatening forces are registered in the "faded heath" and "scanty vegetation", the "perpetual cloud of mist" and the "huge fragments of stone" (II:78). The estate is also the site of her husband's abduction, an event that launches Laura Glenmorris' adventures at another gothic location, the abbey of Kilbrodie. This home of Glenmorris' relations was comprised, in part, of "great masses of ruins" and overseen by the Lady of Kilbrodie, a woman of "evil passions", who at an earlier age "would most undoubtedly have been in danger of being tormented, or killed as a female warlock" (II:100, 103). But here Mrs Glenmorris begins to distinguish the mere "machinery" from concrete physical danger (II:108). "No dreary description", she observes, "drawn from imagination of tombs and caverns haunted by evil spirits, could equal the gloomy horrors of the place, where I was doomed to linger out the few and wretched days of my remaining existence" (II:113). Sounding very much like Wollstonecraft in the opening paragraphs of *Wrongs of Woman*, Smith reminds the reader that the violation here is once again about inheritance, about succession to an estate. Laura Glenmorris and her unborn child are in danger, not from an "English bogie or sprite" but from the competition for property (II:108). For Lady Kilbrodie's son to inherit the Glenmorris estate (Glenmorris is presumed dead), Laura's child must die. While the child is not murdered, it does perish of complications from a premature birth that was brought on by fear and panic at the hands of the Kilbrodies. This terror is a conflation of both genuine danger – an intense vying for property – and inventive and purposeful elaborations that are meant to upset Mrs Glenmorris. The child's death then sends Mrs Glenmorris into a state of wandering and isolation that parallels her husband's exile and presages her eventual breakdown. By now the gothic and romantic elements of the narrative have taken over, and the precision of jacobinical analysis appears to have vanished. Laura initially takes her destiny into her own hands, though it is to submit to her fate. But she soon becomes the object of a search and is transformed into the victim of familial predators. Mrs Glenmorris' story, which takes up all of Volume II of the novel, was initially cited by some reviewers as a distracting digression;[23] however, much like the first part of *Caleb Williams*, it provides a paradigm of familial tyranny that will be rewritten in the latter part of the novel. In the process, the gothic machinery will become indistinguishable from institutional persecutions.

In the last two volumes of the novel, Smith thoroughly immerses the reader in the "gothic" world of finance and law as they are implicated in "family business". In fact, not long after Mrs Glenmorris concludes her narrative with advice about the importance of love and honour, over and above property concerns in marriage, George Delmont is lured into his own family predicament, which is occasioned by a financial crisis. Having heard Mrs Glenmorris' narrative, the reader is prepared for another tale of terror and torment, and it is precisely the operations of familial tyranny in her story that set up our ability to believe what is to follow. George Delmont's response to his brother's predicament and the ongoing legal maneuvering of his family's estate parallel and compound the efforts by Laura Glenmorris and her daughter to secure Medora's share of the DeVerdon family wealth. The gothic paraphernalia is now manifest in the trappings and transactions of law, and the law is rendered inseparable from property – not only land, capital, and investments but also the property in the self. At the very moment that George Delmont implicates himself in his brother's debt, he also entrusts himself to an attorney. George mortgages his estate for half its value, personally binds himself on behalf of his brother,

Adolphus, to answer any claims against him, and allows the lawyer to work on recovering their legacy from Lord Castledane's estate. Likewise, when Mrs Glenmorris attempts to gain Meodra's rightful inheritance, she is thrust into the arms of attorneys, "a race of men, who live ostensibly and avowedly on contention and pecuniary disputes" and "who exist on the follies and fears of mankind, which they therefore encourage and perpetuate" (III:40). These "monsters 'of the great Babel'" are the ghosts, the English bogies and sprites, that now haunt Laura Glenmorris' existence (III:41).

Smith's wholehearted indictment of the legal profession, as mentioned above, is partly attributable to her personal experiences as an executor to her father-in-law's will. But her condemnation moves well beyond the level of chronic disgruntlement. Within her depiction of the legal profession as a school of scoundrels is the heart of her critique of the contract and a crystallization of her focus on the family. The duplicitousness, equivocation, and deft manipulation of binding agreements by various representatives of the law entrap people – invoking as much fear as enforced confinement to the ruins of an abbey. Yet an even more provocative consequence of Smith's depiction of the law is that it renders "the contract" suspect. What could such promises mean if they are susceptible to endless interpretation and bartering, if they are trapped in a state of perpetual deferral? Moreover, what are the politics of keeping a lawsuit open, of suspending final judgment? One manifestation of the glorious uncertainty of the law and the benefit of that incertitude is in the obliqueness of legal language. Verbal circuitousness works to the advantage of those who wish all to remain indeterminate and thereby static. To clarify, define, and ultimately reveal "truth", was to invite change because the consequent truth was the dire need for individual, inalienable rights as protection against the encroachments of legal institutions and protection against the perpetual indecisiveness that would accompany the contract.

Smith also illustrates the law's obsession with property, specifically in the execution of Lord Castledane's will, which is all about "the estates, fortunes, assets and effects, sums of money in government securities, mortgages or bonds, or lands, domains, forests, woods, coppices, parks, warrens, marshes, heaths, orchards, gardens, or paddocks, commons, rights of common, fee farm and copyholds, ... (III:56–57). For Smith, regardless of the specific branch, the operations of law are always about property. Not only does certain legislation protect property, one's very relationship to law is determined by the proprietorship of the self, or lack of it. Burke himself was well aware of this conjunction. In *Reflections*, he registers alarm that for "the national assembly of France, possession is nothing; law and usage are nothing". According to Burke, possession, law, and usage, all working in concert, equal and justify "the doctrine of prescription", which is, itself, "a part of the law of nature".[24] Property, then, is safely embedded in the triad that constitutes prescription, and it is strengthened by that which protects it: law and custom. In addition, like property (and because of it), prescription requires "security from invasion".[25] Attempts, therefore, to stall claims made against family fortunes are maneuvers to contain the franchise, to protect possession, law, and usage.

In *The Young Philosopher*, the omnipresence of law is manifest in its ability to dictate the action of the last two volumes of the novel. It is also underscored by what appears to be a conspiracy, perpetrated by various representatives of the legal profession, who are personally involved in protecting the concentration of wealth in the family and are not averse to imagining how they might themselves profit by it. In the gruesome machinations of the law, overtly (and covertly) driven by financial interests, the two story lines of the novel unite. Midway through the third volume, we discover that the same legal villains – Gorges, Loadsworth, and Brownjohn – are involved in the affairs of both the Glenmorrises and the Delmonts. In each case, their intent is the same: to keep the parties from obtaining their rightful portion of an inheritance and to maintain the integrity of the family fortune. The law, moreover, works intimately with the family to prevent a mutual destabilization. Without the law, familial interests would be vulnerable to "infiltration" by individuals; and without the family, the law would lose much of its *raison d'etre* and its operational support. The "formidable phalanx" of family and law works against the reformer and any efforts to create a new form of the family (III:109).

Smith's representation of radicalism at the end of the 1790s is marked by suffering, sacrifice, and exile. The euphoria of the political visionary has given way to the fatigue of the embattled reformer. Early in the novel, George Delmont speaks with a jaded though prescient voice when he acknowledges that "we are always to be the slaves of the world; the world, of which after all the sacrifices we make, so few obtain the suffrage, and that suffrage when obtained, is not only so fragile, that the least reverse of fortune deprives us of it" (I:227–28). Even though the Glenmorrises are successful in obtaining the property that is rightfully their daughter's and she marries for love rather than money, we are left at the end of the novel with a sense of defeat. By the fourth and final volume of *The Young Philosopher*, all members of the new family are estranged and dispersed. Mrs Glenmorris is "wandering about an absolute maniac, raving for her daughter, and execrating the cruelty of Lady Mary" (IV:335). Mr Glenmorris is confined to Fleet prison, "arrested for a debt due before he left England" (IV:334). Medora has vanished; she has been "carried away by a stratagem from the hotel where she lodged" (IV:75). And George Delmont is travelling about in search of Medora and her mother.

The uneasiness in Smith's conclusion is largely a function of the fate of Laura Glenmorris, the woman who bears the brunt of legal and familial torment. Hovering in the background of Smith's portrayal is her personal identification with suffering. In a letter written near the end of her life, Smith compares her destiny to "the fabled punishment of Sysiphus or the Danaïds – My whole life is pass'd in baffled toil and unavailing solicitude".[26] Furthermore, in her preface to *The Young Philosopher*, Smith represents herself as an expert on suffering, as one who has experienced "all the evils arising from oppression, from fraud and chicane" (I:iii–iv). Mrs Glenmorris' fate, however, strikes an especially profound chord because she once held the promise of change and through her we see the unraveling of a reformer. When she falters, in her own succumbing to "too acute sensibility", and she stumbles under the weight of rigorous persecution, we witness the grim results of the encounter between a free-thinker and the institutions of civil society.

The final scene of the novel sets the stage for a conclusive discussion of the state of radicalism by two representative *philosophes*, Mr Armitage and Mr Glenmorris. Notably, neither Mrs Glenmorris, through whom we have most closely witnessed the actual suffering of reformers, nor George Delmont, the young philosopher of the title, participates in this exchange that elucidates the pros and cons of exile to America. The Godwinian Mr Armitage, who encourages the Glenmorrises to stay in England, warns of "false pride". To Glenmorris, he counsels, "You feel yourself out of your place in England, because you have not power, or great affluence (which in fact is power); but is not that a sensation a little bordering on the sentiment, 'Better to reign in hell than serve in heaven'" (IV:391). Throughout the novel, Mr Armitage has been a voice of experience, wisdom, and generosity, but Glenmorris has center stage in this final scene, and he expounds on why emigration to America is the only answer, at least for now. Glenmorris' justification is largely twofold: an intolerance of English society and a commitment to anti-nationalism. Both Armitage and Glenmorris observe that in Britain property is power, yet Glenmorris cannot rid himself of the debilitating frustration incurred at seeing the "frightful contrast between luxury and wretchedness" and daily occurrences of "injustice" and "misery" (IV:391). When the Glenmorrises leave England, they symbolically and literally abandon the struggle for the property that will give them power. Glenmorris' reasons for embracing America are wrapped in hope and in the imagination. Hence, his discourse on America is abstract and imbued with aesthetics. In the immense physical expanse, in the uncertainty of wilderness, and in the power afforded by bringing the purest arts of civility, "without its misery and its vices", Glenmorris found "le vrai beau" ("the great simple") and *sublimity* (IV:201). Beauty and pleasure are derived from being in a place "where human life [is] in progressive improvement" (IV:201–02). Again, the clean, classical lines of the philosophical imperative are embraced as they lie in contrast to the grotesque, to the "spectacle of court figures in hoops and periwigs" (IV:392). This final portrait of two prominent *philosophes* debating the future direction of reform efforts is a somewhat deceptively concise culmination of a narrative that resonates with confusion and displacement. Far more powerful than the picture of this final discussion is the image that prevails through much of the novel, that of Mrs Glenmorris, lost, mad, nearly undone by her persecutors, and ultimately uncertain of recovery. She is the one who champions the reconstructed family, and (though ultimately they receive Medora's fortune as a gift) she ends the pursuit of property.

Maria Edgeworth, *Castle Rackrent*

Maria Edgeworth's *Castle Rackrent*, published anonymously in January 1800, is a somewhat unusual novel to find in the category of "English Jacobin". Yet Edgeworth's portrayal of a community in crisis, of rampant corruption and pervasive chaos, offers an additional representation of "things as they are" in need of reform. Although her specific case is Ireland, her analysis of the crisis extends beyond the confines of that nation, which, quite importantly, was on the brink of union with Great Britain. Edgeworth broaches questions of individual integrity that pertain to any citizen about to receive the authority of proprietorship in society. She investigates land management, property transactions, the misuse of wealth and privilege, and the manipulations of a legal system based on ambiguous law. She also examines moral conduct and addresses a dimension of the legal subject in a social contract that requires moral agency. Edgeworth's portrayal of life in Castle Rackrent is infused with humour. But the novel ends in a state of uncertainty because the new generation of landowners is more corrupt than the last and there is no one prepared to receive the mantle of reform. The New Jerusalem remains out of reach.

Edgeworth joined forces with her father to provide an explanatory glossary for *Castle Rackrent* in 1799.[27] In the novel's advertisement, Edgeworth explains that the purpose of the glossary is to educate the English reader in the language of the Irish people. Ernest Baker suggests that Edgeworth, contemplating the union of Great Britain and Ireland,[28] considered it her social duty to help acquaint the English with Irish customs and manners.[29] The effect of the glossary, however, is not only an infusion of social didacticism but also the imposition of editorial control that diminishes the authority of "poor Thady", the Irish steward who narrates the story. As Elizabeth Kowaleski-Wallace observes, through both the glossary and extensive footnotes, the author as editor contextualizes Thady's provincial point of view in a more expansive history. The result is that we are exposed to Thady's limitations as a narrator, and we are forced to look beyond his interpretation of events and his loyalty to the Rackrent family.[30] Just how much of the editorial structure was the result of her father's influence remains unknown, but Marilyn Butler, in her biography of Edgeworth, contends that both Maria and Richard Edgeworth used the glossary to distance themselves from Thady's parochialism. They anticipated, as well, that the reader would assume a corresponding critical objectivity and remain untouched by Thady's charm. Edgeworth, Butler explains, "expected us to feel more surprised and more critical, to reject actively his indulgent view of the Rackrents, and supply the correct, the enlightened, moral frame of reference".[31]

Through her story of the Rackrent family, Edgeworth illustrates a crisis of authority which has precipitated a realignment of power. Everyone in *Castle Rackrent* is plagued by moral confusion and is suffering from a lack of clear direction and thoughtful analysis. In the world of Castle Rackrent, promises are broken and debts are left unpaid, love is forsaken while marriages are made for money, life is commodified and death comes matter-of-factly. The text is replete with moral incongruities. When Sir Kit locks his wife in her room for seven years because she refuses to hand over her diamond cross, drinks to her health while she seems to be dying, and entertains women who hope to become the next Lady Rackrent, he has "the voice of the country with him on account of the great spirit and propriety he acted with" (33). In a pair of duels, Sir Kit just as easily spares the life of one man whose wooden leg gets caught in a piece of sod, as he readily shoots another who presumably stands firm. Not only are life and death apparently subject to accidents and a capricious heart, but the very telling of the stories is marked by an inconsistency in judgment or a lack of ethical consideration that leaves us wondering how to "read" these occurrences. The narrator, Thady, who is finally overwhelmed with a sense of moral ambiguity, voices the cumulative frustration of the text. "Well, I was never so put to it in my life, between the womens and my son and my master, and all I felt and thought just now, I could not upon my conscience tell which was the wrong from the right" (93).

Edgeworth's illustration of moral confusion begins in the first part of the novel, written sometime between 1793 and 1796, with a series of rather comical caricatures of Irish landlords who abuse privilege, covet property and waste their lives.[32] Sir Patrick enjoys too many glasses of whiskey punch and is finally overcome by drink. Sir Murtagh, known to have had a lawsuit for every letter in the alphabet, is obsessed by litigation; his passion ends with the bursting of a blood vessel. Sir Kit, who marries for money, is done in by gambling and an unrelenting desire for his wife's diamond cross. Sir Kit dies, further in debt; the estate, his widow finds, has been mortgaged and bonds have been set out against him. Yet underneath these colourful stories of bumbling squires is a serious indictment of inherited wealth and authority.

Edgeworth worked closely with her father in the management of the family estate in Edgeworthstown and eventually acted as his agent while he attended Parliament in Dublin. Her portrait of Irish life, particularly the detailed account of financial transactions, has often been attributed to her active involvement in the administrative affairs of land-ownership. But she herself points to an additional source that reinforces her portrayal. In the epilogue of *Castle Rackent*, Edgeworth refers the reader to Arthur Young's *A Tour of Ireland, 1776–1779*, in which Young records observations on Irish life that range from customs and manners to economic conditions. Much of Edgeworth's depiction of Castle Rackrent and her characterizations of the gentry, absentee landlords, and middlemen are borne out by Young's findings. He describes the condition of Ireland as a general state of "idleness and dissipation", and though he claims that things had improved by the latter part of the eighteenth century, he acknowledges "drinking and duelling" as "two charges which have long been alleged against the gentlemen of Ireland".[33] He discusses in great detail the local economy. Land was frequently leased to a middleman, then "under-let" for exorbitant "rack-rents" out of which the middleman made a profit. The process encouraged neglect and often resulted in poverty and "wretched husbandry".[34] Though Young assesses landlords as "lazy, trifling, inattentive, negligent, *slobbering*, [and] profligate",[35] and though he blames absentees for draining Ireland of money derived from rent, it is middlemen who receive the brunt of his criticisms. Middlemen, Young writes, are "the vermin of the kingdom" and "the most oppressive species of tyrant that ever lent assistance to the destruction of a country". Their involvement will never lead to improvement, Young continues, because if they are non-resident they cannot improve the land and if they are resident they do not.[36]

Since land, rather than industry, was the basis of Ireland's economy, Edgeworth's decision to narrativize the machinations of property transactions goes to the heart of Irish social and political life. While she emphasizes the abuses of wealth and privilege by the community at large, she also specifically addresses the compelling issue of married women's property to reaffirm her point that no one escapes the responsibilities of ownership. Though Sandra Gilbert and Susan Gubar consider *Castle Rackrent* a critique of classical patriarchy, women in Edgeworth's novel are often complicitous in the misuse of wealth.[37] While the Ladies Rackrent all suffer at the hands of their husbands' mercenary interests, they frequently contribute to systemic mismanagement. Sir Murtagh marries the widow Skinflint for her family's fortune. But Lady Rackrent proves to be a complementary wife to Sir Murtagh, a man who was obsessed by the manipulations of law and forbade the mending of fences because he made so much money out of trespassers. Lady Rackrent manages a charity school where poor children might learn to read and write, yet she also uses the children to spin the yarn that is woven and bleached gratis by the weavers on the estate. Her exploitation goes unchallenged because Lady Rackrent is able to get the looms for free from the Linen Board, where she has an interest, and because the tenants fear a lawsuit from Sir Murtagh.

The management of property by the Rackrent wives parallels that of their husbands; however, the outcome of their greed or negligence is not nearly as harsh. While the Lords Rackrent die as a result of their vices, the Ladies Rackrent not only survive, but two of them find economic stability and independence, and the third sues for a jointure that would provide her with an income of her own. All three of the Rackrent women marry for money, pride, or at the whim of a tossed coin. No one is married out of love, and none of them bear children. Still, in the first part of the novel, the wives of Sir Murtagh and Sir Kit outlive their greedy husbands and profit financially from the marriage. Sir Murtagh's unhappiness with Lady Rackrent's spending of formidable sums of private money, gleaned from "weed ashes", "sealing money", and informal extortion (a slight fee for putting in a good word to her husband on behalf of a tenant) leads to an argument in which Sir Murtagh bursts a blood vessel and perishes.[38] After her husband's death, Lady Rackrent has a "fine jointure" settled upon her and leaves the estate, taking most of the household furnishings with her. Sir Kit, having received a report that his wife was dead, begins to sort out the confusion over who is to become his next wife. But he soon dies in a duel with the relative of a disappointed young woman, and in a quick turn of events, his body is wheeled to Lady Rackrent in a hand-barrow.

The first two Ladies Rackrent emerge somewhat victorious, yet for Sir Kit's wife, the glory is not without substantial suffering and pain. Known to us only as "the Jewess", or as Thady calls her, the "heretic Blackamoor", this Lady Rackrent is taunted by her husband and eventually imprisoned. For seven years she is locked in her apartment because she refuses to surrender the last vestige of her independent wealth, her diamond cross, to Sir Kit. Given the outrageousness of this tale, Edgeworth provides a "historical" account of an actual imprisonment that appeared in *The Gentleman's Magazine* in 1789.[39] Lady Cathcart, we are told in a footnote, was locked in her house for more than twenty years, and it was her husband's custom to drink to her health and send his compliments to her each evening at dinner. She too tried to protect her property (in the form of diamonds) from her husband and set about a plot to have it removed to a safe place until she was free. The diamonds were carried by a poor beggar-woman to another trusted person and finally recovered years later when Lady Cathcart was released upon her husband's death. The story of Lady Cathcart both reinforces the plausibility of Lady Rackrent's imprisonment and enhances the impact of her victimization. It ensures that when Thady criticizes her for not giving the diamond cross to her husband, the reader will notice the skewed morality of Thady's assessment: "Her diamond cross was, they say, at the bottom of it all; and it was a shame for her, being his wife, not to show more duty, and to have given it up when he condescended to ask so often for such a bit of a trifle in his distresses, especially when he all along made it no secret he married for money" (36).

Sir Kit's wife ultimately gains her independence: "she had made up her mind to spend the rest of her days upon her own income and jewels in England" (36). Her tale, nonetheless, prepares us for some of the more complex realities of the second part of the novel, written two years after the first and in a decidedly more serious tone. The story of Sir Condy and Isabella Moneygawl (the third and final Lady Rackrent) is somewhat different from that of the earlier couples. We know much more about Isabella and her sentiments than we did about the others. She is the youngest daughter of a wealthy family and, as a young woman, falls "head and ears" in love with Sir Condy. But their relationship is associated, early on, with contrivance and denial. Isabella is involved in theater, and when Sir Condy first dines with her family in "Mount Juliet's town", she is also playing Juliet. Inspired by her role as Shakespeare's passionate heroine, her "love" for Sir Condy proves to be that of a young woman immersed in a romantic defiance of her family's disapproval. When they meet, Sir Condy does not particularly like Isabella and instead declares his feelings for Judy M'Quirk, Thady's great-niece. Yet, while Sir Condy praises himself for being "not a man to mind a fortune" (which later proves to be a double entendre because he is incapable of managing money), he succumbs to pride when he too reacts with defiance to the Moneygawls' dislike of him (45). In a perverse attempt to prove his integrity, Sir Condy tosses a coin to decide whom he should marry, Isabella or Judy. Isabella "wins", so Sir Condy forsakes his love for Judy and does "the honourable thing". He marries Isabella, and she becomes a victim of his pride and her own romanticism.

In their marriage, Isabella and Sir Condy are both guilty of fiscal irresponsibility as they carelessly dissipate what is left of a fortune already decreased by years of mismanagement at the hands of the Rackrents. When eventually faced with financial disaster, Isabella leaves Sir Condy to return to her family's home in Mount Juliet's town. As if in punishment, she suffers a horrible accident while traveling, and is left severely injured and near death. Meanwhile, Sir Condy, in one of his final acts of generosity, has written into his will a 500 pound jointure for his wife, due to be paid before any of the debts on the estate.[40] When Jason, about to become the new owner of *Castle Rackrent*, hears of the jointure, he becomes enraged by an "incumbrance on the land" (76). True to Young's description of the venomous middleman, Jason does all he can to rid the estate of its burden and is temporarily successful. After hearing of Isabella's accident, and not expecting her to live, Sir Condy sells her jointure to Jason. But in yet another twist of events, Isabella recovers, and it is Sir Condy who succumbs to death. Since the jointure is no longer securely in the hands of either Jason or Isabella, like their predecessor, Sir Murtagh, they turn to the courts for clarification. The judicial system, however, has proven to be anything but reliable and enlightening. It promises only more of the ambiguity that pervades the text.

In the realm of Castle Rackrent, women who hold property promise no relief from the misuse of wealth and privilege. Even Judy M'Quirk reveals her mercenary tendencies at the death of Sir Condy and the expected death of Isabella. Her sights set on Jason and his newly acquired fortune, Judy forsakes her love for Sir Condy. "What signifies it to be my Lady Rackrent and no Castle?" she asks, "sure what good is the car and no horse to draw it?" (92). By implicating women in the dissipation of property, Edgeworth de-emphasizes gender difference and holds each person accountable for his or her actions. Yet, at the same time, Edgeworth also foregrounds the gender-defined predicament of women that leaves them victims of greedy acquisition and/or subject to the severe legal limitations of ownership. Sir Kit's wife clings to her diamond cross, but she is painfully aware that she married for money and not for love. Judy M'Quirk, although she sheds a few tears when Sir Condy speaks of imminent death, finally deserts him when he is faced with financial ruin. She does so, however, as one who has already been abandoned by Sir Condy, in spite of his love for her.

The financial independence that widowhood sometimes provided, primarily in the "modern" eighteenth-century form of the *jointure*, occurs in *Castle Rackrent* as the only means of economic security for women. The jointure, as defined by Sir Edward Coke, is "a competent livelihood of freehold for the wife of lands or tenements, &. to take effect presently in possession or profit after the decease of her husband for the life of the wife at the least".[41] As social historians such as H.J. Habakkuk have pointed out, a widow could live quite comfortably on a jointure settlement. And according to Coke and Blackstone, the system of jointure was an improvement over the system of dower that guaranteed a widow one third of her husband's real property upon his death and had traditionally governed women's property under common law. Susan Staves, however, claims that the replacement of the dower with the jointure did not necessarily result in an advancement of property rights for women, and it was not a simple "substitution" of forms. What was once a *right* of dower became a *gift* of jointure. Staves also observes that because a settlement of jointure was a negotiation finalized in the form of a contract, it has often been argued that women and their families had an opportunity to ensure fairness in the agreement. But women and their families were frequently not in a position to bargain for a sum that would equal what the bride might have gained in a dower settlement.[42] In *Castle Rackrent*, Sir Condy's arrangement of a jointure for Isabella is indeed presented as a "gift" that is under his control. He may sell it, if he so wishes, or he may respect Isabella's need for future security. In either case, Isabella is at the mercy of Sir Condy's benevolence and loses the promise of a right to certain income. Whereas under a dower system, Isabella would have been assured of at least one third of her husband's property at his death, under a jointure she enjoys no such guarantee. Hence, the novel ends with a pending legal case over Isabella's "right" to a part of her husband's fortune.

The nightmarish web of legal ambiguities and manipulations that surrounds the treatment of women is a manifestion of a much larger crisis of integrity that not only permeates the tale of the Rackrent family but is a focal point of the debate over the "rights of man". In *Reflections*, Burke reveals a preoccupation with the preservation of structures threatened by revolution and reform movements. Likewise, in *Castle Rackrent* (as well as in Edgeworth's other novels), Edgeworth betrays a concern with the dissipation of economic and social resources. The disjunction of intent and action, meaning and word, that indicates a fundamental rift in the relationship between law and ethical practice, creates conditions for the kind of abuse and exploitation that plagues the Rackrent family. Unlike Burke, who in response to the crisis, looks back to posterity for a reintegration of divine and secular principles, Edgeworth joins the other English Jacobin novelists in an attempt to disambiguate "the law" by reconceptualizing the relationship of the individual to society. Faced with the vacancy in social leadership left by a neglectful and ineffective aristocracy, Edgeworth first acknowledges the inevitability of change and then turns her attention to the rational individual, guided by moral law, to fill the void.

Edgeworth's illustration of the crisis of moral, social, and economic integrity that plagues the Rackrents is remarkably similar to Burke's description of the discord that plagues him throughout his *Reflections*. To those who advocate that the social contract be subject to the transient demands of specific political trends and economic conditions, Burke responds,

But if that which is only submission to necessity should be made the object of choice, the law is broken, nature is disobeyed, and the rebellious are outlawed, cast forth, and exiled, from this world of reason, and order, and peace, and virtue, and fruitful penitence, into the antagonist world of madness, discord, vice, confusion, and unavailing sorrow.[43]

The "law" Burke fears will be broken is in his "great primeval contract of eternal society". Because each generation remains answerable to a civil social contract (as a power greater than itself), a social and moral stability is thus guaranteed. The political system, Burke claims, is thus rendered in a "just correspondence and symmetry with the order of the world" – an organic order of growth, depletion and regeneration.[44]

In all its disarray, the Rackrent family not only shatters the order and unity that Burke wished to defend, but it also calls into question the very notion that the architecture of society was ever so ideally structured. The paradigmatic process of inheritance, which in Burke's scheme is the vehicle of both conservation and regeneration, is obstructed by sterility and dissipation in the Rackrent family. Edgeworth's story of the Rackrents begins with a change of a name by an Act of Parliament, thereby indicating that the patrilineal continuity of the family has been broken. Sir Tallyhoo has no direct heir, so he is forced to turn to a cousin, Sir Patrick O'Shaughlin, and a legal adjustment to perpetuate the family name. As Michael McKeon notes, this and other forms of "patrilineal repair" were necessary and fairly common in light of the demographic fact that in a stable eighteenth-century population approximately forty percent of families will be unsuccessful in producing a male heir.[45] When each Rackrent marriage is without issue, the partnership of generations that Burke envisioned appears as a (literally) man-made construct to control the distribution of property, rather than as a sovereign metaphor for the organization of society. Though property in *Castle Rackrent* is maintained and transmitted according to the vertical hierarchy of inheritance laws, the elegant symmetry and balance of nature is missing. The mystery that should inspire our reverence is destroyed by Edgeworth's detailed accounts of the legal machinations behind property transactions. And the great primeval contract is ultimately marred by the need for secular alteration to maintain the image of a constitutional policy patterned after nature.

The portrait Edgeworth paints of the Irish gentry makes it difficult, in a time of moral crisis and social upheaval, merely to look back to a time when "the law" was infused with divine authority in order to recover and sustain the virtue and the integrity that "should have" characterized noble families. Edgeworth provides fictional evidence (some of which is derived from actual reports, such as the story of Lady

Cathcart from *The Gentleman's Magazine*) of why moral stability cannot be left to the laws that had been used not to protect property but rather to exploit proprietorial privilege. Edgeworth's observations challenge "aristocratic ideology" as defined by McKeon in his study of the "destabilization of social categories". Either as the O'Shauglins, derived from the ancient kings of Ireland, or as the contemporary landowning family of the Rackrents, the gentry we confront in Edgeworth's novel figure the decay of the supposed conjunction of external wealth or privilege with an internal moral order that, McKeon explains, justified social stratification and a hierarchical social structure.

While Edgeworth strives to unveil the less than honourable character of an aristocratic family, she also interweaves an even more biting incrimination of the emerging class of middlemen or agents. Burke's expectant fear of the "invasions of ability" and "spectre of innovation" does indeed seem to have materialized in Jason, the calculating and opportunistic son of a steward who is more attentive, watchful, and clever than his aristocratic counterpart, Sir Condy (140). As the narrative progresses, Jason waits in the wings ready to take advantage of the imprudent, negligent Rackrents. He begins to insinuate himself into the Rackrent fortune just as Sir Kit shirks his responsibility and becomes an absentee landlord. Jason, who proves to be a "good scholar" and a "good clerk", is allowed by Sir Kit's agent to copy the rent accounts (22). With the help of Thady, the agent, and a bit of "insider information", he obtains his first piece of property, and having earned the confidences of Sir Kit, eventually replaces the agent and takes the accounts into his own hands. Once Sir Condy becomes heir to the estate, Jason is given additional land, which he promptly leases to under-tenants at a comfortable profit of 200 pounds a year (39). Jason's "takeover" is finally enabled by the debt Sir Condy and Isabella amass through their financial recklessness. By the end of the novel, Jason is the new owner of Castle Rackrent and the Rackrent fortune dwindles to a handful of guineas. The ruthless and devouring Jason embodies the darker side of law divorced from ethical practice and exemplifies the flagrant self-aggrandizement that is legitimated in a culture devoid of any clear moral authority. In Jason's realm, there seems to be no governing principle to which he must submit. He is a lawyer, entrenched in secular legalities and obviously skilled at the orchestration of positive law; but Jason is reprehensibly incompetent when it comes to moral law – to the subjective courtroom of the conscience – because he is willfully ignorant of its demands.

The lawlessness of *Castle Rackrent* is manifest in a singularly degenerate family; however, its consequences and the predicament it represents resonate beyond the borders of its Irish locality. Edgeworth adds her voice to those acknowledging the transformation of society from a vertical structure based on hierarchy and inherited authority to a horizontal one founded on the prototype of a contract that respects natural rights. The crisis of law and ethics that Edgeworth illustrates lays the groundwork for a "new" form of authority embedded in the individual and contingent on the ability to reason. When out of the pervasive moral confusion Thady utters his frustration, he points to the people who are vying for control: women, the landed gentry, and the emerging class of agents and middlemen. But in Edgeworth's text, none of the characters exhibits the competence to rule in shifting constructs of control. Social leadership, *Castle Rackrent* shows in a series of inept aristocrats, will not necessarily come from those with inherited wealth and power; nor will it come from a young man of unguided "ability" such as Jason. In a form of political irony characteristic of English Jacobin fiction, Edgeworth only implies the solution to a crisis of governance through its absence. The lack of morally sound leadership creates a void that must be filled, and Edgeworth's indictment of the family and the process of inheritance moves away from Burke's solution to chaos and toward the individual of contractarianism.

The central role that ownership plays in Edgeworth's novel culminates in the dissipation of wealth by the Rackrents and the "usurpation" of the estate by a familial outsider. There is, however, one form of property that remains intact: Thady's great coat. At the beginning of her story, Edgeworth provides an ample footnote that explains the significance of this singular garment that Thady wears in winter and summer. The cloak, or mantle, she explains, is of "high antiquity ... derived from the Scythians ... [and] a general habit to most nations". Even Spenser, she continues, "knew the convenience of the said mantle, as housing, bedding, and clothing" (7–8). Through the course of the novel, Thady's coat is the only form of property that is not wasted or transferred through various hands. It reappears at the end of the novel intact and still in the possession of its original owner. Furthermore, wrapped in a handkerchief in its pocket is the last handful of guineas that belong to Sir Condy, the final Rackrent heir. The property that belongs simply and strictly to *the person* survives while inherited property is gone.

The great coat is of course the very sort of garment that could get one arrested under the Black Act if it were deemed to be a form of disguise, as occurs in *Caleb Williams*. But in *Castle Rackrent*, the great coat also recollects the Biblical story of Elijah, the prophet and reformer, bestowing his mantle on Elisha, the young man who is to follow in his footsteps. Thady, the Irish narrator, is this story's Elijah; but Elisha remains unknown. There is no one in the world of Castle Rackrent who is prepared to take over. The rapacious Jason Quirk, who as Thady's son would have been the most likely, has been corrupted and is now unworthy. Thady concludes, "Jason won't have the land ... I'm tired wishing anything for this world" (96), and we are left with the same kind of fatigue and uncertainty that preoccupies Smith's novel. The only other form of property in the hands of Thady is the narrative itself, which is a memoir of the Rackrent family that he has "voluntarily undertaken to publish" (7). The narrative is a vital form of property; without being able to pass on the great coat, all that Thady can bequeath is the story. But his ownership is challenged and desta-bilized by Edgeworth's careful contextualization of the story with the glossary and footnotes.

Knowledgeable about the intricacies of land management, Edgeworth was exceptionally aware of the decisive role ownership played in socio-political constructs. In a country (Ireland) where the right of ownership was a particularly volatile issue and property rights were strictly con-trolled and circumscribed, the question of who has a right to the responsibilities of proprietorship had pressing local as well as global implications. Edgeworth was interested in the *quality* of land manage-ment and concerned that leadership be based on talent and merit rather than on status. She aligns herself with contractarians in exposing the corruptions in hereditary privilege, but she takes contact theory into the realm of morality and confronts Burke on his own territory (both morality and Ireland). She confirms his fears of chaos but regards the family whose privileged status is inherited rather than earned as the culprit rather than the saviour of British and Irish society. Bestowing the mantle of reform for both Smith and Edgeworth continues to revolve around property and the rights and privileges accompanying it. The optimism of earlier Jacobin novels is tempered by the reality of struggle and the failures to bring about widespread change; however, the intricacies of property, rights and the law remain enmeshed and inseparable.

Notes

Introduction

1. The designation "English Jacobin" is a controversial one ; however, I have chosen to use "English Jacobin" (or simply "Jacobin") because it is a historically specific term and a customary (and therefore recognizable) name. In addition, I sometimes borrow Michael McKeon's term "progressive narrative" because the texts challenge the constructions of status. See Michael McKeon, *The Origins of the English Novel, 1600–1740* (Baltimore: Johns Hopkins University Press, 1987), 21.
2. Among important and recent analyses of the English Jacobin novel are the following: Angela Keane, *Women Writers and the English Nation in the 1790s* (Cambridge: Cambridge University Press, 2000); Nicola J. Watson, *Revolution and Form of the English Novel* (Oxford: Clarendon Press, 1994); Pamela Clemit, *The Godwinian Novel* (Oxford: Clarendon Press, 1993); Gary Kelly, *Women, Writing, and Revolution, 1790–1827* (Oxford: Clarendon Press, 1993); Mona Scheuermann, *Her Bread to Earn* (Lexington: University Press of Kentucky, 1993); Eleanor Ty, *Unsex'd Revolutionaries* (Toronto: University of Toronto Press, 1993); Mona Scheuermann, *Social Protest in the Eighteenth-Century English Novel* (Columbus: Ohio State University Press, 1985); Gary Kelly, *The English Jacobin Novel, 1780–1805* (Oxford: Clarendon Press, 1976); Marilyn Butler, *Jane Austen and the War of Ideas* (Oxford: Clarendon Press, 1975).
3. The phrase, "things as they are", is taken from the title of William Godwin's novel *Things As They Are: or, the Adventures of Caleb Williams* (London: B. Crosby, 1794).
4. The term "contractarianism" refers to the political theory of John Locke, John Harrington, Algernon Sidney, and Jean-Jacques Rousseau, among others. It conceives of political authority as derived from the consent of the people who have agreed to form a civil society. The governed and the governors are bound by a contract that is based on this consent. The campaign for the rights of man in the 1790s is the late eighteenth-century manifestation of contractarianism. See P.S. Atiyah, *The Rise and Fall of Freedom of Contract* (Oxford: Clarendon Press, 1979), 39–40.
5. Marilyn Butler, ed., *Burke, Paine, Godwin and the Revolutionary Controversy* (Cambridge: Cambridge University Press, 1984), 1–2.
6. William Godwin, *Things As They Are: or, The Adventures of Caleb Williams*, ed. Pamela Clemit, vol. 3 of *Collected Novels and Memoirs of William Godwin* (London: Pickering & Chatto, 1992), 279. All subsequent references will be given parenthetically within the text.
7. Atiyah, 37, 41.
8. *Oxford English Dictionary*, s.v. "enfranchise", "enfranchisement", "alienate".
9. Mary Wollstonecraft, *A Vindication of the Rights of Men*, vol. 5 of *The Works of Mary Wollstonecraft*, ed. Janet Todd and Marilyn Butler (New York: New York University Press, 1989), 24.

10. David Lieberman, *The Province of Legislation Determined* (Cambridge: Cambridge University Press, 1989), 1; E.P. Thompson, *Customs in Common* (New York: The New Press, 1993), 34. See also, Elizabeth Mensch, "The History of Mainstream Legal Thought", in *The Politics of Law: A Progressive Critique*, ed. David Kairys (New York: Pantheon Press, 1982), 19, 21.

11. Algernon Sidney, *Discourses Concerning Government* (London: John Toland, 1698; Indianapolis: Liberty Classics, 1990), 104.

12. James Harrington, *A System of Politics*, in *The Political Works of James Harrington*, ed. J.G.A. Pocock (Cambridge: Cambridge University Press, 1977), 850.

13. The phrase "equivocal spirit of the law" is from Thomas Holcroft, *A Narrative of Facts, relating to a Prosecution for High Treason* (London: Symonds, 1795), 27. The phrase "glorious uncertainty of the law" was a frequently repeated phrase in the eighteenth century. It was, for example, a toast offered to judges and counsel in Serjeant's Hall at a dinner given in honour of Lord Mansfield when he was elevated to the peerage (as Baron Mansfield) and to the office of Lord Chief Justice in 1756. It was also used in numerous political tracts in the 1790s. See, for instance, Joseph Priestley, *Letters to the Right Honourable Edmund Burke* (London: J. Johnson, 1791), 14.

14. Jeremy Bentham, *A Comment on the Commentaries* in *Collected Works of Jeremy Bentham*, ed. J.H. Burns and H.L.A. Hart (London: Athlone Press, 1977), 6, 58–59.

15. Peter Brooks and Paul Gewirtz, *Law's Stories: Narrative and Rhetoric in the Law* (New Haven: Yale University Press, 1996), 2–22.

16. John Barrell, *Imagining the King's Death* (Oxford: Oxford University Press, 2000), 137–40.

17. Barrell, 1. See also, Albert Goodwin, *The Friends of Liberty: The English Democratic Movement in the Age of the French Revolution* (Cambridge: Harvard University Press, 1979), 171–207; James T. Boulton, *The Language of Politics in the Age of Wilkes and Burke* (London: Routledge and Kegan Paul, 1963), 1–7; Olivia Smith, *The Politics of Language, 1791–1819* (Oxford: Clarendon Press, 1984), 35–109; Andrew McCann, *Cultural Politics in the 1790s: Literature, Radicalism, and the Public Sphere* (New York: St. Martin's Press, 1999), 1–32.

18. Carole Pateman, *The Sexual Contract* (Stanford: Stanford University Press, 1988), 1, 7.

19. E.P. Thompson notes the inappropriateness of the term "Jacobin" for British reformers; they much more closely resembled "the sans culottes of the Paris 'sections'", See E.P. Thompson, *The Making of the English Working Class* (New York: Vintage Books, 1963), 156. See also, Gary Kelly, *English Jacobin Novel*, 7.

20. *Anti-Jacobin; or Weekly Examiner*, 5th ed. (London: Printed for J. Hatchard, 1803), 1:7. The *Anti-Jacobin* was published from 1797–98.

21. Goodwin, 20.

22. Gordon J. Schochet, *Patriarchalism in Political Thought* (London: Basil Blackwell, 1975), 64–65.

23. M.O. Grenby notes the difficulty of defining "Jacobinism" from the perspective of the Anti-Jacobin movement. "Jacobinism", he suggests, "was simply a label for all that conservatives found detestable within society".

See M.O. Grenby, *The Anti-Jacobin Novel: British Conservatism and the French Revolution* (Cambridge: Cambridge University Press, 2001), 8.

24. *Anti-Jacobin Review and Magazine* 3 (May 1799), 93. The *Anti-Jacobin Review* was published from 1798–1821.

25. Seamus Deane *The French Revolution and Enlightenment in England, 1789–1832* (Cambridge: Harvard University Press, 1988), 162; Roy Porter, *The Creation of the Modern World* (New York: W.W. Norton, 2000), 6–12; Goodwin, 20–21.

26. Goodwin, 81–87.

27. Dr Richard Price, *A Discourse on the Love of our Country* (London: Woodstock Books, 1992), 50.

28. Quoted in Carl B. Cone, *Burke and the Nature of Politics: The Age of the French Revolution* (Louisville: University of Kentucky Press, 1964), 301.

29. Quoted in Deane, 162–63.

30. Adam Smith, *Lectures on Jurisprudence* (Indianapolis: Liberty Classics, 1982), 5.

31. Frans de Bruyn, *The Literary Genres of Edmund Burke* (Oxford: Clarendon Press, 1996) 6, 14.

32. Robert Cover, "Nomos and Narrative" in *Narrative, Violence and the Law: The Essays of Robert Cover*, ed. Martha Minow, Michael Ryan, and Austin Sarat (Ann Arbor: University of Michigan Press, 1992), 95–96.

Chapter 1   Narrativizing a Critique of the Contract

1. Cover, 105.

2. Cover, 101–102.

3. Mark Philp, "Introduction" to *The French Revolution and British Popular Politics* (Cambridge: Cambridge University Press, 1991), 1–17.

4. Edmund Burke, *Reflections on the Revolution in France* (London: J. Dodsley, 1790), 144.

5. Ian Balfour, "Promises, Promises: Social and Other Contracts in the English Jacobins (Godwin/Inchbald)", in *New Romanticisms: Theory and Critical Practice*, ed. David L. Clark and Donald C. Goellnicht (Toronto: University of Toronto Press, 1994), 225.

6. William Godwin, *Enquiry Concerning Political Justice*, vol. 3 of *Political and Philosophical Writings of William Godwin*, ed. Mark Philp (London: William Pickering, 1993), 83.

7. Godwin, *Political Justice*, 84.

8. Mark Philp, *Godwin's Political Justice* (Ithaca: Cornell University Press, 1986), 16–26. See also, Godwin, *Political Justice*, 72–80.

9. McKeon, 1–64.

10. The preface was added to the second and following editions. Godwin's explanation for the omission of the preface from the first edition was "the alarms of booksellers", precipitated by the atmosphere of fear that was created by the London Treason Trials of 1794. Godwin, *Caleb Williams*, 279–280.

11. Fredric Jameson, *The Political Unconscious* (Ithaca: Cornell University Press, 1981), 20.

12. See Jürgen Habermas, *The Structural Transformation of the Public Sphere*, trans. Thomas Burger (Cambridge: MIT Press, 1991), 57–88.

13. Godwin, *Political Justice*, 2.
14. Mary Wollstonecraft, *The Wrongs of Woman: or, Maria*, vol. 1 of *The Works of Mary Wollstonecraft*, ed. Janet Todd and Marilyn Butler (New York: New York University Press, 1989), 83. All subsequent references will be given parenthetically within the text.
15. See Gary Kelly, "Women Novelists and the French Revolution Debate: Novelizing the Revolution/Revolutionizing the Novel", *Eighteenth-Century Fiction* 6 (July 1994):369–88; McKeon, 51–52; Ian Watt, *The Rise of the Novel* (London: Chatto & Windus, 1957), 42–49.
16. Mary Hays, *Memoirs of Emma Courtney* (London: Printed for G.G. & J. Robinson, 1796; London: Oxford University Press, 1996), 3. All subsequent references will be given parenthetically within the text.
17. From Holcroft's review of Robert Bage's *Man As He Is*. See *The Monthly Review*, 2d ser., 10 (March 1793):297.
18. Thomas Holcroft, *The Memoirs of Bryan Perdue* (London: Longman, Hurt, Rees, and Orme, 1805), iii.
19. J. Paul Hunter, *Before Novels* (New York: W.W. Norton & Co., 1990), 225–47.
20. Hunter, 245.
21. James Boyd White, *Justice as Translation* (Chicago: University of Chicago Press, 1990), ix.
22. *The British Critic* 6 (July 1795):94.
23. *The Monthly Review*, 2d ser., 11 (June 1793):254.
24. *The Monthly Review*, 2d ser., 9 (November 1792):337–38.
25. See Holcroft's review of Eliza Kirkam Mathews, *The Count de Hoensdern; a German tale*, 2 vols. (Dublin: Wogan, et al., 1793) in *The Monthly Review*, 2d ser., 12 (November 1793):338.
26. Martha Minow, "Partial Justice: Law and Minorities", in *The Fate of Law* (Ann Arbor: University of Michigan Press, 1993), 15–77; Robin West, *Narrative, Authority and Law* (Ann Arbor: University of Michigan Press, 1993), 20–23.
27. Maria Edgeworth, *Castle Rackrent* (Oxford: Oxford University Press, 1964), 1–2. All subsequent references will be given parenthetically within the text.
28. Hunter connects the interest in witnessing to the prevailing Protestant culture (particularly that of the Calvinists) and its "need to record the self extensively and analytically". See Hunter, 303–4.
29. Hunter, 303–4.
30. Georg Lukács, *The Theory of the Novel*, trans. Anna Bostock (Cambridge: MIT Press, 1971), 77–78. For Lukács the inner form of the novel is about the journeying of the problematic individual and the outward form is "biography".
31. See Patricia Meyer Spacks, *Imagining A Self* (Cambridge: Harvard University Press, 1976), 1.
32. For a conservative example, see Elizabeth Hamilton's *Memoirs of Modern Philosophers* (London: G.G. and J. Robinson, 1800).
33. Hunter, 338–41.
34. Spacks, 73.
35. Mikhail M. Bakhtin, *The Dialogic Imagination*, trans. Caryl Emerson and Michael Holquist (Austin: University of Texas Press, 1981), 124–25.
36. Felicity Nussbaum, *The Autobiographical Subject* (Baltimore: Johns Hopkins University Press, 1989), 136.

37. See Chapter 2 for a full discussion of "inherited rights".
38. *The Anti-Jacobin Review and Magazine* 3 (May 1799):55.
39. Nancy Armstrong, *Desire and Domestic Fiction* (Oxford: Oxford University Press, 1987), 3.
40. Armstrong, 29.
41. McKeon, 173.
42. Bakhtin, 177.
43. Ronald Paulson, *Representations of Revolutions (1789–1820)* (New Haven: Yale University Press, 1983), 1, 3.
44. Paulson, 4.
45. Thomas Paine, *The Rights of Man, Part I*, in *Thomas Paine: Political Writings*, ed. Bruce Kuklick (Cambridge: Cambridge University Press, 1989), 77.
46. Holcroft, *Narrative of Facts*, 1.
47. Quoted in C.K. Ogden, *Bentham's Theory of Fictions* (London: Kegan Paul, Trench, Trubner & Co., 1932), xvii.
48. Paine, 64.

Chapter 2   Debating Rights, Property, and the Law

1. The dates of composition for *Patriarcha* have been widely disputed. Peter Laslett has suggested that the text was composed between 1635 and 1642. See Peter Laslett, Introduction to *Patriarcha and other Political Works*, by Sir Robert Filmer (Oxford: Basil Blackwell, 1949), 3–5. Johann Sommerville believes the composition dates to be earlier: the first two chapters of *Patriarcha* written in the 1620s, and the third in 1630. See Johann P. Sommerville, Introduction to *Patriarcha and Other Writings* by Sir Robert Filmer (Cambridge: Cambridge University Press, 1991), xxxiv.
2. Sir Robert Filmer, *Patriarcha: A Defence of the Natural Power of Kings against the Unnatural Liberty of the People*, in *Patriarcha and Other Writings*, ed. Johann P. Sommerville (Cambridge: Cambridge University Press, 1991), 12.
3. "Genetic" refers to a theory of government that locates authority in the origin of its formation. See Schochet, 8–9.
4. Sir Robert Filmer, *Observations Concerning The Originall of Government*, in *Patriarcha and Other Writings*, ed. Johann P. Sommerville (Cambridge: Cambridge University Press, 1991), 225–26.
5. Filmer, *Patriarcha*, 35; see also Sir Robert Filmer, *The Free-holder's Grand Inquest Touching Our Soveraigne Lord the King and his Parliament*, in *Patriarcha and Other Writings*, ed. Johann P. Sommerville (Cambridge: Cambridge University Press, 1991), 99–100.
6. Sir Robert Filmer, *The Anarchy of a Limited or Mixed Monarchy*, in *Patriarcha and Other Writings*, ed. Johann P. Sommerville (Cambridge: Cambridge University Press, 1991), 149–50.
7. Among examples of precursors to Filmer's views on patriarchy, Sommerville cites Jean Bodin's *Six Livres de la Republique* (1576), Hadrian Saravia's *De Imperandi Authoritate* (1593), John Buckeridge's *De potestate papae in rebus temporalibus* (1614) and *A sermon preached before his Maiestie at Whitehall* (1618). See Sommerville, xv–xx. See also James Daly, *Sir Robert*

Filmer and English Political Thought (Toronto: University of Toronto Press, 1979), 3–27.

8. Jean-Jacques Rousseau, *Discourse on Political Economy*, in *Rousseau's Political Writings*, ed. Alan Ritter and Julia Conway Bondanella, trans. Julia Conway Bondanella (New York: W.W. Norton & Co., 1988), 61.

9. It is important to note here that not all royalists used the analogy of father and king to justify monarchy. Sommerville, xviii–xix.

10. Rousseau's consideration of "the people" has its roots in seventeenth-century Parliamentarian and republican thought. See Christopher Hill, *Intellectual Origins of the English Revolution* (Oxford: Clarendon Press, 1965), 196.

11. Richard Tuck cites texts in the early and high Middle Ages as important antecedents to the works of Grotius, Selden, Locke, et al. See Richard Tuck, *Natural Rights Theories* (Cambridge: Cambridge University Press, 1979).

12. John Locke, *Two Treatises of Government*, ed. Peter Laslett (Cambridge: Cambridge University Press, 1988), 356.

13. I am indebted to Bill Walker for introducing me to the importance of religious toleration in *Two Treatises* and for pointing out the necessity of reading *Two Treatises* in conjunction with *A Letter Concerning Toleration*. See William Walker, *Locke, Literary Criticism, and Philosophy* (Cambridge: Cambridge University Press, 1994).

14. Thomas Davies, ed., *Committees for the Repeal of the Test and Corporation Acts* (London: London Record Society, 1978).

15. Sir William Holdsworth, *A History of English Law* (London: Methuen & Co., 1966), 6:181–201.

16. *A Letter Concerning Toleration* is a translation of a letter Locke addressed to Philip von Limborch in Latin in 1685–86. The original title was *Epistola de tolerantia*. See Richard Ashcraft, *Revolutionary Politics and Locke's Two Treatises of Government* (Princeton: Princeton University Press, 1986), 475.

17. John Locke, *Letter Concerning Toleration* (London: Printed for Awnsham Churchill, 1689; Indianapolis: Hackett Publishing, 1983), 28.

18. Locke, *Letter*, 38.

19. James Tully, *An Approach to Political Philosophy: Locke in Contexts* (Cambridge: Cambridge University Press, 1993), 47–62.

20. Locke, *Two Treatises*, 414–15.

21. Locke, *Two Treatises*, 381–82.

22. Jean-Jacques Rousseau, *On Social Contract*, in *Rousseau's Political Writings*, ed. Alan Ritter and Julia Conway Bondanella, trans. Julia Conway Bondanella (New York: W.W. Norton & Co., 1988), 88–89.

23. Locke, *Two Treatises*, 381.

24. In discussions of the self in contract theory, I use the pronoun "he" because Locke, Rousseau, Paine, et al. specifically had men in mind when they wrote about the individual.

25. "Civil society" refers to existence in a society or civilization of "men", distinct from a state of nature. See Marvin B. Becker, *The Emergence of Civil Society in the Eighteenth Century* (Bloomington: Indiana University Press, 1994).

26. Locke, *Two Treatises*, 357.

27. Sidney, 320.

28. Sidney, 78.
29. Sidney, 83.
30. Emphasis added. Sidney, 100.
31. Sidney, 98, 192.
32. Sidney, 192–93.
33. C.B. Macpherson, *The Political Theory of Possessive Individualism* (Oxford: Clarendon Press, 1962), 107–59.
34. Keith Thomas, "The Levellers and the Franchise", in *The Interregnum: The Quest for Settlement*, ed. G.E. Aylmer (New York: Macmillan, 1974), 60–63.
35. *Puritanism and Liberty*, ed. A.S.P. Woodhouse (London: J.M. Dent & Sons, 1992), 53.
36. Thomas, 68–69.
37. *Puritanism and Liberty*, 53, 83.
38. Christopher Hill, *The Century of Revolution, 1603–1714* (New York: W.W. Norton, 1980), 110–11.
39. Richard Gleissner, "The Levellers and Natural Law: The Putney Debates of 1647", *Journal of British Studies* 20 (1980):74–89.
40. *Puritanism and Liberty*, 53.
41. *Puritanism and Liberty*, 54.
42. Priestley's response to Burke's *Reflections*, in particular, strongly endorses major tenents of contractarianism. See Joseph Priestley, *Letters to the Right Honourable Edmund Burke* (London: J. Johnson, 1791).
43. Priestley, *Letters to ... Burke*, 41.
44. Priestley, *Letters to ... Burke*, 51.
45. Priestley, *Letters to ... Burke*, 56.
46. Joseph Priestley, *An Essay on the First Principles of Government; and on the Nature of Political, Civil, and Religious Liberty* (London: Dodsley, Cadell and Johnson, 1768), 16.
47. Priestley, *First Principles of Government*, 20–21.
48. Priestley, *First Principles of Government*, 21–22.
49. Catharine Macaulay makes a similar argument for a limited franchise. See Catharine Macaulay, *Observations on the Relfections of the Right Hon. Edmund Burke in a Letter to the Right Hon. The Earl of Stanhope* (London: C. Dilly, 1790).
50. James Tully, *A Discourse on Property* (Cambridge: Cambridge University Press, 1980), 63.
51. Locke, *Two Treatises*, 287–88.
52. Locke, *Two Treatises*, 383.
53. Tully, *Discourse on Property*, 61. C.B. Macpherson, however, tends to emphasize liberty as a "possession" rather than a right. See Macpherson, *Possessive Individualism*.
54. Macpherson, 215–16. Macpherson's point is supported by Carole Pateman's observation that the "character of the historical state of nature and the relationships of its inhabitants ... closely resemble those of a developing capitalist market economy". See Carole Pateman, *The Problem of Political Obligation* (Chichester: John Wiley & Sons, 1979), 65–68.
55. Richard Ashcraft argues that Locke's theory of property must be read in the context of its "theological underpinnings". Ashcraft, 257, 263–66.
56. Tully, *Political Philosophy*, 77.

57. Locke, *Two Treatises*, 350–51.
58. Locke, *Two Treatises*, 383.
59. See Burke, *Reflections*; John Bowles, *Dialogues on the Rights of Britons, between a Farmer, a Sailor, and a Manufacturer* (London: T. Longman, 1792); and John Bowles, *A Protest Against Thomas Paine's "Rights of Man"* (London: T. Longman, 1792).
60. Locke, *Two Treatises*, 383.
61. Locke, *Two Treatises*, 277.
62. J.G.A. Pocock refers to Harrington as a "classical republican, and England's premier civic humanist". *The Political Works of James Harrington*, ed. J.G.A. Pocock (Cambridge: Cambridge University Press, 1977), 15.
63. Harrington, *Oceana*, 199.
64. Harrington, *Oceana*, 163–64.
65. J.G.A. Pocock, ed., *Three British Revolutions* (Princeton: Princeton University Press, 1980).
66. Harrington, *Oceana*, 199.
67. Harrington, *Oceana*, 203–4.
68. Christopher Hill, *Puritanism and Revolution* (London: Secker and Warburg, 1958), 301; Macpherson, 162; Pocock, *Harrington*, 51.
69. While Dr Price's sermon is commonly cited as the beginning of the rights debate of the 1790s, Marilyn Butler observes that between 1760 and 1790 there had been a succession of attempts to extend the franchise and a number of pamphlets written in favour of, or against, altering Parliamentary boundaries, repeal of the Test and Corporation Acts, slavery in the West Indies, civil and religious liberties, etc. Butler, ed., *Revolution Controversy*, 3–4.
70. Eleanor Nicholes points to the disagreements over the repeal of the Test and Corporation Acts as a primary catalyst for Burke's fevered response to Price in *Reflections*. Eleanor Louise Nicholes, Introduction to *A Vindication of the Rights of Men*, by Mary Wollstonecraft (London: J. Johnson, 1790; Gainesville: Scholars' Facsimiles & Reprints, 1960), v.–xix. See also Deane, 13–14; Cone, 300–313.
71. Goodwin, 81.
72. The Corporation Act (13 Charles II, Stat.2, c.1) was passed in 1661 and the Test Act (25 Charles II, c.2) was passed in 1673. Both required sacramental tests to prove affiliation with the Church of England before one could be elected to a corporation office or any civil or military office. See Thomas Davis, ed., *Committees for the Repeal of the Test and Corporation Acts: Minutes 1786–90 and 1827–8* (London: London Record Society, 1978).
73. Cone, 301–6.
74. Nicholes, xii–xv.
75. Burke's concept of inherited rights can be traced back to Henry de Bracton's thirteenth–century treatise *De legibus et consuetudinibus Angliae* ("On the laws and customs of England"). The essay is more frequently known under the simpler title, *Bracton*. See J.H. Baker, *An Introduction to English Legal History*, 3rd ed. (London: Butterworths, 1990), 201, 532–33.
76. Burke, *Reflections*, 47–48.
77. Baron de Montesquieu, *The Spirit of the Laws*, trans. Thomas Nugent (New York: Hafner Press, 1949), 2:62–63.

78. Blackstone subcategorizes "hereditaments" as "corporeal" and "incorporeal" (this last term defined as anticipated financial gain such as rents, annuities, tithes, or continued privileges such as offices or advowsons). Sir William Blackstone, *Commentaries on the Laws of England* (Dublin, 1771), 1:107–108, 2:20–21, 2:2.

79. Burke, *Reflections*, 49.

80. Stephen Prickett, *England and the French Revolution* (London: Macmillan Education Ltd., 1989), 43.

81. Cone, 330.

82. Burke, *Reflections*, 144.

83. Cone, 318. The French National Assembly ignored the authority of prescription, and Burke regarded this as one of the numerous threats of the Revolution. Burke considered prescription to be a natural law, and a threat to prescription endangered the security of property.

84. Burke, *Reflections*, 87.

85. Sir James Mackintosh argues that Burke's comment "[w]hatever each man can do without trespasing on others, he has a right to do for himself ..." is actually an endorsement of the concept of natural rights. See Sir James Mackintosh, *Vindiciae Gallicae. Defence of the French Revolution and its English Admirers, against the Accusations of the Right Hon. Edmund Burke*, in *The Miscellaneous Works of the Right Honourable Sir James Mackintosh*, ed. R.J. Mackintosh (Philadelphia: Carey and Hart, 1846), 437.

86. Burke, *Reflections*, 87.

87. Burke, *Reflections*, 90–91.

88. Burke, *Reflections*, 87–88.

89. Burke, *Reflections*, 21–22.

90. Burke, *Reflections*, 48–49.

91. Burke, *Reflections*, 75–76.

92. Holdsworth, 11:275–276.

93. Burke, *Reflections*, 48.

94. Burke, *Reflections*, 76.

95. According to Peter J. Stanlis, there were at least four hundred responses to Burke's *Reflections*. See Peter J. Stanlis, *Edmund Burke: The Enlightenment and Revolution* (New Brunswick: Transaction Publishers, 1991), 39–41. See also, Carl Cone "Pamphlet Replies to Burke's Reflections", *The Southwestern Social Science Quarterly*, 26 (June 1945):22–34 and Thomas W. Copeland and Milton Shumway Smith, *A Checklist of the Correspondence of Edmund Burke* (Cambridge: Cambridge University Press, 1955).

96. Butler, ed., *Revolution Controversy*, 4–5; Alfred Cobban, ed., *The Debate on the French Revolution, 1789–1800* (London: Nicholas Kaye, 1950), 2–6; Deane, 158–175.

97. Cobban, 95, 119.

98. Butler, ed., *Revolution Controversy*, 4.

99. Butler, ed., *Revolution Controversy*, 5.

100. Deane, 164.

101. Virginia Sapiro, *A Vindication of Political Virtue* (Chicago: University of Chicago Press, 1992).

102. Wollstonecraft, *Vindication of the Rights of Men*, 9.

103. Wollstonecraft, *Vindication of the Rights of Men*, 7, 14.
104. Wollstonecraft, *Vindication of the Rights of Men*, 20.
105. Wollstonecraft, *Vindication of the Rights of Men*, 10–14.
106. Wollstonecraft, *Vindication of the Rights of Men*, 11–12.
107. Wollstonecraft, *Vindication of the Rights of Men*, 13, 14–15.
108. Wollstonecraft, *Vindication of the Rights of Men*, 22.
109. Wollstonecraft, *Vindication of the Rights of Men*, 23–24.
110. Cobban, 92.
111. Mackintosh, 404–5.
112. Mackintosh, 405.
113. Mackintosh, 424.
114. Mackintosh, 424.
115. Mackintosh, 421.
116. Mackintosh, 436.
117. Mackintosh, 437.
118. Paine, *Rights of Man*, 77.
119. Paine, *Rights of Man*, 77–78.
120. Thomas Paine, *The Trial of Thomas Paine for a Libel ... December 18, 1793* (Boston: I. Thomas and E.T. Andrews, 1793); Gregory Claeys, *Thomas Paine: Social and Political Thought* (Boston: Unwin Hyman, 1989), 26–29.
121. Paine, *Rights of Man*, 80–81.
122. Paine, *Rights of Man*, 58.
123. Paine, *Rights of Man*, 81.
124. Paine, *Rights of Man*, 78.
125. Paine, *Rights of Man*, 79.
126. Paine, *Rights of Man*, 139.
127. Paine, *Rights of Man*, 109.
128. Paine, *Rights of Man*, 77.
129. Peter Gabel and Jay M. Feinman, "Contract Law as Ideology", in *The Politics of Law: A Progressive Critique*, ed. David Kairys (New York: Pantheon Press, 1982), 172–73. See also Atiyah, *The Rise and Fall of Freedom of Contract*; Marianne Constable, *The Law of the Other* (Chicago: University of Chicago Press, 1994); Zillah R. Eisenstein, *The Female Body and the Law* (Berkeley: University of California Press, 1988); Pateman, *The Sexual Contract*; Roberto Mangabeira Unger, *The Critical Legal Studies Movement* (Cambridge: Harvard University Press, 1983).
130. Gabel and Feinman, 173–75.

Chapter 3 Envisaging the New Citizen

1. Butler, *Jane Austen and the War of Ideas*, 7–28.
2. Godwin, *Political Justice*, 27.
3. Godwin, *Political Justice*, 30.
4. Godwin, *Political Justice*, 34.
5. Thomas Holcroft, "A Letter to the Right Honourable William Windham, on the Intemperance and Dangerous Tendency of his Public Conduct" (London: Symonds, 1795), 49. For a response to Holcroft's "Letter", see William Belcher, *Holcroft's Folly* (London, [1795?]).

6. Holcroft, *Narrative of Facts*, 3–4.
7. Wollstonecraft, *Vindication of the Rights of Men*, 53.
8. Godwin, *Political Justice*, 20–21.
9. Earl of Shaftesbury, *Characteristicks of Men, Manners, Opinions, Times*, 3 vols. (London: 1711), 2:9.
10. Shaftesbury, 2:15–16.
11. Shaftesbury, 2:45.
12. Wollstonecraft, *Vindication of the Rights of Men*, 31.
13. Godwin, *Political Justice*, 10.
14. Godwin, *Political Justice*, 2.
15. Godwin, *Political Justice*, 13.
16. Shaftesbury, 2:64.
17. Shaftesbury, 2:23.
18. Frances Hutcheson, *A System of Moral Philosophy* (New York: Augustus M. Kelley, 1968), 40.
19. Hutcheson, 50.
20. William Hazlitt, *Memoirs of the Late Thomas Holcroft* (London, 1816), 2:1.
21. *The Monthly Review*, 2d ser., 10 (March 1793): 297.
22. Hazlitt, 3:292.
23. *The Monthly Review*, 2d. ser., 9 (November 1792):337.
24. Butler, *Jane Austen*, 48.
25. Hazlitt, 2:4.
26. Patricia Meyer Spacks, *Desire and Truth* (Chicago: University of Chicago Press, 1990), 178.
27. In his letter to Windham, Holcroft claims that he has no desire to charge Windham with "intentional guilt"; instead he blames "your ignorance, your errors, your passions". See Holcroft, "Letter to the Right Honourable William Windham", 7.
28. Thomas Holcroft, *Anna St Ives* (London: Oxford University Press, 1973), 209. All subsequent references will be given parenthetically within the text.
29. *Oxford English Dictionary*, s.v. "improvement". For a thorough and helpful discussion of the meaning of "improvement" in the eighteenth century, see De Bruyn, 67–89.
30. De Bruyn, 3, 59–61.
31. De Bruyn, 70.
32. Godwin, *Political Justice*, 50.
33. Evan Radcliffe, "Revolutionary Writing, Moral Philosophy, and Universal Benevolence in the Eighteenth Century", *Journal of the History of Ideas* 54 (April 1993):221.
34. C.B. Jones, *Radical Sensibility* (London: Routledge Press, 1993), 30–31.
35. Adam Smith, *The Theory of Moral Sentiments*, 6th ed. (London, 1790; Indianapolis: Liberty Classics, 1982), 52.
36. Smith, *Moral Sentiments*, 53.
37. Adam Smith quoted in Jones, 31.
38. Radcliffe, 221–40.
39. Radcliffe, 221.
40. Lynn Hunt, *The Family Romance of the French Revolution* (Berkeley: University of California Press, 1992), 87.

41. Bakhtin, 263.
42. Loraine Fletcher, *Charlotte Smith: A Critical Biography* (New York: St Martin's Press, 1998), 142.
43. Charlotte Smith, *Desmond*, 3 vols. (London: G.G.J. and J. Robinson, 1792), I:111. All subsequent references will be given parenthetically within the text
44. Georges Lefebvre, *The French Revolution*, trans. Elizabeth Moss Evanson (London: Routledge Press, 1962), 1:180. Fletcher, 142.
45. Helen Maria Williams' *Letters written from France in the Summer of 1790* was followed by *Letters from France* (1792–6), *Letters from France* (1795–6), and *Letters on the Events which have passed in France since the Restoration in 1815* (1819). When Mary Wollstonecraft was in France, from December of 1792 until April of 1795, she wrote the first of what was to be a series of letters for Joseph Johnson. It was entitled "Letter on the Present Character of the French Nation" and dated 15 February 1793. Johnson, however, never published the letter. See Janet Todd, *Mary Wollstonecraft: A Revolutionary Life* (New York: Columbia University Press, 2000), 207–08, 475 n. 5.
46. Watson, 36. Carrol L. Fry also suggests that Smith borrowed from Williams's *Letters*. See Carrol L. Fry, *Charlotte Smith* (New York: Twayne Publishers, 1996), 70.
47. Janet Gurkin Altman, *Epistolarity: Approaches to a Form* (Columbus: Ohio State University Press, 1982), 87–89.
48. See Antje Blank and Janet Todd, "Introduction" to Charlotte Smith, *Desmond* (London: Pickering and Chatto, 1997), xi–xxxix; Alison Conway, "Nationalism, Revolution, and the Female Body: Charlotte Smith's *Desmond*", *Women's Studies* 24 (1995):399; Watson, 36; Ty, 130–142; Pat Elliott, "Charlotte Smith's Feminism: A Study of *Emmeline* and *Desmond*", *Living by the Pen: Early British Women Writers*, ed. Dale Spender (New York: Teachers College Press, 1992), 91–112; Diana Bowstead, "Charlotte Smith's *Desmond*: The Epistolary Novel as Ideological Argument", *Fetter'd or Free?: British Women Novelists, 1670–1815*, ed. Mary Anne Schofield and Cecilia Macheski (Athens: Ohio University Press, 1986), 237–263.
49. *The Monthly Review*, 2d ser., 9 (1792): 406. In addition, *The London Review* comments on the narrative's "morality" that is "blended so easily and delicately with the sentiments of liberty". See *The European Magazine and London Review* 22 (1792): 23.
50. The Comte d'Hauteville is often the voice of Burke, though he does not refer directly to Burke or his work. See for example, *Desmond*, vol. I, 232–33 and *Reflections*, 144.
51. Desmond does not mention Wollstonecraft's *Vindication of the Rights of Men* directly, but he quotes from it in this extended political discussion in vol. II, Letter X (II:124). See Smith, *Desmond*, ed. Antje Blank and Janet Todd, 425 n. 39.
52. Burke, *Reflections*, 144.
53. There are several examples of "mirroring" or "doubling" in *Desmond* that link England and France. Geraldine (Waverly) and Josephine (Boisbelle) are the primary and most frequently analyzed instance. For a discussion linking

Geraldine and Josephine to Rousseau's Julie, see Watson, 37. For a provocative and persuasive reading of Josephine as "the erotically decadent female body" that must "wither away" as it is displaced by Geraldine, the representative of the "ungendered mind", see Conway, 395.

54. In this quality of foresight, Bethel does remind one of Burke, as Blank and Todd suggest (see n. 59); however, Bethel seems too sympathetic a character in the novel to represent the central figure of political attack.

55. See *The Critical Review*, 2d ser., 6 (1792): 99; *The Monthly Review*, 2d ser., 9 (1792): 412; *The European Magazine and London Review* 22 (1792): 23.

56. Altman, 201.

57. Bruce Redford makes a similar point about the familiar letter and the categories of history and fiction, or in the case of his discussion, the "natural" and the "fictive". See Bruce Redford, *The Converse of the Pen* (Chicago: University of Chicago Press, 1986), 13.

58. Redford, 5.

59. Blank and Todd portray this epistolary novel as a series of "letters" to Burke, one of the many responses to the statesman following the publication of his *Reflections* but the first in novel form. They liken Bethel to Burke and Desmond himself to de Pont, the addressee of Burke's "letter" that is the essay *Reflections*. See Blank and Todd, xxiii–xxvi.

60. Mary Favret, *The Romantic Correspondence: Women, Politics, and the Fiction of Letters* (Cambridge: Cambridge University Press, 1992).

61. For an extended discussion on the motif of "meeting" in the Greek romance and in the contemporary novel, see Bakhtin, 97–98.

62. Altman, 13.

63. Redford, 9–10.

64. James Boaden, *Memoirs of Mrs Inchbald* (London: Richard Bentley, 1833), 1:315, 328.

65. Boaden, 1:346.

66. See Elizabeth Hamilton's *Memoirs of Modern Philosophers* (1800), Jane West's *A Tale of the Times* (1799), Isaac d'Israeli, *Vaurien; or Sketches of the Times* (1797), Charles Lloyd, *Edmund Oliver* (1798), and Henry James Pye, *The Democrat* (1795).

67. Kelly, *English Jacobin Novel*, 96.

68. Kelly, *English Jacobin Novel*, 98; *Anti-Jacobin Review and Magazine* 5 (February 1800):152.

69. Ty, 102.

70. Kelly, *English Jacobin Novel*, 94.

71. Jones, 69.

72. Wollstonecraft, *Vindication of the Rights of Men*, 8.

73. Elizabeth Inchbald, *Nature and Art* (Philadelphia: Printed for H. & P. Rice by Snowden and McCorkle, 1796), 1: 3–4. All subsequent references will be given parenthetically within the text.

74. Jean-Jacques Rousseau, *La Nouvelle Héloïse*, trans. Judith H. McDowell (University Park: Pennsylvania State University Press, 1968), 391, 393.

75. In some later editions, "Hannah" Primrose is called "Agnes" Primrose.

76. Marcel Mauss, *The Gift*, trans. W.D. Halls (New York: W.W. Norton & Co., 1990), 3, 65.

77. Kelly, *English Jacobin Novel*, 98.

78. Hermes, in addition to being a messenger, was the god of commerce and the market, a "protector of traders". See Edith Hamilton, *Mythology* (New York: Warner Books, 1942), 34

79. Oliver Elton, *A Survey of English Literature, 1780–1830* (London: Edward Arnold, 1912), 182.

80. McKeon, 218–22.

81. Robert Bage, *Hermsprong; or Man As He Is Not* (London, 1796; Oxford: Oxford University Press, 1985), 166. All subsequent references will be given parenthetically within the text.

82. Burke, *Reflections*, 29.

83. Chris Tennant, "Primitives, indigenous rights and international institutions: International engagement with indigenous peoples, 1945–1992" (Paper delivered at the "Law and Literature Seminar", Center for Literary and Cultural Studies, Harvard University, Cambridge, Mass., 13 April 1993), 22.

84. The "son of nobody" (*filius nullius*) is the legal term for an illegitimate child. This status reflects an illegitimate child's inability to inherit property. See Blackstone, I:447.

85. Cone, 130–39.

86. Burke, *Reflections*, 75.

87. Quoted from Adam Smith's *Theory of Moral Sentiments*, II. ii. 3.4., by Andrew Skinner, Introduction to *The Wealth of Nations*, Books I–III, by Adam Smith (London: Penguin Books, 1974), 28.

88. Wollstonecraft, *Vindication of the Rights of Men*, 45–47.

89. Blackstone, 1:122. Blackstone defines "private wrongs" as those infringements of particular rights concerning individuals only, also referred to as "civil injuries". These rights are both the rights of persons and the rights of things, the former defined as rights annexed to the persons of men, the latter, rights one may acquire over external objects. Caroline could be regarded as the subject of Lord Grondale's rights of persons or things; in either case she would be subsumed in the property of another.

90. Blackstone, 1:122–123. Blackstone defines "public wrongs" as a violation of public rights, or rights of the community. He refers to these wrongs as "crimes and misdemeanors".

91. Frederick Engels, *The Origin of the Family, Private Property and the State* (London: Lawrence and Wishart, 1972), 78, 265; Lawrence Stone, *The Family, Sex and Marriage in England 1500–1800* (New York: Harper & Row, 1977), 61, 88.

92. Marc Shell, *Money, Language, and Thought* (Berkeley: University of California Press, 1982), 63.

93. Shell, 63–64.

Chapter 4 Acquiring Political Agency

1. Schochet, *Patriarchalism in Political Thought*, 10–16.

2. Filmer's notion of patriarchalism was "in vogue" primarily between 1679 and 1681. Laslett, 54.

3. S.D. Amussen, "Gender, Family and the Social Order, 1560–1725", in *Order and Disorder in Early Modern England*, ed. Anthony Fletcher and John Stevenson, 196–217 (New York: Cambridge University Press, 1985), 196.

4. Filmer, *Patriarcha*, 10.
5. Linda J. Nicholson, *Gender and History* (New York: Columbia University Press, 1986), 142.
6. Filmer, *Patriarcha*, 12.
7. Filmer, *Patriarcha*, 2–3, 6–7.
8. Locke, *Two Treatises*, 161.
9. Stone, 153–54.
10. Locke, *Two Treatises*, 268.
11. Laslett, Introduction to *Two Treatises*, 12–13.
12. Locke, *Two Treatises*, 267.
13. Locke, *Two Treatises*, 166.
14. Locke, *Two Treatises*, 161.
15. Locke, *Two Treatises*, 174.
16. Locke, *Two Treatises*, 173–74.
17. Sidney, 16.
18. Sidney, 46–48.
19. Sidney, 12.
20. Sidney, 75.
21. Sidney, 90.
22. Rousseau, *Political Economy*, 59–60.
23. Jean-Jacques Rousseau, *Émile*, trans. Barbara Foxley (London: J.M. Dent & Sons, 1992), 326.
24. Rousseau, *Émile*, 330, 335.
25. Rousseau, *Émile*, 328.
26. Rousseau, *Émile*, 332.
27. Rousseau, *Émile*, 325.
28. Rousseau, *Émile*, 340.
29. Pateman, *The Sexual Contract*, 3.
30. Pateman, *The Sexual Contract*, 14.
31. *Monthly Review*, 2d ser., 15 (October 1794), 153.
32. *British Critic* 4 (July 1794), 70–71.
33. The narration of *Caleb Williams* shifts in the course of the novel. The story is partly told by another servant, Mr Collins (Volume 1), and partly by Caleb himself (Volumes 2 and 3). For more on the narrative structure of the novel, see Gerard A. Barker, "The Narrative Mode of *Caleb Williams* and Resolutions", *Studies in the Novel* 25 (Spring 1993):1–15.
34. *British Critic* 6 (July 1795), 94.
35. *British Critic* 6 (August 1795): 213.
36. Leon Radzinowicz, *A History of English Criminal Law and its Administration from 1750* (New York: Macmillan & Co., 1948), 580–81.
37. E.P. Thompson, *Whigs and Hunters* (London: Penguin Books, 1975), 21–27.
38. Thompson, *Whigs and Hunters*, 270.
39. Thompson, *Whigs and Hunters*, 22.
40. Thompson cites the episode of Tyrrel and the Hawkinses in *Caleb Williams* as an example of the state's or a private prosecutor's ability to use the Black Act when it wished to exact the harshest punishment. See Thompson, *Whigs and Hunters*, 247.
41. Thompson, *Whigs and Hunters*, 64.
42. Thompson, *Whigs and Hunters*, 197.

43. Thompson, *Whigs and Hunters*, 206.
44. Paine, *Rights of Man*, 55.
45. Baker, 532–35.
46. Barker, 5.
47. Clemit, 48–9, 67–8.
48. Baker, 530.
49. Caleb's father dies when he is eighteen; his mother is already dead. Emily's parents abandon her when she is three.
50. Godwin, *Political Justice*, 413.
51. Godwin, *Political Justice*, 25.
52. Godwin, *Political Justice*, 26.
53. Godwin, *Political Justice*, 412.
54. Montesquieu, 6.
55. Godwin, *Political Justice*, 72–73.
56. Godwin, *Political Justice*, 76.
57. Godwin, *Political Justice*, 2.
58. William Hazlitt sees Caleb as a secondary character to Falkland. See *Spirit of the Age* (1825; London: Collins Publishers, 1969), 47. See also, Andrew J. Scheiber, "Falkland's Story: *Caleb Williams'* Other Voice", *Studies in the Novel*, 17 (Fall 1985):255–66.
59. See *Shelley's Poetry and Prose*, ed. Donald H. Reiman and Sharon B. Powers (New York: W.W. Norton & Co., 1977), 482–83.
60. Kelly, *The English Jacobin Novel*, 201.
61. Clemit, 53.
62. Burke, *Reflections*, 113.
63. Montesquieu, 25.
64. Godwin, *Political Justice*, 53.
65. Godwin, *Political Justice*, 427, 432.
66. Godwin, *Political Justice*, 428.
67. Godwin, *Political Justice*, 441.
68. Bage, *Hermsprong*, 107.
69. Alex Gold, Jr., "It's Only Love: The Politics of Passion in Godwin's *Caleb Williams*", *Texas Studies in Literature and Language* 19 (1977):135–60.
70. Rousseau, *Political Economy*, 86.
71. "Jones" becomes "Gines" in the second edition (and subsequent editions).
72. Mark Philp, "Caleb Williams and the Treason Trials" in *Godwin's Political Justice* (Ithaca: Cornell University Press, 1986), 103–119.
73. See Barrell, 1.
74. See *Monthly Magazine* 1 (June 1796):385–387; 2 (July 1796):469–70; 3 (March 1797):193–95; 3 (May 1797):358–60; 3 (March 1797):193–95; 4 (Sept 1797):180–81.
75. Gina Luria, "Mary Hays: A Critical Biography" (Ph.D. diss., New York University, 1972).
76. See Mary Hays, *Letters and Essays, Moral and Miscellaneous* (New York: Garland Publishing, 1974), v–x.
77. *Critical Review* 19 (Jan. 1797):109–11. Other reviews of *Emma Courtney* were published in the following periodicals: *Analytical Review* 25 (Feb. 1797):174, 178; *Monthly Review*, 2d ser., 22 (Apr. 1797):443–49; *British Critic* 9 (Mar. 1797):314–15.

78. Kelly, *Women, Writing, and Revolution*, 80–81, 83, 95, 109.
79. *Monthly Magazine* 1 (June 1796):387.
80. Locke, *Two Treatises*, 8–14.
81. Sidney, 39.
82. Paine, *Rights of Man*, 137; Blackstone, I:438.
83. See Genevieve Lloyd, *The Man of Reason* (Minneapolis: University of Minnesota Press, 1984), ix.
84. J.M.S. Tompkins, *The Polite Marriage* (Cambridge: Cambridge University Press, 1938),162.
85. Gina Luria, Introduction to *Letters, and Essays Moral and Miscellaneous*, by Mary Hays (New York: Garland Publishing, Inc., 1974), 5–15.
86. Tompkins, *Polite Marriage*, 158–59.
87. Kelly, *Women, Writing, and Revolution*, 93–94.
88. Christine S. Cozzens, "The Magic Circle: Elizabeth Inchbald, Mary Hays, and Mary Wollstonecraft and the Politics of Domestic Fiction" (Ph.D. diss., University of California at Los Angeles, 1987), 153–161; Gina Luria, Introduction to *Appeal to the Men of Great Britain in Behalf of Women*, by Mary Hays (New York: Garland Publishing, 1974), 5–15; Janet Todd, *The Signs of Angellica* (New York: Columbia University Press, 1989), 236–52. Hays's compassionate obituary for Wollstonecraft appeared in the *Monthly Magazine* 4 (September 1797):232–33.
89. Katharine M. Rogers, "The Contribution of Mary Hays", *Prose Studies* 10 (September 1987):133, 139.
90. "Metaphysics" were derided in numerous issues of the *Anti-Jacobin; or Weekly Examiner* and in conservative novels. Hays received particular ridicule in Hamilton's *Memoirs of Modern Philosophers* as "Bridgetina Botherim", and in Lloyd's *Edmund Oliver* as "Gertrude Sinclair", a tragic woman destroyed by the new philosophy.
91. *Monthly Magazine* 1 (June 1796):387.
92. *Monthly Magazine* 2 (July 1796):469.
93. Paine, *The Rights of Man*, 79.
94. Burton R. Pollin, "Mary Hays on Women's Rights in the Monthly Magazine", *Etudes Anglaises* 24 (1971):271–82.
95. Immanuel Kant, "What is Enlightenment?" in *The Enlightenment*, ed. Peter Gray (New York: Simon and Schuster, 1973), 384.
96. Cone, 2:330; Courtney, 162; Lovell, 330.
97. Blackstone, I:111–127.
98. Blackstone, I:121, 126.
99. Claude Adrien Helvétius, *A Treatise on Man*, trans. W. Hooper (London: Albion Press, 1810), 2–3.
100. Helvétius, 4.
101. Mary Hays, *Appeal to the Men of Great Britain in Behalf of Women* (New York: Garland Publishing, 1974). See also Kelly, *Women, Writing, and Revolution*, 113.
102. See Carol Gilligan, *In a Different Voice* (Cambridge: Harvard University Press, 1982); Armstrong; Gillian Brown, *Domestic Individualism* (Berkeley: University of California Press, 1990).
103. Janet Todd speaks to this point in *Signs of Angellica*, 204–5.
104. Todd, *Signs*, 244.

105. Kelly, *Women,Writing and Revolution*, 3–29.
106. Burke, *Reflections*, 75.
107. Kelly, *Women, Writing, and Revolution*, 4–5.
108. Mary Wollstonecraft, *A Vindication of the Rights of Woman*, vol. 5 of *The Works of Mary Wollstonecraft*, ed. Janet Todd and Marilyn Butler (New York: New York University Press, 1989), 70.
109. Mary Poovey, *The Proper Lady and the Woman Writer* (Chicago: University of Chicago Press, 1984), 109. For an emphasis on sensibility in Wollstonecraft's writing, see also: Mitzi Myers, "Reform or Ruin: A Revolution in Female Manners", in *A Vindication of the Rights of Woman*, ed. Carol H. Poston (New York: W.W. Norton, 1988); Janet Todd, *Women's Friendship in Literature* (New York: Columbia University Press, 1980); Syndy McMillen Conger, "The Sentimental Logic of Wollstonecraft's Prose", *Prose Studies* 10 (September 1987):143–58; Mary Jacobus, *Reading Woman* (New York: Columbia University Press, 1986).
110. Locke, *Two Treatises*, 268.
111. Blackstone, I:442.
112. Through the Court of Chancery (equity), women could arrange for separate property. See Susan Staves, *Married Women's Separate Property in England, 1660–1833* (Cambridge: Harvard University Press, 1990), 199.
113. Blackstone, I:442.
114. Gary Kelly, *Revolutionary Feminism* (New York: St. Martin's Press, 1992), 140–70. See also, Sapiro, 32–41.
115. Montesquieu, in *The Spirit of the Laws*, explains the facets of marriage that correspond to canon law or civil law, respectively. According to William Blackstone, the distinction also appears in English law. The ownership of property is clearly linked with the ability to function in the public sphere. See Blackstone, II:68.
116. In thirteenth-century France, the *communauté* was more of an actual partnership than in the eighteenth century. Both spouses, for example, had to endorse property transactions and were mutually liable to suits for debt. See Adrienne Rogers, "Women and the Law", in *French Women and the Age of Enlightenment*, ed. Samia I. Spencer (Bloomington: Indiana University Press, 1984), 35.
117. Rogers, 33–36.
118. Montesquieu, 3.
119. Rogers, 43–44.
120. *Déclaration des droits de l'homme et du citoyen* ([Paris]: [s.n.], [c.1791]).
121. Hufton, 3–4.
122. Susan Snaider Lanser, *Fictions of Authority* (Ithaca: Cornell University Press, 1992), 231.
123. Anne K. Mellor, *Romanticism and Gender* (New York: Routledge Press, 1993), 69.
124. Paine, *Rights of Man*, 55.
125. Stone, 613.
126. Stone, 630. See also *Laws Respecting Women* (London: J. Johnson, 1777), 401–02.
127. Stone, 502, 532.
128. Hunt, 66.

129. Catharine A. MacKinnon, *Feminism Unmodified* (Cambridge: Harvard University Press, 1987), 48.
130. Stone, 646–47.
131. Catharine A. MacKinnon, *Toward a Feminist Theory of the State* (Cambridge: Harvard University Press, 1989), 113.
132. Wollstonecraft, *Vindication of the Rights of Woman*, 66.
133. Sapiro, 196.
134. Wollstonecraft, *Vindication of the Rights of Men*, 58.
135. Stone, 331; Staves, 162–95.
136. Stone, 332. See also *Laws Respecting Women*, 54.
137. Holdsworth, 12:523.
138. *Laws Respecting Women*, 53–54.
139. A woman could serve as an attorney for her husband because this service was regarded as a "representation" of "her lord" (Blackstone I:442). Though it is not true in any legal sense, Maria refers to Darnford as the man she considers her husband, and it is for him she is acting as "absent" counsel in this courtroom scene.
140. Blackstone, I:443.
141. Kelly, *Women, Writing, and Revolution*, 9–13, 17.
142. Stone, 38.
143. Blackstone, I:440–442.
144. Teresa Michals, "'That Sole and Despotic Dominion': Slaves, Wives, and Game in Blackstone's *Commentaries*", *Eighteenth-Century Studies* 27 (Winter 1993–94):195–98.
145. Eva Figes, *Sex & Subterfuge* (New York: Persea Books, 1982), 57.
146. Tilottama Rajan, "Wollstonecraft and Godwin: Reading the Secrets of the Political Novel", *Studies in Romanticism* 27 (Summer 1988):233.
147. Blackstone, III:268.
148. Wollstonecraft, *A Vindication of the Rights of Men*, 41.
149. Ty, 38.
150. Claudia Johnson, "Mary Wollstonecraft's Novels", *The Cambridge Companion to Mary Wollstonecraft* (Cambridge: Cambridge University Press, 2002), 203–04.
151. Seyla Benhabib, *Situating the Self* (New York: Routledge Press, 1992), 152.
152. For further discussion on the social construction of "woman", see MacKinnon, *Feminism Unmodified*, 21, 23, 49.

Chapter 5   Bestowing the Mantle

1. Thompson, *Making of the English Working Class*, 132–33.
2. Barrell, 190.
3. Roy Porter, *English Society in the Eighteenth Century*, 2nd ed. (New York: Penguin Press, 1990), 348.
4. Goodwin, 387–88.
5. Goodwin, 454.
6. Holdsworth, vol. 13, 173.
7. Thompson, *Making of the English Working Class*, 451.
8. Thompson, *Making of the English Working Class*, 134.

9. The "ill fit" of Smith's title to the novel itself is frequently cited by reviewers and critics. See, for example, *The Analytical Review* 28 (July 1798):73–77. See also, Elizabeth Kraft, "Introduction" to Charlotte Smith, *The Young Philosopher* (London, 1798; Lexington: University of Kentucky Press, 1999), ix–xxxii. In her preface, Charlotte Smith herself recognized the title is a "misnomer" (iv).

10. *The Anti-Jacobin Review and Magazine*, 1 (August 1798), 187.

11. *The Critical Review*, 24 (September 1798), 82. See also *The Analytical Review* 28 (July 1798), 74 and *The Monthly Review* 28 (March 1799), 346–47.

12. Sir Walter Scott, "Charlotte Smith" in *Biographical Memoirs*, vol. 1 (Paris: A.&W. Galignani, 1830), 19. The information in Scott's entry on Charlotte Smith was provided by her sister Catherine Dorset.

13. Fletcher, 337.

14. See, in particular, Charlotte Smith to Thomas Cadell, Jr. and William Davies 22 June, 1797, in which she begins her letter with reference to her father-in-law's will and her frustration with the courts. Beinecke Rare Book and Manuscript Library, Yale University.

15. Fletcher, 62–63. Florence May Anna Hilbish, "Charlotte Smith: Poet and Novelist (1749–1806)" (Ph.D. diss., University of Pennsylvania, 1941), 86.

16. Scott, *Biographical Memoirs*, 22–23.

17. Charlotte Smith, *The Young Philosopher: A Novel* (London: T. Cadell, Jun. and W. Davies, 1798), I:247. All subsequent references will be given parenthetically within the text.

18. John Locke, *An Essay Concerning Humane Understanding* (London: Everyman's Library, 1977), 33, 35. Paine, *Rights of Man*, 55, 58, 77.

19. Rousseau, *Emile*, 59, 131–33.

20. Burke, *Reflections*, 114.

21. Burke, *Reflections*, 91.

22. Burke, *Reflections*, 75.

23. See, for example, *The Critical Review* 24 (September 1798), 79–80.

24. Burke, *Reflections*, 223. Burke credits Jean Domat, a French lawyer, with the placement of prescription within the sphere of natural law.

25. Burke, *Reflections*, 223.

26. Charlotte Smith to Mrs Rose, 2 July 1805, Beinecke Rare Book and Manuscript Library, Yale University.

27. Marilyn Butler, *Maria Edgeworth: A Literary Biography* (Oxford: Clarendon Press, 1972), 353.

28. The Union of Ireland and Great Britain occurred in January of 1801. See *Companion to Irish History, 1603–1921: from the Submission of Tyrone to Partition*, ed. Peter R. Newman (New York: Facts on File, 1991), 206–7.

29. Ernest Baker, "Edgeworth and the English Novel", in *Family Chronicles: Maria Edgeworth's "Castle Rackrent"*, ed. Coilin Owens (Dublin: Wolfhound Press, 1987), 33.

30. Elizabeth Kowaleski-Wallace, *Their Fathers' Daughters* (New York: Oxford University Press, 1991), 158–59.

31. Butler, *Maria Edgeworth*, 358.

32. Marilyn Butler, "The Sources and Composition of *Castle Rackrent*", in *Family Chronicles: Maria Edgeworth's Castle Rackrent*, ed. Coilin Owens (Dublin: Wolfhound Press, 1987), 23.

33. Arthur Young, *Arthur Young's Tour in Ireland* (London: George Bell & Sons, 1892), 2:30.
34. Young, 2:24–34, 460–48.
35. J.C. Beckett, *The Making of Modern Ireland 1603–1923* (New York: Alfred A. Knopf, 1966), 176.
36. Young, 2:26, 27, 53.
37. Sandra M. Gilbert and Susan Gubar, *The Madwoman in the Attic* (New Haven: Yale University Press, 1979), 146–54.
38. Edgeworth, 107.
39. *The Gentleman's Magazine*, 59:766–67.
40. A jointure of 500 pounds per year was an average settlement for the gentry. See Staves, 95.
41. Edward Coke, *The First Part of the Institutes of the Laws of England; or A Commentary upon Littleton*, 19th ed., 2 vols. (London, 1832; reprint, New York: Garland Press, 1979), 1:36b.
42. Staves, 95–104.
43. Burke, *Reflections*, 144–45.
44. Burke, *Reflections*, 48.
45. McKeon, 132.

Bibliography

Primary sources

Bage, Robert. *Hermsprong; or Man As He Is Not.* Oxford: Oxford University Press, 1985.

Belcher, William. *Holcroft's Folly.* London, [1795?].

Bentham, Jeremy. *A Comment on the Commentaries.* Edited by J.H. Burns and H.L.A. Hart. *Collected Works of Jeremy Bentham.* London: Athlone Press, 1977.

Blackstone, Sir William. *Commentaries on the Laws of England.* 4 vols. 1765–69. Reprint. Chicago: University of Chicago Press, 1979.

Bowles, John. *Dialogues on the Rights of Britons, between a Farmer, a Sailor, and a Manufacturer.* London: T. Longman, 1792.

——. *A Protest Against Thomas Paine's "Rights of Man".* London: T. Longman, 1792.

Burke, Edmund. *Reflections on the Revolution in France.* London: J. Dodsley, 1790.

Coke, Sir Edward. *The First Part of the Institutes of the Laws of England; or A Commentary upon Littleton.* 2 vols. 1832. Reprint. New York: Garland Press, 1979.

Déclaration des droits de l'homme et du citoyen. [Paris]: [s.n.], [c.1791].

Edgeworth, Maria. *Castle Rackrent.* Oxford: Oxford University Press, 1964.

Filmer, Sir Robert. *Patriarcha and Other Writings.* Edited by Johann P. Sommerville Cambridge: Cambridge University Press, 1991.

Godwin, William. *Enquiry Concerning Political Justice.* Edited by Mark Philp. vol. 3, *Political and Philosophical Writings of William Godwin.* London: Pickering and Chatto, 1993.

——. *Things As They Are: or, The Adventures of Caleb Williams.* Edited by Pamela Clemit. vol. 3, *Collected Novels and Memoirs of William Godwin.* London: Pickering and Chatto, 1992.

Harrington, James. *The Political Works of James Harrington.* Edited by J.G.A. Pocock. Cambridge: Cambridge University Press, 1977.

Hazlitt, William. *Memoirs of the Late Thomas Holcroft.* 2 vols. London: T. Longman, 1816.

——. *Spirit of the Age.* London: Collins Publishers, 1969.

Hays, Mary. *Appeal to the Men of Great Britain in Behalf of Women.* New York: Garland Publishing, 1974.

——. *Letters and Essays, Moral and Miscellaneous.* New York: Garland Publishing, 1974.

——. *Memoirs of Emma Courtney.* London: Oxford University Press, 1996.

Helvétius, Claude Adrien. *A Treatise on Man.* Translated by W. Hooper. London: Albion Press, 1810.

Holcroft, Thomas. *Anna St. Ives.* London: Oxford University Press, 1973.

——. *A Letter to the Right Honourable William Windham, on the Intemperance and Dangerous Tendency of his Public Conduct.* London: Symonds, 1795.

——. *Memoirs of Bryan Perdue.* London: Longman, Hurt, Rees, and Orme, 1805.

——. *A Narrative of Facts, relating to a Prosecution for High Treason.* London: Symonds, 1795.

Hutcheson, Frances. *A System of Moral Philosophy.* New York: Augustus M. Kelley, 1968.

Inchbald, Elizabeth. *Nature and Art.* Philadelphia: Snowden and McCorkle, 1796.

Kant, Immanuel. "What is Enlightenment?" In *The Enlightenment.* Edited by Peter Gray. New York: Simon and Schuster, 1973.

Laws Respecting Women. London: J. Johnson, 1777.

Locke, John. *An Essay Concerning Humane Understanding.* London: Everyman's Library, 1977.

——. *Letter Concerning Toleration.* Indianapolis: Hackett Publishing, 1983.

——. *Two Treatises of Government.* Edited by Peter Laslett. Cambridge: Cambridge University Press, 1988.

Macaulay, Catharine. *Observations on the Reflections of the Right Hon. Edmund Burke in a Letter to the Right Hon. the Earl of Stanhope.* London: C. Dilly, 1790.

Mackintosh, Sir James. *Vindiciae Gallicae. Defence of the French Revolution and its English Admirers, against the Accusations of the Right Hon. Edmund Burke.* In *The Miscellaneous Works of the Right Honourable Sir James Mackintosh.* Edited by R.J. Mackintosh. Philadelphia: Carey and Hart, 1846.

Mauss, Marcel. *The Gift.* Translated by W.D. Halls. New York: W.W. Norton & Co., 1990.

Montesquieu, Baron de [Charles de Secondat]. *The Spirit of the Laws.* Translated by Thomas Nugent. New York: Hafner Press, 1949.

Paine, Thomas. *The Rights of Man, Part I.* In *Thomas Paine: Political Writings.* Edited by Bruce Kuklick. Cambridge: Cambridge University Press, 1989.

Price, Dr. Richard. *A Discourse on the love of our country.* London: Woodstock Books, 1992.

Priestley, Joseph. *Letters to the Right Honourable Edmund Burke.* London: J. Johnson, 1791.

——. *An Essay on the First Principles of Government; and on the Nature of Political, Civil, and Religious Liberty.* London: Dodsley, Cadell and Johnson, 1768.

Rousseau, Jean-Jacques. *Émile.* Translated by Barbara Foxley. London: J.M. Dent & Sons, 1992.

——. *La Nouvelle Héloïse.* Translated by Judith H. McDowell. University Park: Pennsylvania State University Press, 1968.

——. *Rousseau's Political Writings.* Edited by Alan Ritter and Julia Conway Bondanella. Translated by Julia Conway Bondanella. New York: W.W. Norton & Co., 1988.

Scott, Sir Walter. "Charlotte Smith". In *Biographical Memoirs.* vol. 3. Paris: A. & W. Galignani, 1830.

Shaftesbury, Earl of [Anthony Ashley Cooper]. *Characteristicks of Men, Manners, Opinions, Times.* 3 vols. London: 1711.

Sidney, Algernon. *Discourses Concerning Government.* Indianapolis: Liberty Classics, 1990.

Smith, Adam. *Lectures on Jurisprudence.* Indianapolis: Liberty Classics, 1982.

——. *The Theory of Moral Sentiments.* Indianapolis: Liberty Classics, 1982.

Smith, Charlotte. *Desmond.* 3 vols. London: G.G.J. and J. Robinson, 1792.

——. *The Young Philosopher: A Novel.* 4 vols. London: T. Cadell, Jun. and W. Davies, 1798.

Wollstonecraft, Mary. *A Vindication of the Rights of Men*. Edited by Janet Todd and Marilyn Butler. vol. 5, *The Works of Mary Wollstonecraft*. New York: New York University Press, 1989.
——. *A Vindication of the Rights of Woman*. Edited by Janet Todd and Marilyn Butler. vol. 5, *The Works of Mary Wollstonecraft*. New York: New York University Press, 1989.
——. *The Wrongs of Woman: or, Maria*. Edited by Janet Todd and Marilyn Butler. vol. 1, *The Works of Mary Wollstonecraft*. New York: New York University Press, 1989.

Secondary sources

Altman, Janet Gurkin. *Epistolarity: Approaches to a Form*. Columbus: Ohio State University Press, 1982.
Amussen, S.D. "Gender, Family and the Social Order, 1560–1725". In *Order and Disorder in Early Modern England*. Edited by Anthony Fletcher and John Stevenson. Cambridge: Cambridge University Press, 1985.
Armstrong, Nancy. *Desire and Domestic Fiction*. Oxford: Oxford University Press, 1987.
Ashcraft, Richard. *Revolutionary Politics and Locke's Two Treatises of Government*. Princeton: Princeton University Press, 1986.
Atiyah, P.S. *The Rise and Fall of Freedom of Contract*. Oxford: Clarendon Press, 1979.
Baker, Ernest. "Edgeworth and the English Novel". In *Family Chronicles: Maria Edgeworth's "Castle Rackrent"*. Edited by Collin Owens. Dublin: Wolfhound Press, 1987.
Baker, J.H. *An Introduction to English Legal History*. London: Butterworths, 1990.
Bakhtin, Mikhail M. *The Dialogic Imagination*. Translated by Caryl Emerson and Michael Holquist. Austin: University of Texas Press, 1981.
Balfour, Ian. "Promises, Promises: Social and Other Contracts in the English Jacobins (Godwin/Inchbald)". In *New Romanticisms: Theory and Critical Practice*. Edited by David L. Clark and Donald C. Goellnicht. Toronto: University of Toronto Press, 1994.
Barker, Gerard A. "The Narrative Mode of *Caleb Williams* and Resolutions". *Studies in the Novel* 25 (Spring 1993):1–15.
Barrell, John. *Imagining the King's Death*. Oxford: Oxford University Press, 2000.
Becker, Marvin B. *The Emergence of Civil Society in the Eighteenth Century*. Bloomington: Indiana University Press, 1994.
Beckett, J.C. *The Making of Modern Ireland 1603–1923*. New York: Alfred A. Knopf, 1966.
Benhabib, Seyla. *Situating the Self*. New York: Routledge Press, 1992.
Blank, Antje and Janet Todd. Introduction to Charlotte Smith, *Desmond*. London: Pickering and Chatto, 1997.
Boaden, James. *Memoirs of Mrs. Inchbald*. London: Richard Bentley, 1833.
Boulton, James T. *The Language of Politics in the Age of Wilkes and Burke*. London: Routledge and Kegan Paul, 1963.
Bowstead, Diana. "Charlotte Smith's *Desmond*: The Epistolary Novel as Ideological Argument". *Fetter'd or Free?: British Women Novelists, 1670–1815*.

Edited by Mary Anne Schofield and Cecilia Macheski. Athens: Ohio University Press, 1986.

Brooks, Peter and Paul Gewirtz. *Law's Stories: Narrative and Rhetoric in the Law*. New Haven: Yale University Press, 1996.

Brown, Gillian. *Domestic Individualism*. Berkeley: University of California Press, 1990.

Butler, Marilyn, ed. *Burke, Paine, Godwin and the Revolutionary Controversy*. Cambridge: Cambridge University Press, 1984.

———. *Jane Austen and the War of Ideas*. London: Clarendon Press, 1975.

———. *Maria Edgeworth: A Literary Biography*. Oxford: Clarendon Press, 1972.

———. "The Sources and Composition of *Castle Rackrent*". *Family Chronicles: Maria Edgeworth's Castle Rackrent*. Edited by Coilin Owens. Dublin: Wolfhound Press, 1987.

Claeys, Gregory. *Thomas Paine: Social and Political Thought*. Boston: Unwin Hyman, 1989.

Clemit, Pamela. *The Godwinian Novel*. Oxford: Clarendon Press, 1993.

Cobban, Alfred, ed. *The Debate on the French Revolution, 1789–1800*. London: Nicholas Kaye, 1950.

Cone, Carl B. *Burke and the Nature of Politics: The Age of the French Revolution*. Louisville: University of Kentucky Press, 1964.

———. "Pamphlet Replies to Burke's Reflections". *The Southwestern Social Science Quarterly*, 26 (June 1945):22–34.

Conger, Syndy McMillen. "The Sentimental Logic of Wollstonecraft's Prose". *Prose Studies* 10 (September 1987):143–58.

Constable, Marianne. *The Law of the Other*. Chicago: University of Chicago Press, 1994.

Conway, Alison. "Nationalism, Revolution, and the Female Body: Charlotte Smith's *Desmond*". *Women's Studies* 24 (1995):395–415.

Copeland, Thomas W. and Milton Shumway Smith. *A Checklist of the Correspondence of Edmund Burke*. Cambridge: Cambridge University Press, 1955.

Courtney, C.P. *Montesquieu and Burke*. Oxford: Basil Blackwell, 1963.

Cover, Robert. "Nomos and Narrative". In *Narrative, Violence and the Law: The Essays of Robert Cover*. Edited by Martha Minow, Michael Ryan, and Austin Sarat. Ann Arbor: University of Michigan Press, 1992.

Cozzens, Christine S. "The Magic Circle: Elizabeth Inchbald, Mary Hays, and Mary Wollstonecraft and the Politics of Domestic Fiction". Ph.D. diss., University of California at Los Angeles, 1987.

Cronin, John. *The Anglo-Irish Novel*. Totowa: Barnes & Noble, 1980.

Daly, James. *Sir Robert Filmer and English Political Thought*. Toronto: University of Toronto Press, 1979.

Davies, Thomas, ed. *Committees for the Repeal of the Test and Corporation Acts*. London: London Record Society, 1978.

Davis, Thomas ed., *Committees for the Repeal of the Test and Corporation Acts: Minutes 1786–90 and 1827–8*. London: London Record Society, 1978.

Deane, Seamus. *The French Revolution and Enlightenment in England, 1789–1832*. Cambridge: Harvard University Press, 1988.

De Bruyn, Frans. *The Literary Genres of Edmund Burke*. Oxford: Clarendon Press, 1996.

Eisenstein, Zillah R. *The Female Body and the Law*. Berkeley: University of California Press, 1988.

Elliott, Pat. "Charlotte Smith's Feminism: A Study of Emmeline and Desmond". In *Living by the Pen: Early British Women Writers*. Edited by Dale Spender. New York: Teachers College Press, 1992.

Engels, Frederick. *The Origin of the Family, Private Property and the State*. London: Lawrence and Wishart, 1972.

Favret, Mary. *The Romantic Correspondence: Women, Politics, and the Fiction of Letters*. Cambridge: Cambridge University Press, 1992.

Figes, Eva. *Sex & Subterfuge*. New York: Persea Books, 1982.

Fletcher, Loraine. *Charlotte Smith: A Critical Biography*. New York: St. Martin's Press, 1998.

Fry, Carrol L. *Charlotte Smith*. New York: Twayne Publishers, 1996.

Gabel, Peter and Jay M. Feinman. "Contract Law as Ideology". In *The Politics of Law: A Progressive Critique*. Edited by David Kairys. New York: Pantheon Press, 1982.

Gilbert, Sandra M. and Susan Gubar. *The Madwoman in the Attic*. New Haven: Yale University Press, 1979.

Gilligan, Carol. *In a Different Voice*. Cambridge: Harvard University Press, 1982.

Gleissner, Richard. "The Levellers and Natural Law: The Putney Debates of 1647". *Journal of British Studies* 20 (1980):74–89.

Gold, Alex Jr. "It's Only Love: The Politics of Passion in Godwin's *Caleb Williams*". *Texas Studies in Literature and Language* 19 (1977):135–60.

Goodwin, Albert. *The Friends of Liberty: The English Democratic Movement in the Age of the French Revolution*. Cambridge: Harvard University Press, 1979.

Grenby, M.O. *The Anti-Jacobin Novel: British Conservatism and the French Revolution*. Cambridge: Cambridge University Press, 2001.

Habermas, Jürgen. *The Structural Transformation of the Public Sphere*. Translated by Thomas Burger. Cambridge: MIT Press, 1991.

Hilbish, Florence May Anna. "Charlotte Smith: Poet and Novelist (1749–1806)". Ph.D. diss., University of Pennsylvania, 1941.

Hill, Christopher. *The Century of Revolution, 1603–1714*. New York: W.W. Norton, 1980.

——. *Intellectual Origins of the English Revolution*. Oxford: Clarendon Press, 1965.

——. *Puritanism and Revolution*. London: Secker and Warburg, 1958.

Holdsworth, Sir William. *A History of English Law*. London: Methuen & Co., 1966.

Hufton, Olwen H. *Women and the Limits of Citizenship in the French Revolution*. Toronto: University of Toronto Press, 1992.

Hunt, Lynn. *The Family Romance of the French Revolution*. Berkeley: University of California Press, 1992.

Hunter, J. Paul. *Before Novels*. New York: W.W. Norton & Co., 1990.

Jacobus, Mary. *Reading Woman*. New York: Columbia University Press, 1986.

Jameson, Fredric. *The Political Unconscious*. Ithaca: Cornell University Press, 1981.

Johnson, Claudia. "Mary Wollstonecraft's Novels". *The Cambridge Companion to Mary Wollstonecraft*. Cambridge: Cambridge University Press, 2002.

Jones, C.B. *Radical Sensibility*. London: Routledge Press, 1993.

Keane, Angela. *Women Writers and the English Nation in the 1790s*. Cambridge: Cambridge University Press, 2000.

Kelly, Gary. *The English Jacobin Novel, 1780–1805.* London: Clarendon Press, 1976.
———. *Revolutionary Feminism.* New York: St. Martin's Press, 1992.
———. "Women Novelists and the French Revolution Debate: Novelizing the Revolution/Revolutionizing the Novel". *Eighteenth-Century Fiction* 6 (July 1994):369–88.
———. *Women, Writing, and Revolution, 1790–1827.* Oxford: Clarendon Press, 1993.
Kowaleski-Wallace, Elizabeth. *Their Fathers' Daughters.* New York: Oxford University Press, 1991.
Lanser, Susan Snaider. *Fictions of Authority.* Ithaca: Cornell University Press, 1992.
Laslett, Peter. Introduction to *Patriarcha and other Political Works,* by Sir Robert Filmer. Oxford: Basil Blackwell, 1949.
Lefebvre, Georges. *The French Revolution.* Translated by Elizabeth Moss Evanson. London: Routledge Press, 1962.
Lieberman, David. *The Province of Legislation Determined.* Cambridge: Cambridge University Press, 1989.
Lloyd, Genevieve. *The Man of Reason.* Minneapolis: University of Minnesota Press, 1984.
Lovell, Colin Rhys. *English Constitutional and Legal History.* New York: Oxford University Press, 1962.
Lukács, Georg. *The Theory of the Novel.* Translated by Anna Bostock. Cambridge: MIT Press, 1971.
Luria, Gina. Introduction to *Appeal to the Men of Great Britain in Behalf of Women,* by Mary Hays. New York: Garland Publishing, 1974.
———. Introduction to *Letters, and Essays Moral and Miscellaneous,* by Mary Hays. New York: Garland Publishing, Inc., 1974.
———. "Mary Hays: A Critical Biography". Ph.D. diss., New York University, 1972.
MacKinnon, Catharine A. *Feminism Unmodified.* Cambridge: Harvard University Press, 1987.
———. *Toward a Feminist Theory of the State.* Cambridge: Harvard University Press, 1989.
Macpherson, C.B. *The Political Theory of Possessive Individualism.* Oxford: Clarendon Press, 1962.
Maitland, Frederic W. and Francis C. Montague. *A Sketch of English Legal History.* New York: AMS Press, 1978.
Marshall, Peter H. *William Godwin.* New Haven: Yale University Press, 1984.
McCann, Andrew. *Cultural Politics in the 1790s: Literature, Radicalism, and the Public Sphere.* New York: St. Martin's Press, 1999.
McKeon, Michael. *The Origins of the English Novel, 1600–1740.* Baltimore: Johns Hopkins University Press, 1987.
Mellor, Anne K. *Romanticism and Gender.* New York: Routledge Press, 1993.
Mensch, Elizabeth. "The History of Mainstream Legal Thought". In *The Politics of Law: A Progressive Critique.* Edited by David Kairys. New York: Pantheon Press, 1982.
Michals, Teresa. "That Sole and Despotic Dominion: Slaves, Wives, and Game in Blackstone's *Commentaries*". *Eighteenth-Century Studies* 27 (Winter 1993–94): 195–216.

Minow, Martha. "Partial Justice: Law and Minorities". In *The Fate of Law*. Ann Arbor: University of Michigan Press, 1993.

Myers, Mitzi. "Reform or Ruin: A Revolution in Female Manners". In *A Vindication of the Rights of Woman*. Edited by Carol H. Poston. New York: W.W. Norton, 1988.

Newman, Peter R., ed. *Companion to Irish History, 1603–1921: from the Submission of Tyrone to Partition*. New York: Facts on File, 1991.

Nicholes, Eleanor Louise. Introduction to *A Vindication of the Rights of Men*, by Mary Wollstonecraft. London: J. Johnson, 1790; Gainesville: Scholars' Facsimiles & Reprints, 1960.

Nicholson, Linda J. *Gender and History*. New York: Columbia University Press, 1986.

Nussbaum, Felicity. *The Autobiographical Subject*. Baltimore: Johns Hopkins University Press, 1989.

Ogden, C.K. *Bentham's Theory of Fictions*. London: Kegan Paul, Trench, Trubner & Co., 1932.

Pateman, Carole. *The Problem of Political Obligation*. Chichester: John Wiley & Sons, 1979.

———. *The Sexual Contract*. Stanford: Stanford University Press, 1988.

Paulson, Ronald. *Representations of Revolutions (1789–1820)*. New Haven: Yale University Press, 1983.

Philp, Mark. "Caleb Williams and the Treason Trials". In *Godwin's Political Justice*. Ithaca: Cornell University Press, 1986.

———. *The French Revolution and British Popular Politics*. Cambridge: Cambridge University Press, 1991.

———. *Godwin's Political Justice*. Ithaca: Cornell University Press, 1986.

Pocock, J.G.A. ed. *Three British Revolutions*. Princeton: Princeton University Press, 1980.

Pollin, Burton R. "Mary Hays on Women's Rights in the Monthly Magazine". *Etudes Anglaises* 24 (1971):271–82.

Poovey, Mary. *The Proper Lady and the Woman Writer*. Chicago: University of Chicago Press, 1984.

Porter, Roy. *The Creation of the Modern World*. New York: W.W. Norton, 2000.

———. *English Society in the Eighteenth Century*. New York: Penguin Press, 1990.

Prickett, Stephen. *England and the French Revolution*. London: Macmillan, 1989.

Radcliffe, Evan. "Revolutionary Writing, Moral Philosophy, and Universal Benevolence in the Eighteenth Century". *Journal of the History of Ideas* 54 (April 1993):221–40.

Radzinowicz, Leon. *A History of English Criminal Law and its Administration from 1750*. New York: Macmillan & Co., 1948.

Rajan, Tilottama. "Wollstonecraft and Godwin: Reading the Secrets of the Political Novel". *Studies in Romanticism* 27 (Summer 1988):221–51.

Redford, Bruce. *The Converse of the Pen*. Chicago: University of Chicago Press, 1986.

Rogers, Adrienne. "Women and the Law". In *French Women and the Age of Enlightenment*. Edited by Samia I. Spencer. Bloomington: Indiana University Press, 1984.

Rogers, Katharine M. "The Contribution of Mary Hays". *Prose Studies* 10 (September 1987):131–42.

Sapiro, Virginia. *A Vindication of Political Virtue*. Chicago: University of Chicago Press, 1992.

Scheiber, Andrew J. "Falkland's Story: *Caleb Williams'* Other Voice". *Studies in the Novel*, 17 (Fall 1985):255–66.

Scheuermann, Mona. *Her Bread to Earn*. Lexington: University Press of Kentucky, 1993.

——. *Social Protest in the Eighteenth-Century English Novel*. Columbus: Ohio State University Press, 1985.

Schochet, Gordon J. *Patriarchalism in Political Thought*. London: Basil Blackwell, 1975.

Skinner, Andrew. Introduction to *The Wealth of Nations*, Books I–III, by Adam Smith. London: Penguin Books, 1974.

Shell, Marc. *Money, Language, and Thought*. Berkeley: University of California Press, 1982.

Smith, Olivia. *The Politics of Language, 1791–1819*. Oxford: Clarendon Press, 1984.

Sommerville, Johann P. Introduction to *Patriarcha and Other Writings* by Sir Robert Filmer. Cambridge: Cambridge University Press, 1991.

Spacks, Patricia Meyer. *Desire and Truth*. Chicago: University of Chicago Press, 1990.

——. *Imagining A Self*. Cambridge: Harvard University Press, 1976.

Stanlis, Peter J. *Edmund Burke: The Enlightenment and Revolution*. New Brunswick: Transaction Publishers, 1991.

Staves, Susan. *Married Women's Separate Property in England, 1660–1833*. Cambridge: Harvard University Press, 1990.

Stone, Lawrence. *The Family, Sex and Marriage in England 1500–1800*. New York: Harper & Row, 1977.

Tennant, Chris. "Primitives, indigenous rights and international institutions: International engagement with indigenous peoples, 1945–1992". Paper presented at the "Law and Literature Seminar", Center for Literary and Cultural Studies, Harvard University, Cambridge, Mass., 13 April 1993.

Thomas, Keith. "The Levellers and the Franchise". In *The Interregnum: The Quest for Settlement*. Edited by G.E. Aylmer. New York: Macmillan, 1974.

Thompson, E.P. *Customs in Common*. New York: The New Press, 1993.

——. *The Making of the English Working Class*. New York: Vintage Books, 1963.

——. *Whigs and Hunters*. London: Penguin Books, 1975.

Todd, Janet. *Mary Wollstonecraft: A Revolutionary Life*. New York: Columbia University Press, 2000.

——. *The Signs of Angellica*. New York: Columbia University Press, 1989.

——. *Women's Friendship in Literature*. New York: Columbia University Press, 1980.

Tompkins, J.M.S. *The Polite Marriage*. Cambridge: Cambridge University Press, 1938.

Tuck, Richard. *Natural Rights Theories*. Cambridge: Cambridge University Press, 1979.

Tully, James. *An Approach to Political Philosophy: Locke in Contexts*. Cambridge: Cambridge University Press, 1993.

——. *A Discourse on Property*. Cambridge: Cambridge University Press, 1980.

Ty, Eleanor. *Unsex'd Revolutionaries*. Toronto: University of Toronto Press, 1993.

Unger, Roberto Mangabeira. *The Critical Legal Studies Movement.* Cambridge: Harvard University Press, 1986.

Walker, William. *Locke, Literary Criticism, and Philosophy.* Cambridge: Cambridge University Press, 1994.

Watson, Nicola J. *Revolution and Form of the English Novel.* London: Oxford University Press, 1994.

Watt, Ian. *The Rise of the Novel.* London: Chatto & Windus, 1957.

West, Robin. *Narrative, Authority and Law.* Ann Arbor: University of Michigan Press, 1993.

White, James Boyd. *Justice as Translation.* Chicago: University of Chicago Press, 1990.

Woodhouse, A.S.P., ed. *Puritanism and Liberty.* London: J.M. Dent & Sons, 1992.

Young, Arthur. *Arthur Young's Tour in Ireland.* London: George Bell & Sons, 1892.

Index

Adams, Daniel, 154
Altman, Janet, 73, 81
America, 1, 156, 158, 159, 168–69
  Bill of Rights (1789), 2
  Revolution, 7
Analytical Review, 142
Anglican Church, 28, 39
Anti-Jacobin; or Weekly Examiner, 6
Anti-Jacobin Review and Magazine, 6,
  21, 72, 84, 156
Anti-Jacobinism, 6–7, 69, 119
Arabian Tales, 16
Armstrong, Nancy, 21
Ashcraft, Richard, 35

Bage, Robert, 1, 4, 8
  Hermsprong, 8, 18, 23, 56, 93–103,
    126, 144, 149
  Man As He Is, 8, 61
Baker, J.H., 117
Bakhtin, Mikhail, 20, 22, 71
Balfour, Ian, 13
Benevolence, 91–92, 116
  Universal, 61, 68–69
Benhabib, Seyla, 152
Bentham, Jeremy, 4–5, 24
Biography, 18–19
Blackstone, Sir William, 40, 46–47, 66
  127, 131, 134, 141–42, 150–51,
  175, 189 n. 78, 194 nn. 89, 90,
  198 n. 115
  Commentaries, 40, 151
British Critic, 16, 111, 112
Burke, Edmund
  on abstractions, 47
  and the ancient constitution, 2,
    143
  in *Caleb Williams*, 124
  and chivalry, 52, 124
  conservation of state, 96, 177, 178
  and improvement, 65
  on law, 134, 143, 166–67, 176–77
  and literary forms, 10

on national security, 138–39, 162,
  167
and prescription, 97, 138, 162, 167,
  189 n.83
on property, 80, 139, 177
Reflections, 10, 24, 39–44, 46, 49,
  51, 75–76, 82, 85, 124, 147,
  151, 167, 176
on rights, 2, 20, 34, 39–44, 51,
  75,122, 143–44, 162
on the social contract, 12, 25, 41,
  54
Butler, Marilyn, 45, 56, 62, 170

Castle of St Vallery, 16
Catholicism, 28
Christie, Thomas, 82
Citizenship, 3–5, 22, 56, 61, 62, 71,
  84,
  in *Desmond*, 71, 75, 80
  in *Hermsprong*, 93, 98
  Locke on, 30
  property and, 65
  reason and, 59
  Rousseau on, 27–28
  and sensibility, 85
  and subjectivity, 13, 17
  Wollstonecraft on, 48
  and women, 104, 130
Civil society, 1, 3–5, 10, 12, 13, 30, 33,
  38, 39, 41–42, 54, 106, 186 n. 25
Clemit, Pamela, 117, 124
Coke, Sir Edward, 69, 134, 175
Combination Acts (1799, 1800), 154
Contractarianism, 2–5, 6, 9, 13–14,
  22, 28–39, 44–47, 53, 71–72, 74,
  75, 82, 181 n. 4
  and women, 104–10
Cover, Robert, 11, 12
Critical Review, 130, 156

De Bruyn, Frans, 65
Deane, Seamus, 45